THE WORLD OF ARCHAEOLOGY
General Editor: GLYN DANIEL

The Archaeology of Mesopotamia

SETON LLOYD

The Archaeology of Mesopotamia

*From the Old Stone Age
to the Persian Conquest*

with 174 illustrations

THAMES AND HUDSON

Table I Palaeo   p. 22
Table II 8–2500 BC   27
Table III S. Mesop   36
       5–2500 BC

Library of Congress Catalog card number 78-52961

Filmset and printed in Great Britain by
BAS Printers Limited, Over Wallop, Hampshire

Contents

Preface   9

1 The Land and its Rivers   12

THE TWO REGIONS
THE COASTLINE
THE RIVERS
CLIMATE AND IRRIGATION
SALINIZATION
NORTHERN IRAQ

2 The Twilight of Neolithic Man   21

THE OLD STONE AGE
GARROD AND SOLECKI
AMERICAN EXCAVATORS IN KURDISTAN
THE STATE OF NEOLITHIC RESEARCH
     Jordan and the Levant; Anatolia; Iran
THE IRAQ-JARMO PROJECT

3 The Threshold of Written History   37

THE SEQUENCE OF DISCOVERIES
     Al 'Ubaid; Warka; Eridu; Khafaje
THE 'UBAID PERIOD
     Architecture; Religion; Pottery and Small
     Objects; The Cemetery
THE URUK PERIOD
     Warka; The Anu Area; The Eanna Precinct;
     Tell 'Uqair
BUILDINGS OF THE JEMDET NASR PERIOD
     Warka; Khafaje
THE PROTOLITERATE PERIOD
     The First Writing; Sculpture; Cylinder-seals;
     Pottery
SUMERIAN ANTECEDENTS

4 Illiterate Peoples of Northern Mesopotamia   65

EXCAVATIONS IN THE NORTH
  Arpachiyah; Tepe Gawra; Küyünjik; Hassuna;
  Other Hassuna Sites; Samarra and Sawwan
ARCHITECTURE
  The Pre-Halaf Period; The Samarra Period; The
  Halaf Period; The 'Ubaid Period; The 'Gawra'
  Period; Tell Brak
POTTERY
  Pre-Halaf; Tell Halaf; Northern 'Ubaid; Post-
  'Ubaid
BURIALS
  The 'Gawra' Period
SMALL OBJECTS
  Figurines; Seals
FOREIGN RELATIONS
  Susiana

5 The Early Sumerian Dynasties   88

THE KING-LIST
THE EARLIEST WRITTEN TEXTS
ARCHAEOLOGICAL PHASES
THE 'FLOOD'
EARLY DYNASTIC SITES
  Khafaje; Tell Asmar; Tell Agrab; Ur-of-the-
  Chaldees; Al 'Ubaid; Kish; Lagash; Nippur;
  Ashur and Mari; Shuaira
VARIANTS IN TERMINOLOGY

6 Pre-Sargonid Art and Architecture   111

SCULPTURE
  Statues; Relief Carving
ARCHITECTURE
  Building Methods; Temples; Palaces
CYLINDER-SEALS
METALLURGY AND COMPOSITE CRAFTSMANSHIP
  Inlaid Ornament; Composite Objects
POTTERY

7 The Dynasty of Akkad and the Sumerian Revival   135

SEMITES IN MESOPOTAMIA
SARGON AND HIS SUCCESSORS
ARCHAEOLOGY
  Buildings; Tell Asmar; Khafaje and Brak;
  Sculpture; Cylinder-seals; Gasur

GUTIANS AND LAGASH
   De Sarzec; Telloh; Gudea; Al-Hiba
THE THIRD DYNASTY OF UR
   Buildings at Ur; The Ziggurat; The Terrace;
   The Mausoleum; Temples and Sculpture

8   The 2nd Millennium BC   157

CONFLICTING STATES
BUILDINGS OF THE ISIN–LARSA PERIOD
PRIVATE HOUSES
THE PALACE AT MARI
MURAL PAINTINGS
TELL RIMAH
SCULPTURE
THE KASSITES
MITANNI (NUZI)
THE MIDDLE ASSYRIAN PERIOD
   City of Ashur; Fortifications; Temples and
   Palaces; Some Finds at Ashur; Building
   Practices

9   The Late Assyrian Period   187

IMPERIAL HISTORY
EARLY EXCAVATIONS IN ASSYRIAN CITIES
NIMRUD (KALHU)
KHORSABAD
NINEVEH
AMERICAN EXCAVATIONS AT KHORSABAD
BUILDING CONSTRUCTION
LATE ASSYRIAN SCULPTURE
BRITISH RETURN TO NIMRUD
THE NIMRUD IVORIES

10 Babylon: The Last Mesopotamian   222
**   Monarchy**

A DYNASTIC REVIVAL
THE GERMAN EXCAVATION
THE CITY
BUILDINGS
POSTSCRIPT

Notes on the Text   232

Bibliography   238

Photographic Acknowledgments   244

Index   245

To the memory of Henri Frankfort

Anyone already familiar with the subject of this book may well be disconcerted at first by the extravagant claim implicit in its title, and justifiably feel that it calls for some immediate qualification. Throughout Mesopotamia, archaeological excavations have been in progress almost continuously for more than 100 years, and the literature which their results have engendered is by now sufficient to fill a fair-sized library. From field reports and typological analyses, to epigraphical commentaries and stylistic art studies, every facet is represented of a complex and far-reaching enquiry. Indeed, one has observed without surprise that a recently published bibliography could list over 5,000 relevant books and articles. Since it would then clearly be impossible to summarize even the central themes of all these writings, the purpose of the conspectus which follows has been confined to one specific aspect of the research with which it is concerned, and other minor limitations have been imposed on its coverage. This selective process has in fact primarily been made possible by a conspicuous duality in the categories of evidence provided by excavations in a country where writing was invented at an extremely early age.

The function of archaeology has been rather arbitrarily defined by one writer as 'a way of learning about the past through things instead of words': a ludicrous over-simplification in the case of Egypt or Mesopotamia, where a significant proportion of the 'things' found by excavators have themselves been written documents. On the other hand, the purpose which these documents have served, far from being restricted to the recovery of narrative history, has embraced the much wider task of re-creating in detail the anatomy of ancient civilization. To this remarkable achievement the written texts have largely contributed, by perfecting the recorded patterns of social or economic organization and of intellectual development in literate ages. Yet, where excavations are concerned, it is the vestigial remains of the physical setting in which the documents themselves were written that has completed the revelation of evolving humanity and its adaptation to environmental influences. In a word, our astonishingly wide knowledge of Mesopotamian civilization in 'historical' times is derived in almost equal proportions from two different sources: ancient literature on the one hand and, on the other, the study of material remains. It should also be remembered that these 'historical' ages were preceded by a long era of illiteracy, a formative period in human development of which our increasingly explicit understanding has been derived exclusively from the results of 'spade archaeology'.

As may already have been inferred from these observations, it is with the material remains and with the progress of excavations which have revealed them that this book is intended to be concerned, rather than with the philological contribution. Other limitations have been imposed upon it for a variety of reasons. First, because I have dealt at length with the pioneer activities of early Mesopotamian explorers in another book (*Foundations in the Dust*, Oxford 1947), I have not wished here to become involved in anecdotal accounts of primitive digging in Victorian times. I have preferred that my point of departure should coincide with the first introduction of discipline and method into archaeological procedure. This is well known to have taken place at the turn of the 19th century, and something further should be said about it.

In Mesopotamia, the beginnings of systematic excavation and proper recording must be credited to the two German scholars, Robert Koldewey and Walter Andrae, whose work at Babylon began in 1899. The method which they rapidly perfected of tracing mud-brick walls, enabled them to expose and study the buildings and fortifications in a manner which had never before been attempted. In 1903 Andrae transferred his activities to the old Assyrian capital at Ashur, whose ruins he proceeded to explore in the same ingenious manner. Both excavators continued to deal in this way with buildings immediately beneath the surface; but Andrae went further. Finding that one particular temple showed signs of having been repeatedly rebuilt at successive epochs in the history of the city, he was able to examine the remains at each level in turn, down to an earliest shrine which he attributed to the Sumerians: a people about whom almost nothing was then known. But of even greater importance was the fact that, in doing so, he mastered the art of 'stratified' excavation: a practice whose understanding became the key to effective research in all Mesopotamian settings. In the third decade of the present century, when 'professional' archaeologists of other nationalities began to arrive in Iraq, these German methods were adopted by them to great advantage. Needless to say, they have been elaborated and improved upon as time has gone by; but they can still be seen to have provided the basis for a developing technique of excavation, without which the discoveries recorded in this book could not have been made.

Secondly it has proved necessary, where possible, to restrict my coverage geographically to the frontiers of Iraq. But, since these cannot be taken to correspond in all respects with the limits of ancient Mesopotamia, some exceptions have needed to be made. I was reminded, for instance, that when in 1933 a revised Antiquities Law denied to foreign excavators their share of the 'removable finds', certain French and British archaeological expeditions transferred their activities to sites beyond the Syrian frontier. Since this development led directly to A. Parrot's discovery of Mari and M. E. L. Mallowan's productive campaigns in the Khabur region, their subsequent finds could hardly be excluded from this record. Finally also, it was decided that, historically, my study must conclude with the Persian conquest of Mesopotamia in the 6th century BC because of limitations of space. The archaeology of the

Sasanian, Parthian and Islamic periods – well represented by recent excavations in Iraq – might even require a second volume.

It remains to be said that the book is primarily intended as an introduction to further reading. For this reason, some care has been taken in the bibliography, where more specialized subjects are concerned, to emphasize references to works which are most easily accessible, at the same time giving priority to those in English.

Finally, I am deeply grateful to David and Joan Oates for sparing the time to read my typescript and make suggestions. They are naturally absolved from all responsibility for errors and omissions.

Chapter One

The Land and its Rivers

The name 'Mesopotamia' is an archaism, traditionally more often applied to the setting of ancient history than to a clearly defined geographical area. The Greek translators of the Old Testament thought of it as the homeland of the Patriarch Abraham around the ancient city of Harran, which lies between the middle courses of the Euphrates and Tigris. Strabo also used it to denote only the northern part of the interfluvial lowland, and referred to the southern part as 'Babylonia'. It was Pliny who extended its limits to the Arabian Gulf, making it approximately the equivalent of modern Iraq. But the use of this Arabic name, meaning 'the Cliff', is also slightly equivocal. It was applied by the Arab conquerors only to Babylonia, and requires some explanation. If one approaches the

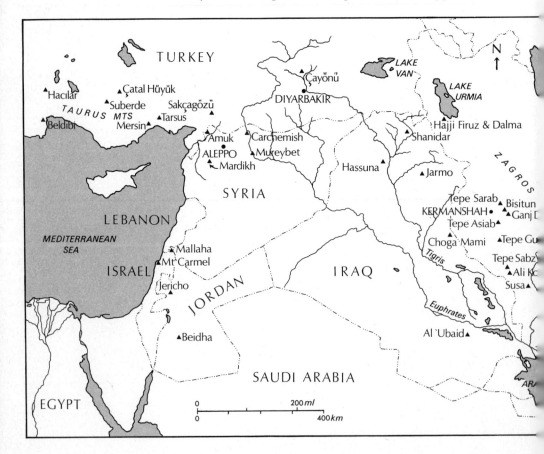

river valley, as they did in the 7th century A D, from the Hamad or high Arabian Desert to the west, one finds oneself suddenly on an escarpment about 30 m above the plain, looking out over the tree-tops of the Euphrates cultivation to that of the Tigris beyond and, in the remoter distance, to the thin line of the Zagros Mountains, which form the eastern limits of Mesopotamia. At Kufah, on the edge of the 'cliff', there is a shrine called *As-Safinah*, 'the Ship', marking the place where Moslems think that the Ark rested.

The Two Regions

Already, these few sentences will have drawn attention to the disparity between northern and southern Mesopotamia, and this will become more apparent if we now consider the geophysical character of the country, its geological formation, climatic peculiarities and all the other environmental elements which combined to make a distinctive pattern in the lives of its earliest inhabitants.[1] As a geographical unit – not yet satisfactorily defined – it consists of a broad and shallow depression, running northwestward from the head of the Gulf, of which geologically it is a prolongation. The allocation of its limits on either side present little difficulty. To the northeast they correspond to the diminishing foothills of the Iranian Mountains, to the southwest, to the

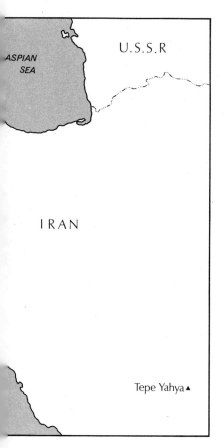

1 Map showing some Near Eastern sites mentioned in the text

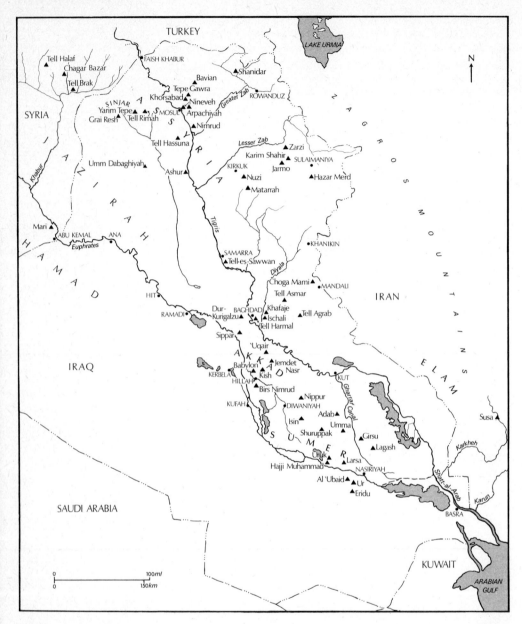

2 Map showing Mesopotamian
sites mentioned in the text

fringes of the tremendous desert which geologists call the 'Arabian
Plateau'. What is less apparent on an ordinary map is a horizontal
dividing-line, running approximately through Hit on the Euphrates and Samarra on the Tigris, which marks the uppermost
limit of the alluvial plain. To the north of this line, the rivers are
separated by a barren limestone plateau called Al-Jazirah, 'the
Island', which restricts the Euphrates to a narrow valley. The
Tigris, however, profiting from its eastern tributaries, passes
through a wide upland of undulating ploughland and pasture: the
productive countryside which was once Assyria. To the south of
the Hit–Samarra line, where the two rivers reach their common

delta, there is an entirely different landscape, a country which is the creation of two rivers. Here, from time immemorial, the Tigris and Euphrates have been depositing alluvium over a bed of sedimentary rock; and this has brought into being an immense and entirely flat plain, of which, from the point of view of potential fertility, there is no equivalent in the whole of the Near East.

The Coastline

Having reached this point in a description of Mesopotamia, we are confronted by one of the most outstanding problems regarding the geological formation of the southern delta. For it has been tempting in the past to consider that a great part of the present alluvial plain has, in the course of time, actually been reclaimed from the sea. Throughout the first half of the present century, the concensus of opinion among historians and geologists alike favoured this interpretation. It was clear of course that any recession of the coastline must have started at a very early period, since the upper two-thirds of the plain is dotted with ancient mounds representing the great cities of Sumer and Akkad, whose history goes back to the earliest human settlements in the 6th millennium BC. But here again there is a line across the country at about the latitude of Nasiriyah, southward of which no mounds are to be seen;[2] and between this line and the present coast there is a wide and sparsely populated region of marshes and lakes. It was supposed therefore that the Gulf, which had once perhaps extended over the whole of the delta, by early historic times had receded as far as the Nasiriyah line; the rivers Karkheh and Karun, flowing westward from Khuzistan, had built forward their own delta, closing off the head of the Gulf and converting it into a huge lake, which the Tigris and Euphrates had since partially contrived to fill in with their own burden of alluvium.

In 1952, however, this easily accepted hypothesis was demolished by two geologists[3] who, after a lengthy investigation with improved equipment, were able to show that the position of the coastline had in fact not varied greatly since the earliest historical times. Their initial observations confirmed the fact that very little of the alluvium carried by the two rivers ever reached the sea, and that the consequent rise in level of the southern plain could be calculated at almost 60 cm in every 100 years. No marshes or lakes in the south could therefore have continued to exist unless this infilling were countered by a corresponding subsidence of the basic rock beneath the delta. The occurrence and approximate rate of this subsidence they were then able to substantiate.

Archaeologists at first found all this a little difficult to reconcile with certain, fully established historical facts. The Sumerian city of Eridu for instance (Tell Abu Shahrain), which, according to Mesopotamian tradition, ranks as 'the oldest city in the world', is explicitly described by ancient writers as 'standing upon the shores of the sea'; and Ur, situated only a few miles away, had quays at which ocean-going vessels discharged their cargoes.[4] Both of these today are almost 100 miles from the seashore; so some acceptable compromise had to be arrived at. One small detail of archaeological evidence has helped to make this possible. In the temple at Eridu, fish-offerings were made to the god Enki, and among them were found bones of a sea-perch species which can only live in the brackish water of tidal estuaries. Perhaps the shallow depression in which Eridu lies was then part of the present lake system which, in its turn, connected by deep channels with the Euphrates estuary. Similarly, Ur would have been served by an ancient course of the Euphrates itself.

The Rivers

Perhaps one should now return to the character of the two rivers, on which the whole economy of the country depends.

The Tigris rises in a small lake (Hazar Gölü), about 100 miles west of Lake Van, and flows down easterly and southeasterly towards Nineveh and the Assyrian uplands. The Euphrates, which is a much longer river (1,780 as opposed to 1,150 miles), has two sources between Van and Erzerum. Both branches flow at first westward, to unite near Elâziğ, where the Keban dam now creates a lake. The main stream then follows a winding course southward, crossing from Turkey into Syria near the ancient city of Carchemish and so eventually into Iraq. At this point it is separated from the Tigris by some 250 miles of steppe country and the two do not draw together again until reaching the neighbourhood of Baghdad and Ramadi. Here the Euphrates is flowing at a level 9 m higher than the Tigris, and a sequence of ancient irrigation canals, draining from one river into the other, in earlier days made the belt of country between them extremely fertile. Beyond this, their streams separate again, and the plain is served by a more complicated system of canals and diversions.

In their passage through Iraq, before reaching the Hit-Samarra Line, the two rivers are flowing through beds which they have themselves cut into hard limestone and shale, so that their courses have hardly changed at all since prehistoric times. For this reason, cities like Carchemish, Nineveh, Nimrud and Ashur are still to be seen, standing as they always have beside the river banks. South of the same line the situation is quite different. Here rivers meander through the alluvial plain, frequently changing course and throwing off side-branches. Also, like all sediment-bearing rivers which flow at a very low gradient, they gradually raise the level of their own beds, so that, for the greater part of the time, they flow at a higher level than the surrounding plain. If, as inevitably happens on occasion, they overflow their banks in floodtime, great permanent lakes and swamps tend to be created, and occasionally the river changes its course. This explains why some of the great cities of the alluvial plains, which once stood beside the Tigris or Euphrates, are now huge desiccated ruinfields, far out in the unwatered desert.

This picture, of the two rivers running between semi-artificial banks rather higher than the surrounding plain, will serve to introduce the subject of irrigation in Mesopotamia, and its primary contribution to the country's economy. For this purpose, water has to be drawn off in such a way that the banks are not damaged or floods released. The system by which this is done is naturally dependent upon the seasonal regime of flooding, itself dictated by climatic conditions.

Climate and Irrigation

Where the climate of Mesopotamia is concerned, it is well to remember that, according to the findings of geologists, there has been no perceptible change since very early times. The country has summer temperatures ranging from 110 to 130 degrees in the shade, and eight months in the year without rainfall. By the end of the dry season, the rivers are reduced to sluggish brown meanders in a waste of dried mud. Then comes the winter, with pale sunshine at midday and cold nights, bringing intermittent rainstorms. But the rivers do not receive their full volume of water until the spring, when the melting snows in the Taurus and Zagros Mountains feed their tributaries. Then come the spring floods which, a generation ago, were considered practically uncontrollable and all through history represented an ominous threat to the inhabitants of the lower plain. Paradoxically also, this happens between April and June, which from an agricultural point of view is too late to water the main crop, usually harvested in April.

This was the climatic regime and seasonal fluctuation with which the ancient farmers of southern Mesopotamia were faced: rain in inadequate quantities at the wrong time; river water, also at the wrong time, and concentrated around the river-beds in almost unmanageable quantities. So in the end the country had to be supplied with water, simply by the contrivances of human ingenuity: a complex system of canals, reservoirs, dykes and regulator-sluices. This needed a great deal of organization and also a great deal of patience. The canals themselves very rapidly filled up their beds with silt, and consequently required repeated dredging. Then, as this process went on, the banks became too high to throw out the spoil, and consequently a new canal had to be dug, parallel to the first. Today, looking at the country from the air, one can see these extraordinary networks of canals, some of them with as many as three parallel channels. The overall impression is that of a single complicated pattern, and this extraordinary sight could lead to the illusion that all these channels have been in use at the same time. In fact, for a previous generation it created an historical picture of Iraq as one vast granary, whose fabulous prosperity survived until it was destroyed by the Mongols in the 13th century AD. This was of course a complete misconception, and a reverse situation has been revealed by agricultural research in recent years. One specialist investigation after another has added to the record of declining productivity, to be explained not by some isolated disaster in comparatively recent times, but by a longstanding and radical deficiency in the basic system of cultivation, going back to a surprisingly early period.[5]

Salinization

Next to the effects of flooding, the most disastrous danger to Mesopotamian agriculture generally has been the salinization of the soil and the consequent practice of what is known as 'extensive cultivation'. Travelling in Iraq today, one cannot fail to see the results of the mishandling of the soil. Wide areas, no longer cultivated, are covered with a white incrustation caused by over-prolonged cultivation. The water comes from the river with a strong saline content and, as it evaporates in the hot sun, the salt is deposited, ruining the fertility of the soil. When this happens to land in an 'extensive economy', the farmer simply transfers his cultivation to new ground and starts irrigating all over again. But an even more serious source of salinization is the rise in level of the ground-water as a result of prolonged irrigation, which pushes the salt up to the surface. Only efficient drainage can counteract this effect; but there is no inducement to go to such lengths as long as 'extensive' agriculture can be practised.

In the late 1950s much new light was thrown on this subject during the course of a study by Thorkild Jacobsen, one of the great Assyriologists of our time.[6] In a variety of cuneiform texts, he found unmistakeable references to the results of salinization, and could study its effects over a long period of history. Jacobsen was able for instance to gather that soil deterioration was particularly serious in the city state of Lagash, where salinization began in about 2400 BC and spread westward towards the Euphrates. A thousand years later, it had reached as far as Babylonia. He was able to calculate that wheat at first accounted for 16% of the total crop. Three centuries later, the percentage had dropped to 2% and, between 2000 and 1700 BC his reports contained no mention of wheat at all. Even the barley, whose greater toleration of salinization had long made it the principal crop, could now be seen to have a greatly reduced yield per acre in many southern districts. Information of this sort gave substance to a picture of diminishing agricultural prosperity, moving continually northward as a result of soil impoverishment in the south. This, he thought, could even account for the sequence of major changes in Mesopotamian history, by which political ascendancy transferred itself first from Sumer to Babylonia and later to the Assyrian kingdom in the north, where the problem of salinization did not arise. Nevertheless, there is much evidence to suggest that the diminution of agricultural productivity during these centuries was only a temporary affair. For Jacobsen and his colleagues, examining the Diyala area east of Baghdad, were able to detect already in the late 3rd millennium BC improved techniques for combating salinization, or at least delaying it. Long experience had resulted in the contrivance of better practices for extracting a maximum yield from the soil. A Sumerian agricultural manual of about 2100 BC even suggested the use of a primitive fallow system and elementary forms of drainage.

It seems therefore that, even if we discard Herodotus' exaggerated account of the harvest in Babylonia at his time, we should be justified in concluding that some sort of recovery took place in the agricultural productivity of southern Mesopotamia during the 2nd and early 1st millennia BC. Undoubtedly there must have been periodic disasters, due to flooding and unpredictable changes in the course of the river-beds. For that matter, the northern provinces too must occasionally have suffered, as they do today, from abnormal shortages of rainwater. But, taken as a whole, Mesopotamia may be said to have been a country rich in agricultural products and well able, during the greater part of its early history, to feed its own population. In addition, it has as a rule been able to barter its surplus cereals for stone, metals and other materials, which had to be obtained by trade with neighbouring countries. Nor was its agricultural productivity limited to grain alone. We learn from ancient texts that as early as the 3rd millennium BC southern Iraq had extensive palm-groves and that dates were already being cultivated by artificial pollination. In fact, flour and dates formed the staple diet of ancient Mesopotamians, though cattle and sheep were also bred and grazed in uncultivated areas, while rivers, lakes, canals and the sea produced fish in abundance. Fruit and vegetables were grown in gardens, sheltered from the sun by palm-trees and irrigated by very simple water-lift devices, of a sort which are still used in Iraq today.

Northern Iraq

We should now complete the geophysical picture of Mesopotamia with a short description of the northern uplands, beyond the Hit-Samarra line. To the west of the barren Al-Jazirah plateau, as we have said, the Euphrates irrigates a narrow strip of agricultural land, punctuated by small market-towns such as Hit, Rawa and Ani. North of the present Syrian border the cultivation widens out into a considerable agricultural province, dependent in early times on the purely Mesopotamian city called Mari. Beyond the Jazirah to the east, the Tigris and its tributaries, Greater Zab, Lesser Zab and Adhaim, form the agricultural arteries of the Assyrian countryside. This is undulating gravel steppe, with rich ploughland in the valleys and a plentiful supply of building stone. The rainfall in an average year is here sufficient to produce a single crop of wheat without irrigation. Only gardens and plantations are artificially watered from the rivers or wells. For much of the year the country is bare, but spring covers it with grass and flowers.[7]

Finally, enfolding Assyria to the east and north is the mountainous country known today as Iraqi Kurdistan: a crescent of highlands, with one corner resting on modern Khanikin and the other on the crossing of the Tigris at modern Faish Khabur, where the Syrian, Iraqi and Turkish frontiers now meet. The country here differs only in minor respects from the eastern *vilayets* of Turkey. There are stone-built villages, terraced into the hillsides, with tall Lombardy poplars and terraced cultivation including vines and tobacco. Large areas of mountainside are covered with scrub-oak or more rarely conifers, and there is much game below the snow-line in winter. We shall later be visiting this area (sometimes called the 'hilly-flanks' zone of Breasted's 'Fertile Crescent'), in search of the earliest human settlement.

After this general description of the background against which archaeological research in Mesopotamia has taken place, a word may be added regarding the historical relationship between its inhabitants and those of the countries by which it was enclosed on either side: of the Syrian desert, that is, and of the tribal areas of the Zagros Mountains. The Sumerians and Babylonians were essentially town-dwellers and peasant folk. Unlike the nomads of the desert and the migratory herdsmen of the Iranian uplands, they preferred to turn their backs on the open spaces and to concentrate upon a settled life among the amenities of the river valleys. In doing so, however, they were seldom free from the attentions of their less fortunate neighbours, whose practice was to interfere with their trade-routes and raid their outlying villages. As we shall see, long chapters in the history of their country are primarily concerned with the struggle to preserve their sedentary way of life and to protect themselves against these avaricious nomads. At times, the active hostility of such raiders became less significant than their peaceful penetration of river-valley society and their eventual establishment of a formidable majority. It was on such occasions that the hegemony of indigenous rulers could be replaced by an alien Dynasty-of-Akkad or by a largely Semitic line of Babylonian kings. These in their turn might in due course be replaced by a tribal invasion from the east or the intrusion of a Kassite aristocracy. Such events are the substance of Mesopotamian history.

Chapter Two

The Twilight of Neolithic Man

The subject with which this chapter is intended primarily to be concerned is the outcome of research into the origins and sociological development of peoples whose descendants comprised the inhabitants of Mesopotamia in historical times. The thread which connects them with humanity of Palaeolithic (Old Stone Age) times is still tenuous and controversial. It cannot however be ignored; and, since we have already set arbitrary limits to the geographical area with which we are dealing, it would be wrong to neglect the evidence that has been found within those frontiers of human occupation preceding the end of the Old Stone Age. Naturally this subject merges with, or rather emerges from, the geological history of southwestern Asia. Yet it is only with its terminal or most recent phases that we need be concerned. It is the order of these phases or the pattern which they are thought to have created which we should perhaps first endeavour to recollect.

The Old Stone Age

The Palaeolithic period then, which saw the evolution of man from ape-like ancestry to the true semblance of *Homo sapiens*, corresponds roughly with the Pleistocene or 'most recent' phase in geological history. It started over 2,000,000 years ago and ended between 20,000 and 12,000 years ago. It was during this period that, at least four times in succession, huge glaciers which were an extension of the polar ice-cap crept southward to cover large parts of Eurasia and North America.[8] The earliest phase of the Old Stone Age, the Lower Palaeolithic, extends from well before 2,000,000 years ago to about 80,000 years ago. In Europe during the latter part of this long era, the first evidence is found of primitive cultures (Abbevillian, Clactonian and Acheulian), material remains of creatures already related to the forebears of modern man. With the Middle Palaeolithic (80,000–30,000 years ago) we shall be more closely concerned in our present context, since in northern Iraq it is represented by cave-occupations of the Mousterian period, and also by human remains which include the bones of Neanderthal man, that strange, extinct offshoot from the tree of human heredity.

The Upper Palaeolithic (30,000–12,000 years ago) will also be of great interest to us here. In Iraqi Kurdistan, as in other parts of the Near East, its remains have been closely studied whenever an opportunity occurred, because they constitute a preface to the great change which took place at the end of the Pleistocene epoch. The phases corresponding to the Aurignacian and Gravettian in Europe,

Table I

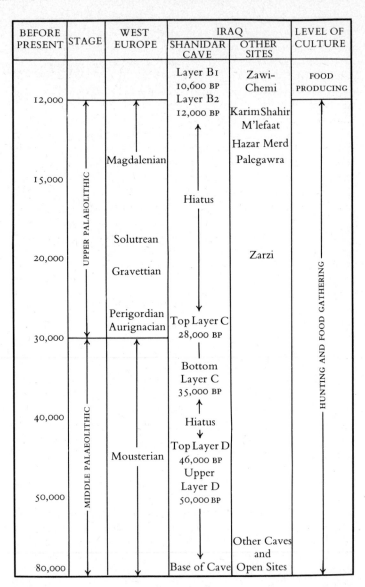

BEFORE PRESENT	STAGE	WEST EUROPE	IRAQ SHANIDAR CAVE	IRAQ OTHER SITES	LEVEL OF CULTURE
			Layer B1 10,600 BP	Zawi-Chemi	FOOD PRODUCING
12,000			Layer B2 12,000 BP	KarimShahir M'lefaat	
				Hazar Merd Palegawra	
15,000		Magdalenian	Hiatus		
20,000		Solutrean		Zarzi	
		Gravettian			
30,000		Perigordian Aurignacian	Top Layer C 28,000 BP		
			Bottom Layer C 35,000 BP		
40,000			Hiatus		
		Mousterian	Top Layer D 46,000 BP Upper Layer D		
50,000			50,000 BP		
				Other Caves and Open Sites	
80,000			Base of Cave		

(UPPER PALAEOLITHIC / MIDDLE PALAEOLITHIC in Stage column; HUNTING AND FOOD GATHERING in Level of Culture column)

Table I Generalized scheme for the Palaeolithic in Europe and the Near East. (After Solecki, 1971)

represented by discoveries on Mount Carmel in Palestine and in Iran at sites ranging from the Zagros Mountains to Lake Urmia, are of interest in themselves, as showing the geographical distribution of these cultures; but the terminal or transitional stage which follows has even greater significance, in that it bridges the gap between the study of man's imperfectly developed ancestors and the fuller revelation of *Homo sapiens* as we know him today, profiting as we may from ampler evidence of his early accomplishments and aspirations. The chronology of this final phase of the Palaeolithic is still a little uncertain. Its terminal limit, however, must be associated with the appearance of the first farming communities at the beginning of the Neolithic period, soon after 10,000 BC.

It is a little difficult to imagine the geological and climatic changes which took place in Western Asia during the Pleistocene, when early man made his appearance for the first time. Some traces of periodic glaciation have been recognized in the high mountains of Anatolia and, to a lesser extent, in western Iran; yet it has become apparent that the encroaching ice-sheet itself did not reach as far as the Near East. On the contrary, throughout most of the Ice Age, moist air from the Mediterranean blew around the lower contours of the mountains in an easterly and southeasterly direction, creating grassy steppes and uplands, which benefited from a comparatively temperate and uniform climate. For the greater part of the time, therefore, the southward-facing lower slopes of the Taurus and Zagros (what has been called the 'upper piedmont zone of foothills and intermontane valleys'), offered good hunting and favourable climatic conditions for Palaeolithic cave-dwellers. It may accordingly have been no great surprise for Old World prehistorians to discover traces of their flint industries in the caves of Iraqi Kurdistan, or for that matter in Palestine, southwest Anatolia or northwest Iran. Nor need it have seemed strange that the cultures of such hunters proved to have affinities with those already recognized in Europe. For all these areas corresponded to a geographical line of migration, which may have been more obvious in Pleistocene times than it is today. Speaking of changes in the inland seas of western Asia at this time, one authority suggests for instance that, during the last glacial age, the accumulation of pluvial waters raised the Caspian Sea something like 76 m above its present level. The Black Sea by contrast was reduced to a brackish lake, cut off from the Mediterranean by a dry Bosphorus, and so leaving an easy connection for early man between Europe and Asia. Further east, however, the Caspian and vast swamps around the Aral Sea inhibited his movements.[9]

Garrod and Solecki

The first Palaeolithic discoveries in northern Iraq were made as early as 1928 by Dorothy A. E. Garrod, whose name afterwards became well known for her more prolonged excavations on Mt Carmel. Her first sounding was made in a cave called Zarzi, near *3* the headwaters of the Lesser Zab river, about 20 miles north of Sulaimaniya. She found undisturbed deposits corresponding to the Gravettian culture in Europe, and Zarzi became the type-site for material of that period.

Garrod's second experiment was in a cave nearer to Sulaimaniya called Hazar Merd, where a brief sounding revealed an earlier flint industry which could be identified as Mousterian, partly by the presence of characteristic unifacial points and scrapers. Garrod was also able to publish a list of contemporary animal remains, identified for her by her colleague Dorothea Blake.[10] After her departure for Palestine, Palaeolithic research in Iraq remained in abeyance until 1949, when a succession of American scholars took up the thread of her investigations. Most successful of all was the work of Ralph S. Solecki in the cave called Shanidar, which he selected from a numerous group on the southern flank of the

3 Map showing major
Palaeolithic sites in northern Iraq

Baradost mountain range, above Rowanduz. His sounding there reached a depth of 13.7 m, and the earliest sequence of occupations (level D) he was able to attribute to a Mousterian phase, with artifacts 'characterising a predominantly flake culture, as opposed to the blade culture of the Upper Palaeolithic (level C) horizon'. But it was here also that, between the years 1953 and 1957, he had the great good fortune to uncover the remains of four human skeletons, unmistakably exhibiting the characteristics of Neanderthal man.[11]

In western Iran, material comparable to that found by Solecki at Shanidar had already been reported by Carleton Coon, an anthropologist from Pennsylvania, in 1949. Following the supposed line of migration we have already mentioned, Coon had come upon a cave site at Bisitun, near Kermanshah, with traces of a Mousterian industry similar to that found at Hazar Merd. He also claimed to have discovered human skeletal material which he described as 'characteristically Neanderthaloid'. Similar parallels were later found by Turkish archaeologists at Beldibi and elsewhere, near the Mediterranean coast of Anatolia; so the pattern of diffusion began to be better defined.

It appears that the two final phases of the Late Palaeolithic in Europe, the Solutrean and the Magdalenian, which accounted among other things for most of the famous rock-paintings of western France, did not reach the Near East. Garrod's assemblage of late Aurignacian or 'extended Gravettian' from Zarzi accordingly came to be regarded as representing the terminal phase of the Old Stone Age in Iraq. Since it already comprised some features of the transitional period which followed, it is perhaps worth examining a little more closely.

American Excavators in Kurdistan

The rather limited range of Garrod's finds at Zarzi were conveniently supplemented by those from a cave at Palegawra, some miles to the southeast, excavated by H. E. Wright and Bruce Howe in 1950, and the combined results consequently give a fuller picture. One important innovation is the use of microlithic flints, a newly refined blade industry which included the first chipped stone arrowheads, in addition to a wide variety of microlithic bladelets, scrapers and burins. Among other stone implements was a polished celt, fragments of querns for grinding and some obsidian (volcanic glass), for which the nearest source would have been the area of Lake Van in eastern Anatolia. There were also beads and pendants of shell. Animal bones showed that the onager or wild ass was the most commonly hunted species; but wild goats, sheep, cattle and gazelle also indicated the nature of the terrain in which 'Baradostian Man' lived. Wood remains included oak, tamarisk, poplar and conifer, all of which are to be found in Kurdistan today. They also provided a convenient radiocarbon date, between 13,060 and 14,210 years ago. The cultural situation envisaged from all this evidence could therefore be treated as a point of departure for the intensified investigation which now took place, of the transition from a Palaeolithic way of life to the vastly changed economy of the Early Neolithic.

It will now be important to recollect the state of this enquiry during the fifth decade of the present century, when R. J. Braidwood of Chicago initiated the Iraq-Jarmo project, supported by an inter-disciplinary team of specialists, whose composition was in itself an innovation.[12] In Iraq at that time, archaeologists of various nationalities had for many years been devoting themselves to the study of pre-Sumerian cultures and the origins of Mesopotamian civilization. Following Leonard Woolley's discovery of primitive marsh-dwellers at the site called Al 'Ubaid and his deep sounding in the prehistoric levels at Ur-of-the-Chaldees, his younger colleague, M. E. L. Mallowan, had made an even deeper penetration beneath the Küyünjik mound at Nineveh, and had recognized a sequence of occupations, throughout which the smelting of copper appeared to have been understood and increasingly practised. It was not however until 1943 that an Iraq Government excavation at Hassuna, on the western periphery of the Assyrian uplands, revealed in its deepest level a nomadic camp-site, which could be regarded stratigraphically as Late Neolithic. The period of some five millennia which separated these remains from the terminal Palaeolithic horizon at Zarzi and Palegawra represented a hiatus in the prehistoric sequence, whose completion became the purpose of Braidwood's expedition during the 1950s.

Braidwood's enterprise in Kurdistan made a number of worthwhile contributions to the solution of the problem in hand. But today it must be considered in terms of the very plentiful information since accumulated from similar investigations in all parts of the Near East. For the moment, therefore, our review cannot be confined to Iraq alone. We must rather examine the pattern created by discoveries at a score or more of ancient sites in the Levant, western Anatolia and Iran. First, however, a word should be said about the term 'Neolithic Revolution', first used by the doyen of British prehistorians, Gordon Childe.

Childe was primarily concerned with the transition from hunting and food-gathering to a food-producing economy. In his time (*c.* 1927 onwards) 'Neolithic' had already long been accepted as a name for the phase in human development during which this change took place. He himself qualified the additional word 'Revolution' by explaining that it should not of course imply any violent upheaval, but 'the culmination of sudden progressive change in the economic structure and social organisation of communities. . .'.[13] Childe accepted the two existing criteria for the Neolithic development – namely, the practice of agriculture and the domestication of animals. He also saw the manufacture of pottery as a hallmark of the period; although the more recent discovery of pre-ceramic food-producing cultures has shown this to be too broad a generalization, in northern Syria at least pottery-making and the collection of wild cereals do seem to have coincided. Yet the most recent assessments of the great 'revolution' have in fact come to suggest an evolutionary rather than a revolutionary process of change, one that was neither rapid in time nor geographically uniform. It has been pointed out, for instance, that 'the earliest species of domesticated animals and plants do not appear in one particular area or at one point of time, but rather at different sites at different times'. Conclusions like these have tended to refute in turn theories propounded by at least one of Childe's successors in the Neolithic field. Braidwood, over a long period, had attempted to define geographically a 'Natural Habitat Zone', in which plant and animal domestication took place, forming a crescent around the 'hilly flanks' of the Zagros and Taurus Mountains with its western point on the Mediterranean. Since many newly discovered sites, showing Neolithic communities practising agriculture and herdsmanship, plainly lie outside this 'zone', this concept has also had to be revised.

The State of Neolithic Research

We should now briefly summarize those excavations in countries of the Near East other than Iraq which have, in the past years, made major contributions to our knowledge of Neolithic cultures and their immediate antecedents. In doing so, we should perhaps start with the Levant where, as long ago as 1928, settlements were found showing the earliest evidence of food production. And here once more we return to the work of Dorothy Garrod, this time in the Wadi-al-Natuf on Mt Carmel. Her 'Natufian' culture, there

BC	LEVANT	ANATOLIA OTHER SITES	ANATOLIA MERSIN	IRAN
2500				Susa Ⓓ a–c
3000			Bronze Age	Susa Ⓒ c, b, a
3000			Uruk-'Ubaid	
3500			'Ubaid XI–XV	Susa Ⓑ
4000	Jericho			Susa Ⓐ (Old Susa I)
4500	PNB / PNA		Fortress XVI	Susiana e
5000	GAP	Hacilar I–IX	Halaf XVII–XIX	Susiana a–d
6000	Beidha / PPNB	Çatal Hüyük O–XII	'Neolithic'	Guran
7000	PPNA	Çayönü		
8000		Mureybet (Syria)		Asiab

Table II Generalized chronology for sites in the Levant, Anatolia and Iran

recognized in caves and shelters, has since served as a point-of-departure for the identification of phases and sub-phases in Neolithic development. But it was also in itself a remarkable revelation of a new way of life, departing in important respects from that of the terminal Palaeolithic which preceded it. The microlithic flint industry was of a sort at that time provisionally described as 'Mesolithic'. Hunting and fishing were the main sources of food; but flint sickle-blades, showing evidence of use, pointed to the reaping of wild wheat or barley. Craftsmanship extended to the carving of animal figures and this was applied to the handles of bone hafts in which the blades were set. Personal ornaments were also found, including headdresses of dentalia and necklaces. Other sites in the Levant, especially Eynan (Ain Mallaha), and Jericho described below, have more recently added new features of this comparatively sophisticated culture, including primitive architecture and evidence of organized religion. In the words of one authority, the Natufians 'founded the earliest permanent settlements in the world'.

JORDAN AND THE LEVANT

At Jericho in Jordan, where the deepest levels of the great 'oasis' city-mound were excavated with such sensational results by Kathleen M. Kenyon between 1952 and 1958, there were two earliest occupations, termed respectively 'Mesolithic' and 'Proto-Neolithic', both corresponding to the Natufian period elsewhere. Kenyon describes the earliest occupants (in about 9000 BC) as hunters and food-gatherers, but a conspicuous feature of their settlement was a stone-built shrine or sanctuary. The Proto-Neolithic was succeeded by two more productive phases, referred to as Pre-Pottery Neolithic (PPN) 'A' and 'B'. The first of these shows a rapid advance in the organization of a communal society. There are circular or rectangular houses, now built of sun-dried bricks whose shape is described as 'hog-backed'. The town, which now covered an area of some 10 acres, was defended by a massive stone wall with a circular tower measuring over 12 m in diameter, and a rock-cut ditch. Understandably, Kenyon conjectured that a defensive system of this sort must imply a surprising degree of social solidarity and leadership: an idea supported by the evidence of organized agriculture and a far-reaching trade in commodities such as obsidian. Radiocarbon dates for this period fall between 8350 and 6770 BC.

The PPNB stage at Jericho, like its predecessor, must have lasted a long period of time, since no less than twenty-six structural phases were distinguished. During this phase, domestic architecture was greatly improved, each house having large intercommunicating rooms. Walls were still of curiously shaped mud-bricks, the floors being carefully paved with gypsum plaster and in some cases covered with reed matting. Again, one symmetrically planned building was thought by Kenyon to be a temple. But the most curious artistic feature of this period were the human skulls, with faces skilfully remodelled in plaster and inlaid eyes. No less than ten of these were found, suggesting some cultic practice for the posthumous commemoration of individuals. For the rest, there

4

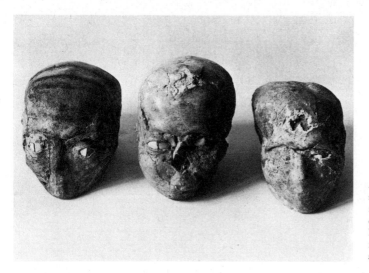

4 Three examples of human skulls, with features carefully modelled in plaster and inlaid eyes of shell, found in the PPNB levels at Jericho (7th millennium BC), perhaps implying a form of ancestor worship

were the bones of wild animals, among which the gazelle was preponderant, and of goats which were plainly domesticated. The carbonized remains of food-grains were also found, the emmer wheat of the previous period having now largely been replaced by einkorn. The Pottery Neolithic phase, which preceded the temporary abandonment of the Jericho settlement, was distinguished as its name implies by the appearance of plain or clumsily painted ceramics, of a sort which are better represented at other sites.

At Jericho, Kenyon's excavation had been hampered to some extent by the limited area of her deep sounding. Soon afterwards, Diana Kirkbride (Mrs Hans Helbaek) had the good fortune to discover a site on the banks of a dry *wadi* to the north of Petra, where the buildings of a Neolithic settlement were accessible directly beneath the surface. At Beidha (Seyl Ahlat) she excavated a wide area during the years between 1958 and 1967, revealing an attractively detailed picture of primitive village life. After a short occupation in the early Natufian period, the site was temporarily deserted and then reoccupied in about 7000 BC by a people corresponding to the later Pre-Pottery inhabitants of Jericho. Their houses, developing from round to rectangular shapes, were constructed with heavily built, dry-stone walling and the rooms repeatedly plastered. Clusters of small rooms were later replaced by larger, single compartments with plastered walls, and pavements a little below ground-level were decorated with lines of coloured paint. A baker's and a butcher's shop were recognized and there was other evidence suggesting a precocious development of specialized trades. Stone implements were variously contrived for every conceivable purpose, while toys or cult-objects were modelled in clay.

The evidence of sites like these in Jordan and the coastal Levant has been supplemented by new and impressive exposures in inland Syria, as yet incompletely published. The implications of at least one have been disconcerting. At Mureybet, 50 miles southeast of Aleppo, M. van Loon and J. Cauvin have excavated a settlement

5 Excavations at Beidha, near Petra, exposing the stone-built houses of a settlement founded in Natufian times, but reoccupied from about 7000 BC onwards by a characteristically Neolithic people

of the 9th millennium BC, where a people living in substantially built clay houses already cultivated einkorn and made pottery (see D. and J. Oates, 1976, p. 74 and *passim*.)

ANATOLIA

If we must now choose from a dozen relevant excavations in modern Turkey, one in particular immediately suggests itself as being likely to provide the Anatolian equivalent of the Pre-Pottery Neolithic at Jericho. This is Çayönü, in the Diyarbakir area, at which Braidwood has more recently been collaborating with a Turkish scholar, Halet Çambel. The material remains here can now be regarded as characteristic of a developing society in its 'aceramic' stage, with an adequate knowledge of agriculture and the exploitation of domestic animals. But it has two unusual characteristics, one of which is architectural. During the second of four phases, the building remains consist of stone foundations or 'sleeper-walls', forming a regular 'grill' with spaces between too small for any purpose other than storage;[14] while, in the third phase, an extraordinary concrete floor was found, decorated in the manner of a 'terrazzo' pavement with a pattern of stone chippings, ground to a smooth surface. A second and equally surprising innovation was the manufacture of simple implements by cold-hammering native copper – the earliest use of metal yet known.

The Çayönü site represents 1000 years of occupation (*c.* 7500 to 6500 BC), immediately preceding the earliest levels of James Mellaart's now-famous settlement at Çatal Hüyük on the Konya Plain, where the record is prolonged through a further 800 or 900 years of spectacular progress and invention.[15]

It would be out of place here to describe in detail the many aspects of the Çatal Hüyük settlement, so well published and publicized in recent years. A township covering more than 15 acres is composed of brick-built houses, arranged contiguously like a honeycomb and entered by ladders from the communal roof-space. Of unique interest are buildings apparently associated with a religious cult, their walls decorated with coloured murals, recalling the cave-paintings of an earlier era, and with the heads or horns of animals. Not only are pottery vessels in general use, but their prototypes in wood or basketwork have survived – no less well preserved than the fragments of woven fabrics which accompany them. Human and animals figures are carved in stone or modelled in clay, weapons and implements fashioned from delicately shaped cores of flint or obsidian. Hunting still takes its place as an important occupation, but the economy is now mainly sustained by agriculture, with a surprising variety of food-plants under cultivation and indications that even irrigation was beginning.

6 The restored interior of a shrine-room in the Neolithic township of Çatal Hüyük, near Konya in Anatolia, ornamented with mural paintings of bulls and a stag-hunt (*c.* 5800 BC). (After Mellaart, 1967)

One would be reluctant to believe that this crescendo of cultural advancement was an isolated phenomenon, unparallelled at this time in other parts of the Near East. Yet, for the present this appears to be the case, and there is little evidence of its having served to accelerate the tempo of development in Neolithic societies elsewhere. Indeed, during the Late Neolithic phase which followed, many of its attainments seem to have been forgotten, and signs are apparent of renewed intellectual inertia. In Turkey, this period is well represented in the deeper levels of sites like Hacılar, Sakçagözü, Mersin and Tarsus, where stone-built houses are associated with characteristic black- or brown-burnished pottery and finely made obsidian artifacts. But its culture seems no more than a prelude to that of the more advanced Chalcolithic period that followed, about which there will be much to say when we return to Mesopotamia.

IRAN

For the moment, however, a few words must finally be said about contemporary developments in Iran. For this purpose we should first mention the particular areas in which discoveries have been made and note their significantly wide distribution. The search for prehistoric origins of Iranian culture hardly began until the 1950s and many contributory discoveries have therefore been made too recently yet to be recorded in the form of definitive publications. An admirable summary published by P. Singh draws mainly on preliminary communications; but in the present context it can be highly recommended. Singh is able to distinguish geographically three clusters of newly discovered sites, which have produced 'cultural assemblages' relevant to the Neolithic enquiry.[16] The first is in the river valleys to the south and east of Kermanshah; the second in the plain of Khuzistan, within a 50-mile radius of Susa, while the third lies to the south and southwest of Lake Reza'iyeh (Urmia) in Azarbaijan. In each of these areas major and minor excavations have taken place, resulting in discoveries which amplify rather than supplement those we have already referred to in Anatolia and the Levant.

Here are some details of primary sites in the above groupings and their contributions to the sequence of Neolithic developments.

First, in the Kermanshah group, Tepe Asiab contains 'the vestige of a semi-permanent settlement of food collectors . . . on the verge of achieving food-production' (estimated date 10,000–7000 BC). A further phase of the early food-collecting culture is seen at Tepe Sarab, where there is still no mud-walled architecture, though the manufacture of pottery, plain and painted, is now in evidence. Another use of baked clay at this site is for various forms of figurine, one of which, known as the 'Sarab Venus', shows particularly skilful modelling. The goat is now domesticated, but there is no proof of the presence of cereals (earliest carbon date 6000 BC). The first signs of solid architecture are found at Ganj Dareh Tepe: mud-brick, rectilinear houses of the 'cluster-type', built against each other, with walls of long plano-convex bricks laid in mortar. The flint industry represents a blade-flake tradition and a total absence of obsidian is still evident. Signs of polishing on some blades suggest the harvesting of grain. Clay figurines already include a 'stalky-headed' type which we shall meet with again in a later setting. (Time bracket of this site, 7300–6900 BC). The 'most carefully excavated site' in this group is Tepe Guran, which again illustrates 'transition from the hut to house and from aceramic to the ceramic stage'. Plain pottery appears at the fourth occupation level and painted or burnished wares later. The stone industry now includes obsidian and, for the first time, marble is used for making vessels by grinding. A notable architectural feature is the making of pavements of feldspar laid in clay which is coloured with red ochre. (Neolithic culture dated 6500–5500 BC).

The second group of sites, in the Deh Luran plain west of Susiana, also creates a sequence of cultural phases, now distinguished by site-names. The first two phases (Bus Mordeh and Ali Kosh), are aceramic, but pottery appears in the third (Jaffar) phase. Together they show that 'the era of early dry farming and caprine domestication, starting from around 7000 BC, was gradually succeeded and replaced by the era of irrigation farming and cattle domestication, which began around 5000 BC'.

The third group of early village cultures, represented by sites such as Hajji Firuz, Dalma and Pisdeli in southwest Azarbaijan, are of a more-nearly Chalcolithic type and have less relevance in the present context. The same may be said of Tepe Yahya, halfway between Kirman and Bandar Abbas, whose remote situation alone serves to emphasize the extended geographical situation of such sites, and may indicate a direction for further exploration.[17]

The Iraq-Jarmo Project

Having attempted a conspectus of major contributions to the Neolithic enquiry, made over a quarter-century by workers in three important areas of western Asia, we are now in a position to appraise the results of similar operations in northern Mesopotamia. For this purpose, we should return to the Iraq-Jarmo project, initiated by Braidwood in the 1950s; and if in doing so we discover that some of his conclusions have in the meanwhile been superseded, we should remember in extenuation the pioneer character of his work at that time.

The results of operations at two of Braidwood's sites may be selected, as taking a modest place in the sequence of cultural developments now so well documented elsewhere. One of these is the open site called Karim Shahir, to the north of Chemchemal in the Kirkuk *Liwa*. This appears to have been one of several sites in the neighbourhood, occupied only as a 'seasonal camp', at a time imprecisely fixed (perhaps contemporary with Kenyon's 'Mesolithic' at Jericho), when the movement from caves and shelters to open settings was becoming more general. Hunting and fishing were the main sources of food and there were no permanent dwellings. Animals were not yet domesticated, and sickle-blades were thought only to have been used in reaping reeds for building purposes. Polished-stone celts and simple clay figurines were among the few positive criteria of emancipation from a Palaeolithic way of life. There is a long gap in time between Karim Shahir and the site of Jarmo itself, where Braidwood excavated on a larger scale between 1948 and 1955. The radiocarbon dates are unsatisfactory; but, in modern charts of chronology, Jarmo occupies a short period before and after the beginning of PPNB at Jericho, with a mean date of about 6750 BC. In Braidwood's terminology, it still takes its place in the category called 'Primary Effective Village Farming Communities'.[18]

The village itself occupied about 3 acres, on an eroded shoulder 7 of conglomerate, overlooking a deep, dry *wadi*. In a total deposit of 7.6 m there were twelve building levels with walls of *pisé* (slabs of clay superimposed on each other), latterly on stone foundations.

Pottery was found in the upper third of these strata, but there were 'baked-in-place' floor-basins throughout. The implications of flint or stone implements for reaping or grinding were confirmed by the presence of food-grains, including emmer wheat and two-row barley. A flint industry comprised both blades and microliths, with a good deal of obsidian from Lake Van in use.

The pottery at Jarmo presented something of an enigma. Rather well-made stone jars in the deeper levels gave way in mid-occupation to a range of clay vessels, competently finished with a burnished slip or painted with simple designs; but their quality seemed to deteriorate nearer to the surface. Braidwood had expected, through this medium, to establish a link with the earliest pottery at Hassuna. In this however he was unsuccessful and the most recent assessment of his painted wares[19] finds a parallel with those at Tepe Guran (one of the best published sites in the Kermanshah group of Iran), thus suggesting an association with the Zagros Mountains, rather than the Mesopotamian lowlands.

34

Braidwood's dating of Jarmo may in fact be taken to suggest a point in time for the abandonment of his settlement near the end of the Late Neolithic elsewhere. If so, the earliest evolution of the Hassuna culture should be sought in the lowlands themselves, where sites like Umm Dabaghiyah and Tell-es-Sawwan already show signs of enlightenment. Here, however, the Neolithic phase merges so amorphously with that until recently called the 'Chalcolithic', that it may better be dealt with in another chapter.

Before leaving Braidwood's site, there is something further to be said about his findings.

We have earlier mentioned the inter-disciplinary element in the group of research-workers which he brought to Iraq in the 1950s. For the first time in the Near East, geologists and climatologists, together with specialists in flora and fauna, were to be found collaborating with archaeologists in their search for the environmental background of ancient man. From their reports, a picture emerged of an ecological situation remarkably different from that of the present day. The contrast which they have revealed between 'then' and 'now' in the physical aspect of northern Iraq is one outstanding result of their work.

As Braidwood says,

During the period which has elapsed since Jarmo was a village, *man* has been the pre-eminent environmental influence, and the effects of his handiwork are to be seen throughout the Near East. In general the role of man, of his agriculture and of his flocks has been destructive, and this without any one man wishing to be destructive.

Here is his description of the countryside in earlier times:

There is much evidence that from central Palestine, round through Syria into eastern Iraq, from late prehistoric into historic times, there stretched a nearly continuous mountain and foothill woodland, in part dense and in part open and park-like. At the higher levels the winter precipitation was heavy; the trees large, thick and spreading and the undergrowth a tangled mass. Here certainly was the primeval forest, limited now to a few steep mountain-sides far from inhabited villages. At lower altitudes we visualise a more open type of deciduous forest, predominantly of oak. . . .

As for the fauna of that time, the evidence from Jarmo suggests a site from which men hunted in the grasslands, in the surrounding woodlands and in the denser forest of the higher ridges. Of the animals whose bones appeared in the excavations, some, such as wild cattle, are entirely extinct. Others such as deer, leopard and bear, dependent on the woodlands, are missing now that the trees are gone. The wild pig, wolf and fox survive in spite of continual hunting, so do the wild goat and gazelle. 'Today', Braidwood says,

throughout much of the once-wooded plain and foothill area of the Chemchemal valley, hardly a shrub remains. The scrub-oak is rarely allowed to reach more than six feet in height before it is hacked away by the charcoal-burners. With the trees and the bush-cover gone, and the grass eaten down to its roots each spring, the soil has largely gone too to silt up the rivers. . . . In winter it washes away on every slope almost as fast as it can form and the rains rage off the land in chocolate torrents.[20]

Here then is the source of the alluvium which created the Mesopotamian plain.

BC	PERIOD		UR	URUK	ERIDU	'UBAID	NIPPUR	KISH	'UQAIR	DIYALA SITES		
										ASMAR	KHAFAJE	AGRAB
	Akkadian		Graves				Buildings	Monument Z		Akkadian Palace	Buildings	Houses
2500	Early Dynastic	IIIb	First Dynasty Royal Tombs	Buildings	Temenos Survives Palaces	Graves Nin-Khursag Temple	Inanna Temple V–VI	Cemetery A	Graves	Single Shrine Temple	Oval Temple III	Shara Temple
		IIIa				Oval Terrace	VII	Palace A Ziggurat			II	
2750		II	Enmerkar				VIII	Houses		Square Temple	Oval Temple I	
		I	Seal Impressions			Earlier Temples	IX–XI	Houses	Sounding Y	Archaic Temple	Sin Temple VI–VII / VIII–IX / X	I–V
3000	Jemdet Nasr		Soundings	White Temple / III	Earlier Temples		XII–XIV		Chapel	Chapel	Sin Temple I–V	
	Late Uruk			Anu Area / Sounding (Eanna) Buildings / IV & V	Temples I–II Temenos Raised	?	XV–XVI		Painted Temple			
3250	Early Uruk			VI–XIV	III–V Walled Temenos		XVII–XX		Earlier Temples ?			
3500	'Ubaid (4)			XV–XVIII / ?	VI–VII Cemetery	Settlement			Settlement			
4000	'Ubaid (3)		Ur/Al 'Ubaid 1, 2 & 3		Temples VIII–XI	?			?			
4500	'Ubaid (2) (Hajji Muhammad)				Levels XII–XIV Hajji Muhammad							
					No Building							
5000	'Ubaid (1) (Eridu)				Temples XV–XVIII Eridu Ware							

Table III Chronology for sites in southern Mesopotamia

Chapter Three

The Threshold of Written History

We must now return to the alluvial plain of southern Mesopotamia and the marshland which separates it from the head of the Persian Gulf in order to follow successive stages in the evolution of Sumerian civilization. In that area, we shall find ourselves dealing with a period of time whose beginning at least is easy to define because it corresponds to the earliest pre-Sumerian settlement of which traces have yet been found, dating from a little before 5000 B C. It ends in about 2900 B C with the foundation of the Sumerian dynasties and the first written references to the names of kings who are now shown to have been historical characters. In the strictest sense, the period could therefore be called prehistoric; but since its final phases cover the earliest use of writing and other major inventions of the Sumerians, the word has seemed inappropriate and other labels have had to be found for the chronological stages in its development.

The Sequence of Discoveries

As early as 1929, among excavators in Mesopotamia, the practice was adopted of naming sub-periods after the sites at which they were first recognized. Later some attempt was made to subdivide or re-group them under names more culturally meaningful. But since by this time the sequence had become a subject for debate among archaeologists of several nationalities, each with his own conception of the stratigraphic implications, a point had been reached where no single system of terminology seemed to be universally accepted. With this difficulty in view, it may be well here first to summarize the original discoveries in their chronological order.

AL 'UBAID

When excavations were resumed in Iraq after the First World War, little was known about the Sumerians and even less about their antecedents. The first indication of prehistoric occupation in the south was found by Leonard Woolley at a small site called Al 'Ubaid, 4 miles to the west of Ur, where H. R. Hall had previously located the brick platform on which a Sumerian temple had once stood. Woolley noticed, as Hall had done, that another part of the mound was covered with sherds of painted pottery and, during a brief excavation there, he was able to associate them with the remains of reed-built houses, which for him created a picture of primitive settlers 'on an island in the marshes'. Later in a deep sounding which he made in the great city-mound of Ur itself, he found the same painted pottery, underlying the Sumerian remains, in a sequence of occupation-levels which suggested that it had been in use over a long period of time. Stylistically he was able to divide this series into three phases, though the terms by which he described them have since been superseded by more recent discoveries.

WARKA

While in the 1920s Woolley was making these discoveries, excavators of other nationalities were experimenting with similar soundings beneath Sumerian cities, of which the most significant was that undertaken by the German Oriental Society under N. Nöldeke and J. Jordan in the great temple-precinct of Eanna at Uruk (modern Warka).[21] Here, eighteen 'archaic' occupation-levels were identified, of which the five earliest (XVIII–XIII) produced pottery corresponding to Woolley's 'Ur 'Ubaid' assemblage. After a short transitional period (XIV–XII), these painted wares disappeared and were replaced by a totally different pottery, often wheel-made and without ornament, except for an occasional red or grey 'slip' with a burnished surface. Apart from the complete repertory of new shapes that now appeared, another notable change could be seen in the complete absence of small objects (such as terracotta figurines, baked-clay sickles and nail-shaped wall-plugs), which had accompanied the painted wares both here and at Ur. Phenomena such as these could be taken to reflect some ethnic change in the city's population.

From level V upwards in the Eanna stratification at Warka, the Germans soon had less reason to rely on the findings in their shaft. Nearby a new excavation had begun which, in the years that followed, was extended over a large part of the precinct.[22] This led by degrees to the astonishing exposure in levels V to III of architectural remains, sculpture, cylinder-seals and inscriptions, through which the marvellous attainments of this pre-dynastic people were first revealed. Meanwhile, a further discovery had been made at a site called Jemdet Nasr, a few miles from Kish, where another Anglo-American expedition under S. Langdon had been excavating on similar lines.[23] Here, the architectural remains were neither well clarified nor well published, but their interest was greatly increased by an entirely new type of painted pottery which accompanied them. This was a polychrome ware, with geometric designs and a distinctively glossy surface. It now appeared to represent the final phase of the pre-dynastic period with which we are dealing.

It was at this stage that a conference of Mesopotamian archaeologists, meeting at Leiden in 1929, agreed upon site-names to designate the three main chronological phases so far recognized in the pre-dynastic sequence. The 'Al 'Ubaid' phase was to cover the whole period associated with painted pottery in the deepest levels at Ur and Warka; the name 'Uruk' could provisionally be applied to the post-'Ubaid, 'archaic' levels in the Warka sounding; and 'Jemdet Nasr' to a final phase, probably recognizable at Warka as well as at the name-site itself. The primary need at that time was for a further exposure and analysis of the lengthy 'Ubaid period. As it proved, it was almost twenty years before this hope was fulfilled.

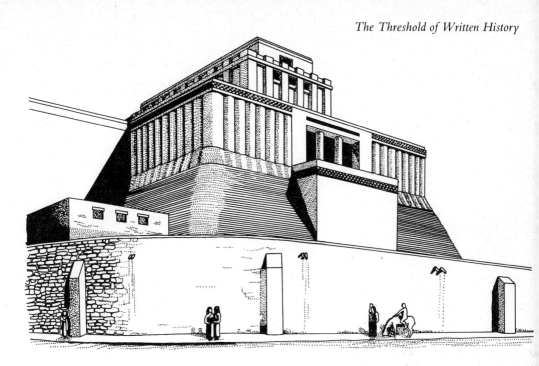

ERIDU

In 1948, F. Safar and S. Lloyd, on behalf of the Iraq Antiquities Directorate, opened a first season of excavations at Eridu (now called Tell Abu Shahrain), which the Sumerians considered to be the oldest city in the world.[24] Here were the remains of a late-Sumerian ziggurat and, beneath one corner of its ruins, the walls of a small temple, dated by pottery to the very end of the ʿUbaid period. This proved to be the latest in a long series of rebuildings, whose plans could be traced in turn through eighteen occupation-levels, down to a primitive chapel founded on a dune of clean sand. The evidence provided by the contents of these buildings was of course invaluable for dating purposes. In particular, successive stages in the development of ʿUbaid pottery could be noted, the earliest of these, the technique and form of the painted vessels so little resembled the standard product of later times that they came provisionally to be known as 'Eridu Ware'. Later we shall see how this and other sub-phases of the Eridu sequence have been assessed and numbered.

The succession of temples at Eridu did not of course end with the ʿUbaid period. A further five rebuildings corresponded to the Uruk period, but of these little remained, save for the brickwork of their repeatedly extended emplacements and fallen fragments of their façade ornament. But here there was a supplementary form of dating evidence. At Eridu, early in the Uruk period, a spreading cluster of subsidiary religious buildings had grown up around the temple. At some point in time this whole complex was abandoned and its rooms filled almost to roof-level with drifting sand. Then (perhaps at the time of Uruk's own great period of architectural invention, in levels V and IV) the whole of these ruins at Eridu had been enclosed in a stone retaining-wall and paved over, to create a raised temenos on which the temple could finally be reconstructed

8 The prehistoric temple at Eridu. An impression of the final rebuilding in Protoliterate times ('Temple I'). Above the stone retaining-wall of the temenos, the platform had survived up to the base of the columned portico. Above this, the reconstruction is based on fallen façade ornament and the appearance of temples elsewhere. (M. E. Weaver after Lloyd)

8

XIV–IX	VIII	VII	VI	V	IVc	IVb	IVa	IIIc	IIIb	IIIa		URUK ARCHAIC LEVELS
EARLY URUK	PROTOLITERATE											Delougaz
WARKAN	PROTOLITERATE											Perkins
EARLY URUK	MIDDLE URUK PROTOLITERATE A			LATE URUK PROTOLITERATE B				PROTOLITERATE C, D JEMDET NASR				Ehrich
XII ← ———————————— URUK								URUK (JEMDET NASR)				Mallowan
PROTOHISTORIC												Moortgat
EARLY URUK	LATE URUK							JEMDET NASR				Lloyd

Table IV Pre-dynastic terminologies according to different authorities

in a really magnificent form. The contents of the old buildings beneath the temenos, when compared with the remains of those afterwards superimposed upon it, now established a primary division of the Uruk period into 'Early' and 'Late' phases.

KHAFAJE

Long before this, during the 1930s, new light of another sort had already been thrown on pre-dynastic chronology by excavations undertaken by the Oriental Institute of the University of Chicago in cities of the ancient state called Eshnunna, in the Diyala region east of modern Baghdad. These had been mainly concerned with the Sumerian dynastic and later periods; but the predecessors of one Sumerian temple at Khafaje had been explored in depth, down to an original foundation at the end of the Uruk period.[25] In publishing the contents of this building, its excavator was the first to realize that this late phase of the Uruk period (levels V and IV at Uruk itself), with its great cultural accomplishments, must be separated, as it afterwards was at Eridu, from the rather undistinguished phase which preceded it (levels XIV–VI at Uruk). He therefore proposed to combine the former with the equally productive Jemdet Nasr phase, making a single period to which he gave the name 'Protoliterate'. This term has in fact never been easily accepted and several alternative systems of dating have since been suggested. For the moment however it may best serve our purpose.[26]

Table IV

In these few paragraphs, then, a preliminary account has been given of the earliest attempts to create a chronological framework for the pre-dynastic period, by rationalizing the stratigraphical evidence

from a number of sources. In doing so, priority has been given to discoveries in southern Mesopotamia, mainly because the cultural sequence established there long provided a system of criteria by which parallel findings in northern Iraq and neighbouring countries could be judged. Before extending our review to such regions, less directly connected as they are with Sumerian origins, it may be well to study in greater detail the character of the southern Mesopotamian cultures already enumerated.

9 The guesthouse (*mudhif*) of a modern Marsh Arab village: a traditional form of reed architecture already to be seen illustrated in carvings of the Protoliterate period. (From Leacroft, 1974)

The 'Ubaid Period

ARCHITECTURE

The text of a Sumerian inscription tells us that Shulgi, a king of the Third Dynasty of Ur, 'cared greatly for the city of Eridu, which was on the shore of the sea'. This description need not be taken too literally. It might, as we have already shown, be concluded that the city was merely connected to the sea by a system of tidal lagoons, and that these formed part of a marshy area, similar to that which today separates the alluvial plain from the head of the Arabian Gulf. In any case, it seems certain that the first inhabitants of Eridu and some other Sumerian sites were themselves marsh-dwellers, living in an environment comparable to that of the modern Marsh Arabs of Iraq. It is not therefore surprising that the earliest (symbolical) representations of architecture on Sumerian cylinder-seals and reliefs depict reed-built structures, resembling in their details the ingeniously designed *mudhifs* or guest-houses to be seen in the marshland villages today.[27] This being so, it is a little disconcerting to find that the earliest identifiable religious buildings, found in level XVI of the temple sounding at Eridu and elsewhere, were already constructed of sun-dried bricks. Admittedly, in another sounding at Eridu, unmistakeable remnants were found of a modest reed structure; but this later proved to have been no more than an outbuilding of a normal mud-brick house.[28]

The prototype 'temple' in level XVI at Eridu was in fact a single compartment, no more than 3 m square; yet its plan already showed features, such as a cult-niche and central offering-table,

9

10

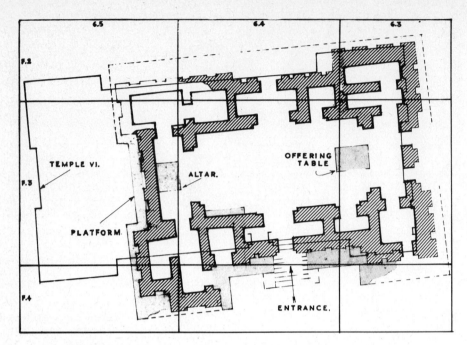

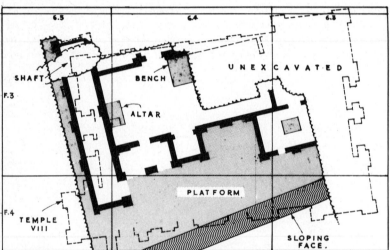

10 Temple plans characteristic of
the three main phases recognized
in the sounding at Eridu: "Ubaid
4' (temple VII) (*top*),
"Ubaid 3' (temple IX (*above*)
and "Ubaid 1' (temple XVI)
(*right*), dated respectively to
c. 3800, 4100 and 4900 B.C.
Temple XVI is no more than a
chapel, but already has a niche
for the altar and offering-table

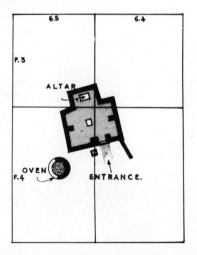

which are characteristic of temples from that time onwards. In the levels immediately above this (XV–XII), the siting of the building seemed to be beyond the reach of the sounding; but it reappeared in level XI and was twice rebuilt (XI–IX) to a more ambitious plan, having a central sanctuary and projecting lateral wings. In this case its extremely narrow brick walls were strengthened at intervals with thicker piers or buttresses, in a manner perhaps reminiscent of earlier reed structures. Next came a sequence of more substantially built and sophisticated temples (VIII–VI), accounting for the remainder of the ʿUbaid period. The long central sanctuary was still entered through a lateral chamber, but it also tended to have more ceremonial doorways at one end and a raised altar at the other. Once more there was a free-standing pedestal for votive offerings, apparently including fish, whose bones were deposited in an adjoining chamber.[29] Façades were now formally decorated with alternating buttresses and recesses, a feature rarely absent from religious buildings from that time onwards.

RELIGION

Having thus already encountered the prototype of Mesopotamian religious buildings, about which so much will presently have to be said, some impression should at once be given of the purpose for which they were built: of the forms of worship and ritual performance for which they provided a setting, and of their significance as a primary expression of abstract thought and spiritual consciousness. At the early stage in their evolution which

11 Temple VII at Eridu after excavation. Overlying it behind can be seen the great bulk of the Third Dynasty ziggurat, built by Shulgi (2095–2048 BC) and in the foreground the extended platforms of Protoliterate temples I–V. The walls are of rectangular mud-bricks

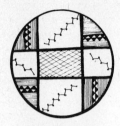

12 Some painted designs used by the makers of 'Eridu ware', the earliest pottery yet found in southern Mesopotamia. These are flat dishes, but tall cups and bowl-shapes were similarly decorated. (Now known as ''Ubaid 1'). (After Lloyd and Safar)

we have so far reached, there is understandably little to be learnt on this subject from their physical or architectural remains as revealed by excavation. A few elementary features can already be recognized by analogy with subsequent developments – we have spoken of an 'altar', 'cult-niche' and 'offering-table'. But a fuller picture of the cults themselves to which the buildings were dedicated, and of the actions by which they were expressed, can only be reconstructed in the light of information provided by the written texts of later times. Here then, in the briefest possible form, are some elements of Sumerian religious worship and ritual performance.

Duties and observances practised in the temple can be grouped under two principal headings: offerings and sacrifices. High amongst the services which the gods required of their worshippers was the provision of food, drink and oil for anointing. According to H. W. F. Saggs (1962), 'The gods enjoyed regular meals . . ., which were placed on tables before the divine images'. Their food included bread in large quantities, the meat of sheep or cattle and drink in the form of beer, which was greatly favoured by the Sumerians. Among provisions listed in later times were honey, ghee, fine oil, milk, dates, figs, salt, cakes, poultry, fish and vegetables.

The meal of the gods was technically a banquet to which other deities were invited and at which the human worshippers and even the dead might be present. The gods themselves received specified parts of the animals, the remainder going to the king, the priests and the temple staff.

Sacrifices were in a different category. These were actually made on special altars or on the roof of the temple, by a qualified priest who cut the animal's throat while reciting an incantation, the welling blood itself being a libation. Other forms of libation are frequently represented in Sumerian art, the wine or other liquid being poured over an altar, on to the ground or over an animal or plant. Saggs writes:

The incense-burner was a very common feature of the temple ritual, and the burning of aromatic woods could be applied either as a purification rite or as a service to the deity, for the gods delighted in sweet odours.

Something more is to be learnt from the names of priests who performed special parts of the ceremonies. Some were concerned especially with incantations, and there were exorcists whose task involved the playing of music. Others dealt with washing and anointing rituals. Finally, in a more important category, were the *Baru* priests, specialists in omen interpretation, who greatly influenced political decisions. It can well be understood that the requirements of these varied religious performances are reflected in the planning and installations of the buildings where they took place.

POTTERY AND SMALL OBJECTS

At each of the levels at Eridu so far mentioned (XVI–VI) pottery was plentiful. The gradual transformation of the early 'Eridu' designs into those associated elsewhere with Al 'Ubaid proved to be separable into four distinct phases, which also conveniently

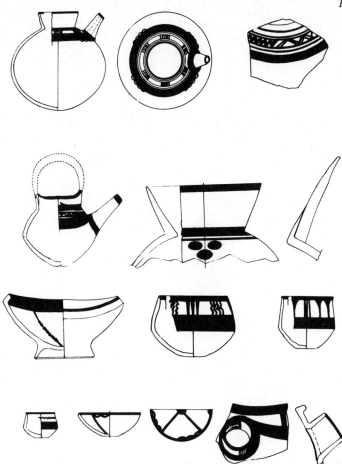

13 Shapes and patterns characteristic of ʿUbaid painted pottery in its latest phase ("ʿUbaid 4"). At this period the ʿUbaidian culture seems to have spread northwestwards as far as Syria and Cilicia. (After Lloyd and Safar, *JNES*, 1923)

corresponded to the major changes in architectural planning, recognized throughout the series of rebuildings. From 'virgin soil' to level XV the early 'Eridu' pottery could be seen to be predominant, 'a fine monochrome, usually chocolate-coloured painted ware, decorated with small-scale rectilinear patterns'. This coincides in time with the modest building activities which culminated in the level XVI chapel, and has been designated 'phase 1'. A second phase accounted for levels XIV–XII above, where no architecture was found, and it was distinguished by the intrusion of an alien pottery, whose peculiar 'wickerwork' patterns had previously been found at a riverside site called Hajji Muhammad, near Warka.[30] 'Phases 3 and 4' corresponded to earlier and later stages in the development of the conventional ʿUbaid culture, which reached its peak at the time of Temples VII and VI, and it is in this stage at Eridu that a new and rich source of evidence becomes available.

12

13

The Cemetery

Fifty metres outside the stone retaining wall, on the southwest side of the raised temple-precinct, a cemetery was found containing perhaps 1000 graves of the late ʿUbaid period; some 200 of these were excavated. The burials were made in rectangular shafts, lined

14 Typical small objects and sherds with figured designs from an ''Ubaid 4' settlement (Tell 'Uqair). The former include sickles, wall-nails, net-weights and socketed axes (all of baked clay), polished celts, a hammer and digging stones

with mud-brick, and their position must have been marked on the surface, since a secondary interment was often made in the same shaft as the first. The body of a dog was occasionally laid across the grave of its master.

The Eridu cemetery, which must be dated to the first half of the 4th millennium BC, represents a fairly advanced stage in the development of funerary practices. As we shall presently see, earlier sites have been found where burials are concentrated in particular areas, often in the vicinity of holy places. But here, for the first time, the number and uniformity of the graves create the impression of a genuine necropolis. The location chosen at Eridu seems to have been just outside the 'Ubaidian settlement and its temple precinct. No corresponding graveyard of any later period has yet been found there, though early excavators at this site, having come upon small deposits of votive pottery within the raised precinct of the Uruk period, did mistake them for human burials (with the bones missing). At Ur, Woolley found a dozen or so 'Ubaid burials in the area which later became the 'Royal Cemetery' – once more, likely to have been just outside the contemporary temple precinct. He observed that, as at Eridu, 'the body was placed on its back, fully extended with its arms by its side or slightly bent so that the hands could be folded across the pelvis', and he comments that 'this was an attitude peculiar to the 'Ubaid people, never to be adopted by any of the subsequent inhabitants of Sumer'. Woolley also recorded the fact that,

Opposite
15, 16 Baked-clay figurines from 'Ubaidian graves at Ur (female) and Eridu (male). The 'coffee-bean eyes', conical headdress and shoulder ornament (tattoo?) are widespread conventions at this and earlier periods (cf. ill. 45)

In two graves, the upper part of the body was covered with a fine red powder, and in one case there lay by the head a lump of red haematite paint. Whether the bodies had been painted it was impossible to say; but there was no doubt that the powder was the same as the paint in the lump. . . .

It is interesting that a similar phenomenon was observed in our own cemetery at Eridu. Almost all the bones were pigmented with a dark orange colour. But as this applied equally to the bodies of dogs – and even in one case to a meat-bone laid beside the mouth of the dog – we are inclined to discount the possibility of a deliberate or ritual pigmentation with ochre, and to attribute the colour to some chemical action of the soil.

The contents of these burials included a rare collection of complete painted pots, matching very closely the contemporary sherds collected from the temple sounding (levels VI and VII). The shapes, painted designs and technical peculiarities of ʿUbaid pottery at this time are of considerable archaeological importance, because the ʿUbaid culture extended itself, now or later, far beyond the frontiers of Mesopotamia to the east and northwest. It is a hand-made ware and its curvilinear or other designs are freely painted with a soft brush, usually in black or dark brown. Foliate patterns often occur and occasionally there are stylized figures of animals or birds. At Eridu, the paint is generally applied over a buff or cream-coloured slip. Elsewhere the slip is more often omitted and the vessel fired at so high a temperature that the clay acquires a dark green colour with the black paint biting deeply into it. The fact that such vessels frequently suffer from over-baking, almost to the point of vitrification, and are often deformed in the process, suggests that these ʿUbaid potters had very little control over their kilns.

The fragmentary vessels found in Woolley's 'reed huts' at Al ʿUbaid itself were in other ways poorly made and seem now to have represented a decadent phase immediately preceding the end of the ʿUbaid period. They, like some examples from level VI at Eridu, show signs of being made on a 'tournette', or hand-turned wheel, thus anticipating the wheel-made pottery of the Uruk period.[31] Surface finds suggest that a deeper penetration would have encountered earlier ʿUbaid occupations.

Objects other than pottery, found to be characteristic of the ʿUbaid period, also have an interest of their own. First and foremost are the painted terracotta figurines, described as 'mother-goddesses' until a male counterpart was found in a woman's tomb at Eridu. Their 'lizard-shaped' heads and bitumen headdresses, which created so much interest when examples were first found by Woolley, can today be recognized as a convention widely accepted in the cult-imagery of the prehistoric Near East. Some earlier stages in the evolution of their design are discussed below in connection with finds made at sites in northern Iraq. In another category are the implements made of baked clay, such as sickles and shaft-hole axes, whose manufacture must have been made practicable by the high temperatures attained in kilns of that time (the sickles were evidently baked in bundles for they are often found adhering to each other in a vitrified mass). In this class also are the large clay nails with bent-back points, used as we think for fixing reed matting to the face of a mud-brick wall. For the rest there are simple artifacts, such as flint knives and hoes or bone implements with bitumen handles, which could belong to any other pre-dynastic phase.

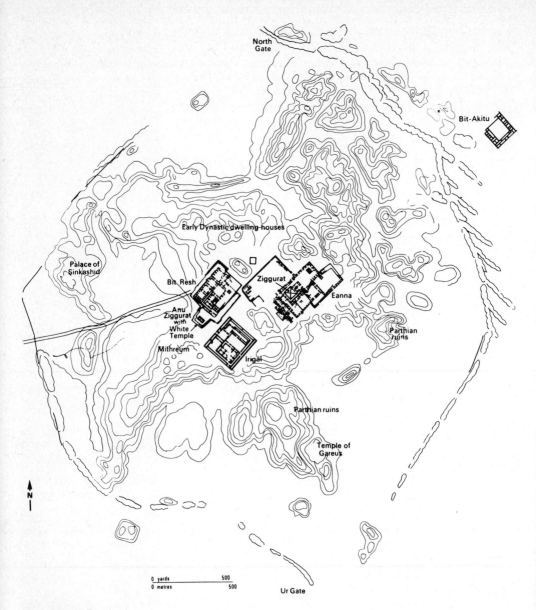

The Uruk Period

WARKA

The most copious source of information about this period has been
the work of German archaeologists, whose excavations at the
name-site have been carried on intermittently for almost half a
century, more recently under the direction of H. J. Lenzen. Uruk,
whose modern name is Warka, is also the 'Erech' of the Old
Testament. In Sumerian literature it is associated with the name of
Gilgamesh, one of the earliest dynastic rulers credited today with
having been an actual historical character. But already in pre-
dynastic times the city is thought to have had an area of some 200
acres, about one third of which was covered with temples and other

public buildings. Soundings in widely separated parts of the site have suggested that even in the 'Ubaid period the settlement had attained an impressive size. In the famous epic of which Gilgamesh was the hero, it is said of him that: 'In Uruk he built walls, a great rampart and the temple of blessed Eanna for the god of the firmament Anu, and for Ishtar the goddess of love'. Sure enough, when the Germans came to excavate the temple area in the centre of the city, they found their work concentrated on two primary building complexes, which they named respectively the 'Anu Ziggurat' and the 'Eanna Precinct'. It was greatly to their advantage that, in both cases, ruins of the pre-dynastic period proved to be accessible at no great depth beneath the surface of the mound.

17

THE ANU AREA

The earliest discoveries in the Anu area are easier to understand today than they were when first made. The building called by its excavators the 'White Temple', whose walls, painted white outside, appeared standing upon an irregular-shaped brick platform, was in fact no more than a late reconstruction of a shrine very much like that at Eridu, in that its origins could, as we now know, be traced back far into the 'Ubaid period.[32] Nevertheless, the planning and arrangement of this final rebuilding, dating from the Jemdet Nasr period (3200–2600 BC), are of special interest, in that all the main characteristics of the 'Ubaid temples are still preserved. Only the area of its platform is greatly increased. Its panelled façades slope inwards at a slight angle and it is approached by an impressive triple stairway. Since no 'platform temple' of a later period than this has survived, we shall presently see that it gains significance as a prototype of the Sumerian ziggurat.

Fifty metres or so to the east of the White Temple were the outer walls of the Eanna Precinct, a broad area of courtyards and terraces surrounding a true ziggurat, dedicated to the goddess Inanna and repeatedly rebuilt in historical times. It was early discovered that this monumental layout had replaced a more ancient complex of religious buildings, dating from the final phases of the pre-dynastic period. We have already seen how the Germans, by means of a 'pilot' sounding in the middle of this area, were able tentatively to construct a chronological sequence for these 'archaic' buildings and to relate them stratigraphically with occupation-levels of an earlier period beneath. During the years that followed, the Eanna excavation was widely extended and the full attention of the excavators was devoted to the task of disentangling their plans.

The problem which this presented can well be imagined if it is realized that such buildings were constructed almost exclusively of perishable mud brick. In the end the excavators were faced with half-a-dozen temples, complete with their various appendages, founded, extended, destroyed, rebuilt and generally overlapping each other, the stumps of their walls often standing no more than a few inches high. If one remembers that the shape and direction of these walls could only be determined by patiently articulating each individual brick, one cannot but regard the clearance of Eanna as a major accomplishment of archaeological technology.

18 A 'cut-open' reconstruction of the 'White Temple' at Warka, standing on its high platform known to the excavators as the 'Anu Ziggurat'. Beneath it they found traces of earlier temples going back in date to the 'Ubaid period. (From Leacroft, 1974)

19 A German architect's reconstruction of the 'Pillar Hall' at Warka ('Uruk IVc', *c.* 3200 BC). Its brick columns, half-columns and walls are entirely covered with coloured cone-mosaic in geometrical patterns. Between the central stairways, a miniature temple is represented. (I. Mackenzie-Kerr after Heinrich, 1932)

THE EANNA PRECINCT

It would be impossible here to describe each individual building in this section of the Warka excavations, or to appraise the reconstructions of their plans, some of which have been ingeniously made from exiguous surviving fragments. Buildings of special interest are not however difficult to select. One of these – better preserved than most – is the so-called 'Pillar Hall' (level IVc), which provided the first *in situ* example of the 'cone-mosaic' façade ornament, so characteristic of the period. It takes the form of a gigantic portico, 30 m wide, comprising a double row of circular, free-standing columns, 2 m in diameter, with corresponding half-columns at either end. This is approached at a lower level through a long rectangular courtyard. The lateral walls of the courtyard too are faced with contiguous half-columns, and from it the colonnade is approached by three separate stairways. The entire surface of columns and side-walls alike is decorated with a mosaic of terracotta cones, thrust into a bed of clay, their coloured ends forming a variety of geometrical patterns. This remarkable architectural composition appears to have created a monumental approach to some building beyond, either uncompleted or totally destroyed. The face of the double stairway in the centre is decorated to resemble in miniature the façade of a building, also ornamented with mosaics.

Cone-mosaic ornament is again more sparingly used on the walls of actual temples built at this period. Their plans seem to adhere to two quite different conventions. One of these is represented by the standard 'tripartite' form, with which we have become familiar at Eridu and again in the White Temple. The second type of plan is a complete innovation, having transepts opening off the sanctuary at one end, with a doorway between them leading to a separate *cella* on the main axis. The finest individual example of this type is to be seen in the restored plan of Temple D in level IVa. Its very dimensions (80 × 55 m) make this building remarkable, while its planning (if the excavator's restoration may be accepted) is an astonishing *tour de force*. The great T-shaped sanctuary is entered through its transepts and surrounded by lateral chambers on all four sides. The outer façades are decorated with elaborate chasing and, on the two longer faces, ornamental niches deeply recessed in the

20

façades alternate with stairway chambers, some accessible from outside. In another example (Temple C) in the same level, a simpler plan of the same sort is extended at the *cella* end to include a second, 'tripartite' element, corresponding exactly in shape and dimensions to the White Temple, as though the building in some way fulfilled a double function.

We shall presently learn that the T-shaped sanctuary, as a feature of temple planning, is not restricted to southern Mesopotamia. Two examples of this same arrangement have been found in northern Assyria, corresponding closely in time to those just described.

One other building of interest – though of doubtful purpose – was the awkwardly named 'Stone Cone Mosaic' temple, built on an isolated site to the west of the main Eanna grouping and assigned in date also to level IV. Enigmatically planned, it was surrounded by a curious, doubly-buttressed protective wall, whose inner face, like the façades of the building itself, had been decorated with a mosaic of cones, in this case shaped out of coloured stone. Stone cones of this sort have been the subject of much speculation, since they appear in considerable quantities, displaced from their original setting, at Eridu, Al ʿUbaid and elsewhere. They have at times been thought of as a more primitive form of ornament, for which terracotta cones were later substituted, in the cause of greater economy. This seems probable, if one considers the variety and

20 Plans, reliably reconstructed, of Temples C and D in the Eanna Precinct at Warka (level IVa, *c.* 3100 BC). In these two buildings the T-shaped sanctuary is an innovation, elsewhere found only in northern Mesopotamia. Annexed to Temple C is a smaller unit, resembling the White Temple. These buildings, the largest of which measures 80 × 55 m, emphasize the precocious ingenuity of Protoliterate architects. (After Lenzen, 1949)

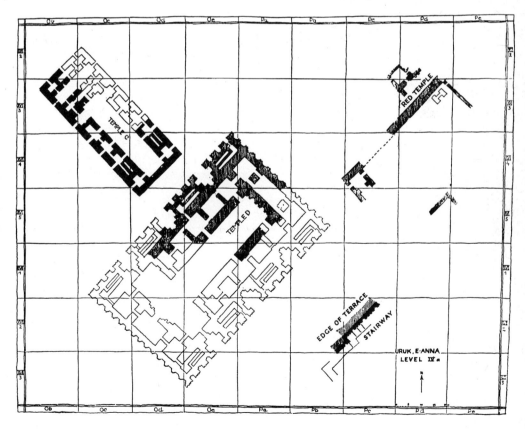

21 Architectural components of a Late Uruk period temple ('Uqair): prismatic bricks (*riemchen*) of clay or gypsum, elements of cone-mosaic façade ornament, rain-water spout and round pedestals of unknown purpose

elaboration of such ornament towards the end of the Uruk period. In some cases, for instance, hollow-ended terracotta cones, up to 30.5 cm in length, formed an ornamental band around the parapet of a temple platform, while in a late building at Eridu similar cones of gypsum were used, their heads sheathed in copper. Sometimes also, figured ornament carved on small plaques of stone was incorporated in the pattern of the mosaic and other devices were used to enliven it.

TELL 'UQAIR

At many sites in lower Mesopotamia, a scatter of these small mosaic components appears on the surface, and can be recognized as a reliable testimony to the occupation of such sites during the Uruk period. One site discovered in this way was Tell 'Uqair, about 50 miles due south of modern Baghdad, excavated by archaeologists from the Iraq Museum, led by F. Safar and S. Lloyd, in 1940–1.[33] On the outer edge of a characteristic 'Ubaid settlement, a slightly higher mound covered the remains of an Uruk-period temple, with a well-preserved platform and some parts of the walls still 22 standing several metres high. The plan in this case precisely matched that of the White Temple at Uruk, except that the ceremonial doorways at one end of the sanctuary were replaced by a high altar on the main axis, approached by a miniature flight of steps. It was, however, through one of the lateral doors that the excavators were (for once) able to enter the building, and it was then immediately discovered that the whole of the internal wall-faces were covered with mural paintings in several colours. A 'dado' of wine-coloured paint was surmounted by a band of geometrical ornament, and above this there was a frieze of human and animal figures, of which only the lower parts had survived. Better preserved was the decoration on the faces of the main altar, which, like the central stairway in the 'Pillar Hall' at Uruk, was painted to represent the façade of a miniature temple with its vertical panels of mosaic. On the sides facing the steps, guardian 23 figures of two spotted leopards were represented in red and black

22 Surviving walls and platform
of the Late Uruk period temple
at Tell ʿUqair. Wall-paintings
in the sanctuary are being
recorded. In the foreground are
remnants of the ground-level
chapel of the Jemdet Nasr
period, where archaic tablets
were found

23 Painted leopard, forming part
of the altar decoration in the
sanctuary of the Late Uruk
period temple at Tell ʿUqair

paint. Apart from the lime-washed façade which had given the White Temple at Uruk its name, and a 'Red Temple' in the Eanna Precinct, of which only a few courses remained standing, this mural painting at ʿUqair was the only example known in a building of the pre-dynastic period, and it continues to be remarkable for that reason.

The Painted Temple at ʿUqair has been provisionally dated to the final phase of the Uruk period (*c.* 2800 BC). Again like the White Temple, its chambers had been packed solid with rather large mud bricks to create a higher platform, on which the shrine could once more be rebuilt on a more ambitious scale. The date at which this took place could not of course be ascertained, but a discovery at the foot of the platform afforded some indication. Here was a small subsidiary chapel, packed with the remains of *ex-voto* vessels: a collection of Jemdet Nasr pottery, finer in quality than any found at the name-site itself. Here, furthermore, chronological evidence of the most reliable sort was provided by the discovery of four clay tablets, which seemed to be items from the temple accounts, inscribed with the pictographic signs typical of the Jemdet Nasr period.

Apart from the ground-plans and wall-ornament of the temples hitherto described, something more can be gathered about their general appearance from the representations of architecture sometimes to be found on Sumerian cylinder-seals and carved reliefs.[34] High up in the space between their lateral buttresses, triangular windows – either real or ornamental – are often shown. But, where internal lighting is concerned, they leave little doubt that the walls of the central sanctuary rose higher than those of the subsidiary chambers, and that accordingly space was left for clerestory windows. In the case of the great temples of the Eanna Precinct, it has sometimes been doubted whether their sanctuaries could ever have been roofed at all. Today, however, most authorities are agreed that suitable timber could probably have been obtained by river transport.

Buildings of the Jemdet Nasr Period

WARKA

We should now remind ourselves of the proposal made in 1942, that the 'Late Uruk period', to which the most impressive buildings in the Eanna Precinct belong, should be combined chronologically with the Jemdet Nasr period to create a new major phase called 'Protoliterate'. Clearly, if this is accepted, no discussion of Protoliterate architecture would be complete without some further reference to buildings of Jemdet Nasr times. So far, only one of these has been mentioned at Uruk itself, namely the final rebuilding of the White Temple; and we should next perhaps glance at contemporary developments in the Eanna Precinct during that period. Here, the great temples of Uruk IV were now in ruins and their sites covered with the confused remains of courtyards and terraces, whose walls were occasionally enriched with panels of mosaic ornament. One curious feature of this layout was the frequent appearance of installations called by the Germans *opferstätten.* These were long plastered troughs, evidently used for incinerating the remnants of sacrificial offerings in the form of animals, birds or fish. Sometimes they were laid out in orderly rows and showed signs of having been re-used many times. They have occasionally been recognized at sites other than Uruk at about this same period. [35]

One actual building, dedicated to some ritual purpose of the same sort, was the so-called *Riemchengebäude,* [36] whose foundations were dug down into the ruins of the earlier 'Stone-Cone-Mosaic' temple on the west periphery of the Precinct. Its innermost chamber, to which there was no apparent access, was entirely surrounded by a corridor, showing signs of some violent conflagration. Within the building, disposed in great confusion as though discarded intentionally, was a rich collection of objects, including 'hundreds of pottery and stone vases, alabaster bowls, copper vessels, clay cones, gold leaf and nails with heads covered in gold leaf, weapons, animal bones and broken components of furniture'. All this was taken by the excavators to imply the ritual destruction of fittings and sanctified objects belonging to some earlier building which had to be demolished.

KHAFAJE

A great deal more, well-published information about the Jemdet Nasr period was obtained from the earliest remains of the so-called 'Sin Temple', dedicated to the moon-god of that name, excavated by Americans in the 1930s at Khafaje in the Diyala region, east of modern Baghdad. [37] This little shrine was a ground-level building, yet its plan closely approximated to that of the White Temple. Only the ceremonial doorways at the ends of its sanctuary were missing. Its five earliest building-levels all fall within the period with which we are concerned, and something will be said about their contents if we now discuss aspects of the Protoliterate period, other than architecture.

The Protoliterate Period

THE FIRST WRITING

Having now watched the crescendo of architectural activity and invention which marked the course of the Protoliterate period, we are able to infer the strength of religious belief by which it was inspired. From buildings alone, however, little can be learnt about the detailed anatomy of Sumerian religion, or about the social background against which it had been conceived. Further information on this subject was of course to be revealed in due course by the written records of later times; but for the moment the elementary forms in which writing was available limited the contribution which could be expected from this source. [38]

The earliest tablets as yet discovered come from level IV at Uruk and use a pictographic script, recognizable as the ancestor of the later cuneiform. [39] The degree of competence which it had already attained suggests that earlier stages in its development may eventually be recognized elsewhere, perhaps in levels correspond-

24

24 Reverse side of a pictographic tablet from Jemdet Nasr (*c.* 3000 BC), giving a list of commodities. Such tablets were at first written in vertical columns, starting top right; later they were turned ninety degrees, anticlockwise, to read horizontally, left to right

ing to Uruk V and VI (which have for that reason been provisionally included in the Protoliterate period). Regarding the language for which this script provided a vehicle, the first texts demonstrably written in Sumerian are found in a Jemdet Nasr setting. Since, however, some authorities have been tempted to conclude that an 'ethnic substructure', in part Semitic, may have existed in Sumer previous to an (hypothetical) immigration of true Sumerians, they would claim that a different language may be expressed in the texts dated to Uruk IV. Speculations of this sort form a part of the long-standing debate on the problem of Sumerian origins (see below).

Some signs used in the Protoliterate script have a recognizable equivalent in the developed cuneiform of later times, and their meaning is accordingly known. Animals such as sheep and goats, cattle and donkeys could all have been expected. Words connected with fishing and hunting also occur, while commerce is implied by the names of merchants. Pottery techniques themselves confirm that the wheel was known, and a 'sledge' mounted on wheels could become a 'chariot'. Other signs suggest metal objects, one of which, the shaft-hole axe, is made in a closed mould. Like the copper sheathing of mosaic cones already mentioned, this would suggest an improved understanding of metallurgy. In a different sphere, it is significant that, although such words occur as 'elder' and 'council', the concept of a 'king' seems still unfamiliar. Such rudimentary scraps of information are fortunately supplemented by the subjects depicted in sculpture and designs in relief carving.

SCULPTURE

In sculpture surviving from the Protoliterate period, the scenes depicted are predominantly religious. At this point, therefore, a digression may not be out of place regarding the character and composition of the Sumerian pantheon.

From the earliest written formulations of religious belief, the names of three male gods, Anu, Enlil and Enki emerge as dominating figures. Anu, the sky-god, whose temple we have noticed at Uruk, was originally recognized as the highest power in the universe and sovereign of all the gods. Later in Sumerian history, he seems to have been replaced in this capacity, first by Enlil, patron god of Nippur and secondly by Marduk, tutelary deity of Babylon. Enki of Eridu was in a class by himself as god of wisdom and learning. Generally speaking, though the whole country worshipped a common pantheon, each individual city retained its own patron god and its own set of legends. For the rest, in the words of George Roux,

The heavens were populated with hundreds of supremely powerful, man-like beings, and each of these gods was assigned to a particular task or a particular sphere of activity. One god for instance might have charge of the sky, another of the air, a third of the sweet waters, and so forth, down to humbler deities responsible for the plough, the brick, the flint or the pickaxe.

These gods had the physical appearance as well as all the qualities and defects of human beings. 'In brief', as Roux concludes, 'they represented the best and the worst of human nature on a superhuman scale'.

Examples of those associated with particular cities, who became also the object of a general cult, include the moon-god, Nanna (Sin) of Ur and his son, Utu (Shamash) of Sippar and Larsa; Ninurta, the warrior-god; Nin-khursag (Nintu), mother and wife of Enlil; Inanna (Ishtar), goddess of love and her husband Dumuzi (Tammuz). Inanna is of course the Great Mother, worshipped throughout the land, to whom the Eanna precinct at Uruk was dedicated: a female principle of creativity, expressing godhead through fecundity. As for Dumuzi, Roux points out that, though undoubtedly associated in the Sumerian mind with productivity in the vegetable and animal world, so that his union with Inanna must symbolize fertility, the theory which long associated him with the 'dying and resurrected' god of Frazer's *The Golden Bough* has more recently been rejected. Other minor gods and goddesses are too numerous to mention.

A well-known stone vase from Warka, 90 cm high, has three   *25* registers of figures very finely carved in relief. Above, the goddess Inanna appears in front of two reed bundles terminating in loops   *26* and streamers, which are her perpetual symbol, and a ritually naked priest offers her a basket of fruit. Behind this the relief is damaged, but a small fragment remains of a figure which may well be that of a 'king' or leader, and an attendant supports the tasselled girdle which he is perhaps about to present. Inanna is supported by minor deities, mounted on model temples and appropriate beasts, with other symbols including a pair of vases like that on which they are carved. In the second register, naked priests bring further offerings and in the third, beasts and plants represent her two 'kingdoms'. Another sacred symbol present here, is the stylized rosette with

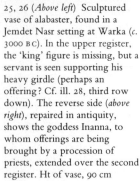

25, 26 (*Above left*) Sculptured vase of alabaster, found in a Jemdet Nasr setting at Warka (*c.* 3000 B C). In the upper register, the 'king' figure is missing, but a servant is seen supporting his heavy girdle (perhaps an offering? Cf. ill. 28, third row down). The reverse side (*above right*), repaired in antiquity, shows the goddess Inanna, to whom offerings are being brought by a procession of priests, extended over the second register. Ht of vase, 90 cm

eight petals. Again, on the sculptured sides of a stone trough in the British Museum, sheep and rams from the 'sacred herd' return to her temple, here represented as a marsh-dweller's reed building, and from it their lambs emerge to meet them. This also is a scene perpetually repeated, for example on the faces of a stone bowl from Khafaje, where cattle replace sheep, and much later in an architectural relief from the Early Dynastic temple at Al ʿUbaid.

Secular subjects are less common. There is the fragmentary stela of black granite from Warka, carved with difficulty, to show two scenes in which the same 'king' figure hunts lions; and there is the extraordinary life-size head in limestone, found in a Jemdet Nasr setting, but dated stylistically to Uruk IV. It is only a component part of a composite figure, the remainder of which could have been made from other materials such as wood and bitumen. The eye and eyebrow inlays are missing, as is the metal-foil covering of the hair. With these restored, the head looks a little outlandish; but the bare stone mask, as found, is strikingly beautiful. Animals carved in the round – a couchant ram from Warka and a wild boar from Ur – seem to have been ornaments attached by metal to larger contrivances, while stone vases also are sometimes decorated with animals – lions or bulls – carved partly in the round and partly in relief. Dating from the Jemdet Nasr period at Warká, there are crudely carved 'king' figures, foreshadowing the *ex-voto* 'personal' statues of Early Dynastic times. Nearer still to these is a single votive statue of a woman from Khafaje. Of the same period are jars of animal form with an opening on top, usually of dark-coloured stone. These are often decorated with coloured inlays in geometrical patterns.

CYLINDER-SEALS

Another innovation which runs parallel to the pictographic writing of Protoliterate times is the cylinder-seal, a device used for establishing ownership or recording an agreement. These small objects of stone or shell, pierced through the centre for suspension, were delicately carved on their curved sides with a variety of devices or designs, to create a tiny frieze of ornament when rolled over soft clay.[41] They have been found in great numbers and their impressions on tablets or clay jar-stoppers are even more plentiful.

The cylinder-seal is a device which makes its first appearance in levels V and IV at Uruk.[42] In the examples dating from this period, therefore, we should expect to see the Sumerian craftsman's first, and perhaps awkward, experiments in an extremely difficult form of carving. On the contrary, though it is clear that he had not yet completely mastered the intricacies of repetitive design, the variety of his subjects and the ingenuity of their decorative treatment testify to an achievement seldom rivalled during the centuries that followed. Already his work has the quality of relief carving, rather than mere linear drawing, as is shown by the vigorous modelling and articulation of the individual figures.

28

The pictorial themes and mythical symbols contributing to the composition of these designs have been the subject of much study and are today partly understood. Most evident in the religious scenes is the invocation of two deities never personally depicted, but symbolized by ideograms implying their attributes. There is a god who, like the biblical Tammuz, personifies the generative force in nature, graphically represented by certain animals and plants. Other symbols of the god include an eagle, sometimes lion-headed, and a snake. Equally prominent is Inanna, whose curiously shaped emblem (identified by some as the 'gatepost' of a reed-built temple), afterwards became her name-sign in pictographic writing. A decorative combination of these symbols alone can provide the subject of a seal design. Alternatively, when the performance of some religious ritual – sacrifice or oblation – is portrayed, human figures appear. A bearded man with diadem and 'chignon', wearing a long folded skirt and attended by a naked or kilted priest, can be identified as a 'king'. He brings ritual objects to a reed-built

27 Carved alabaster trough in the British Museum, of the Protoliterate period. Animals of Inanna's 'sacred herd' beside a reed-built byre, surmounted by her 'doorpost' symbols. Ht 20 cm

28 Cylinder-seals of the Uruk period. The 'king' figure appears, feeding Inanna's beasts or facing her portable shrine on a reed boat. Priests bring ceremonial gifts (one of them by boat) to a reed-built temple with unidentified 'ring-pillar' symbols. Ibexes and other beasts provide alternative motifs

temple or presides over the ceremonial feeding of sacred cattle. Flocks and herds make frequent appearances and are defended against lions by such figures as the 'bull-man' and 'lion-headed eagle', familiar features of Sumerian imagery in later times. Game animals also appear: boars, stags, ibex and moufflon, and from their shapes heraldic patterns are composed to supplement the seal-cutters repertory of designs. Occasionally there are secular subjects, including the 'king' figure, either hunting or at war.

Types of stone favoured by the seal-cutters are often of a sort unobtainable in Mesopotamia and suggest trade connections with neighbouring countries.

all sorts unobtainable in Mesopotamia!

29 During the Jemdet Nasr period, there was a slight deterioration in the care and precision with which seals were carved. The drill, for instance, which had previously been used sparingly and its effects when possible concealed, now became conspicuous and the modelling of animal figures declined in accomplishment. A new

form of seal also appeared, longer in proportion to its diameter and entirely covered with sharply defined geometric ornament.

POTTERY

While tracing successive phases in the evolution of pre-dynastic culture, mention has frequently been made of pottery, stressing its significance as stratigraphical evidence. The pottery of the Protoliterate period is for the most part undecorated. Its technical peculiarities have been the subject of much specialized study, which would not here be possible to summarize. One exception to this generalization however is the fine painted ware which appeared towards the end of the Jemdet Nasr period.[43] The commonest *30* form of vessel decorated in this way is a stoutly proportioned jar, with a broad shoulder and rimmed neck. Geometric ornament in red and yellow is usually confined to the shoulder, sometimes forming panels in which animals, foliage or even human figures appear. The remaining surface is covered with plum-coloured paint, forming a glossy surface. This distinctive ware has provided a useful criterion for dating, when found in alien settings.

29 Cylinder-seals of the Jemdet Nasr period. In those with animal motifs (above), the quality of the carving is impaired by the use of a bow-drill. The geometrical designs below are peculiar to this phase of seal-cutting

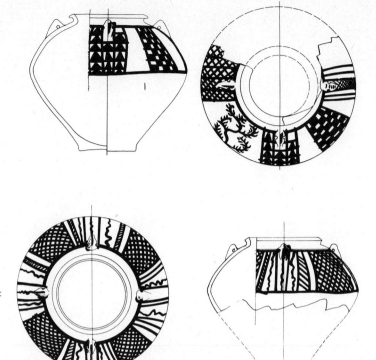

30 Painted pottery of the Jemdet Nasr period. Designs are in plum-red, yellow and black, mostly on the shoulders of jars, and the vessels are given an attractive 'glossy' finish. (After Lloyd and Safar, 1943)

Parallels between pottery of the pre-dynastic period in Mesopotamia and that of contemporary cultures in Iran and elsewhere will be discussed later under a separate heading; but the subject of early relations between Mesopotamia and Egypt may be mentioned here. In doing so, we are concerned less with pottery than with certain cultural developments, apparently shared at this time between the two great centres of incipient civilization. Several aspects of this subject have been ably examined by scholars in recent times.[44] One aspect is the influence of the earliest Mesopotamian brick temples on the design of pre-dynastic 'mastaba' architecture in Egypt. Another is the contention that hieroglyphic writing in Egypt was stimulated by a knowledge of Sumerian or pre-Sumerian experiments in the same field. This has today been made to seem less improbable by the discovery of pictographic writing, similar to that of Mesopotamia, in settings as remotely placed as Romania on the one hand,[45] and the frontiers of Baluchistan on the other.[46] But the most tangible evidence of communication between the two countries at such an early period is the discovery of Jemdet Nasr cylinder-seals in graves at Naqada in Egypt, indicating some form of trade connection, whose existence at that time still requires further investigation.

Sumerian Antecedents

Finally, we must return to the problem of Sumerian origins, which has in the past been the subject of so much deliberation among scholars. Here there has been a conspicuous conflict between the reasoning of philologists on the one hand and the conclusions of archaeologists on the other. Broadly, the problem arises from uncertainty regarding the exact point in the sequence of pre-dynastic 'periods' at which the inhabitants of lower Mesopotamia can rightly be called 'Sumerians'. It has been said that 'the innovations of the Protoliterate period established the identity which Mesopotamian civilization retained throughout its long history', and this was at one time accepted as a strong argument for the 'arrival' of the Sumerians at the beginning of that period. The epigraphists' contention to this effect is largely based on a single premise – namely that some of the older Mesopotamian cities mentioned in historical texts and founded before the Protoliterate period could be thought to have non-Sumerian names. This has been used to justify a whole tissue of speculation about the hypothetical migration of earlier, perhaps Semitic peoples throughout the Near East.[47] Archaeologists, on the other hand, point to the uncertainty of the original premise and to the absence of proof that these names were actually in use before the invention of writing. Finally, they are impressed by the overwhelming evidence for cultural continuity between the 'Ubaid and the Uruk periods.[48]

The evidence alone for continuity of religious beliefs and practices to an archaeologist seem particularly convincing. Three sites already mentioned make impressive contributions to the argument. The sequences at Al 'Ubaid itself, Tell 'Uqair and Eridu start chronologically with a conventional 'Ubaid settlement and,

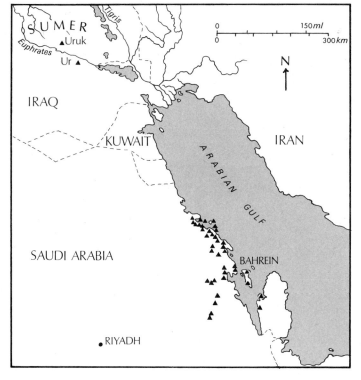

31 Map showing the known distribution of 'Ubaidian sites in the Arabian Gulf. (S. Ebrahim after J. Oates, 1976)

by analogy with Eridu, the two former may also be assumed to have had an ʿUbaid-period temple, frequently rebuilt. At these two sites, the settlements themselves were abandoned at a point in time corresponding to the end of the so-called ʿUbaid period. Not so, however, the temple which, like that at Eridu, was repeatedly rebuilt and enlarged throughout the Protoliterate period. At ʿUbaid itself it was again rebuilt in Early Dynastic times and at Eridu its ruins were chosen as the site for a ziggurat by the Third Dynasty kings of Ur. One also observes that, both at ʿUbaid and at ʿUqair, the old ʿUbaidian settlement mound was used as a cemetery by the Sumerians of Dynastic times.[49]

With this situation in mind, the substitution at any time of alien immigrants for the indigenous population becomes an improbable hypothesis.

A final question remains, regarding the original provenance of the first settlers in southern Mesopotamia. Much interest has now been aroused by the discovery of a thriving enclave of ʿUbaidian settlements along the southern shore of the Arabian Gulf and inland west of Bahrein.[50] Their earliest appearance in this quarter is at present dated to the middle phase of the ʿUbaid period. More recently, however, neutron activation evidence has become available, showing that the pottery in use by these settlers was in fact imported from Sumer, to which their relationship must accordingly have been that of colonists or traders. Speculation regarding an 'earlier home' of the ʿUbaidian culture would thus appear to become increasingly pointless.

31

Chapter Four

Illiterate Peoples of Northern Mesopotamia

During the previous chapter our attention has been concentrated on the results of excavations in the southern Mesopotamian plain, and on the evidence which they produced of cultural developments during the pre-dynastic period. We must next turn to consider parallel researches which had been taking place among the uplands of northern Iraq, and examine the rather different sequence of events which they revealed. In doing so, we shall find that our thread of association with the evolving civilization of the Sumerians may become increasingly tenuous, while cultural influences from beyond the frontiers of Mesopotamia correspondingly gain in importance. For this reason, the term 'pre-dynastic' will clearly no longer be appropriate and, for the period intervening between the Neolithic and Early Bronze Ages, when the smelting of metal began to be understood, the name 'Chalcolithic' should perhaps be substituted, as has been usual in other countries of western Asia.[51]

Once more then in this case, it may be well to sketch the sequence of discoveries, before discussing in detail the succession of cultural phases which they have made it possible to establish.

Table V

Excavations in the North

ARPACHIYAH

In Assyria the initial investigation of prehistoric settlements was undertaken simultaneously by British and American archaeologists during the early 1930s. As a point-of-departure one would select the small site called Arpachiyah, 4 miles to the northeast of Nineveh, excavated by M. E. L. Mallowan in 1933.[52] Here on the surface Mallowan found a little village composed of rather poor huts built of *pisé* clay. But he noticed that the pottery which they contained could be recognized as a northern variant of the ʿUbaid painted wares previously found in Babylonia. There was a wider variety in the colours used – brown, red and even purple paint being more common than black; but the designs and the shapes remained substantially the same. This was confirmed when, outside the village, a cemetery was found containing more than forty graves, containing many complete vessels, some of them unbroken. Also, in the houses themselves were found incised terracotta beads and bent clay nails, both generally characteristic of ʿUbaid sites in the south. Finally, Mallowan found one open-cast copper axe suggesting that, though still rare, copper was already in use side-by-side with the usual flint implements, as one would expect in a Chalcolithic setting.

65

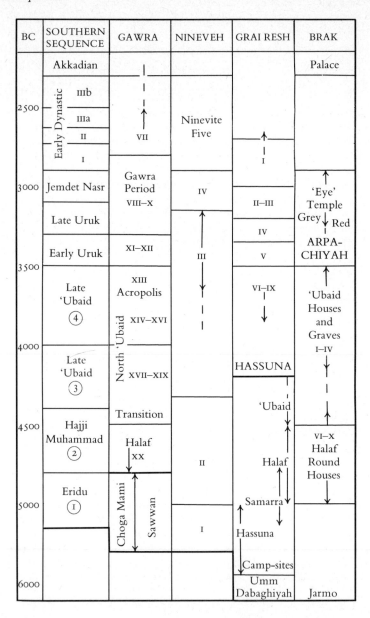

BC	SOUTHERN SEQUENCE	GAWRA	NINEVEH	GRAI RESH	BRAK
	Akkadian	I			Palace
2500	Early Dynastic IIIb / IIIa / II / I	VII	Ninevite Five	I	
3000	Jemdet Nasr	Gawra Period VIII–X	IV	II–III	'Eye' Temple Grey / Red
	Late Uruk			IV	
3500	Early Uruk	XI–XII	III	V	ARPA-CHIYAH
	Late 'Ubaid (4)	XIII Acropolis / XIV–XVI (North 'Ubaid)		VI–IX	'Ubaid Houses and Graves I–IV
4000	Late 'Ubaid (3)	XVII–XIX		HASSUNA	
	Hajji Muhammad (2)	Transition		'Ubaid	
4500		Halaf XX (Choga Mami / Sawwan)	II	Halaf	VI–X Halaf Round Houses
5000	Eridu (1)		I	Samarra / Hassuna	
				Camp-sites	
6000				Umm Dabaghiyah	Jarmo

Table V Chronology for sites in northern Mesopotamia

Similar houses were found in four successive building levels (1–4 down); but Mallowan did not think that these represented more than five or six generations, because the graves in the cemetery did not overlap, suggesting that the positions of the oldest graves were still remembered when the latest ones were dug. In level 5 the character of the pottery began to change, and throughout the remainder of his excavation (6–10), he found himself dealing with an entirely different culture, characterized by a finely finished and brilliant ware, painted for the most part in several colours. This pottery was already known by the name 'Tell Halaf'. It had first been found by the German excavator, Baron Max von Oppenheim, before the First World War, at a site of that name on the Turko-Syrian frontier. But von Oppenheim had encountered it while excavating the great Iron Age palace of an Aramaean prince, in the city called Guzana – piles of painted potsherds, thrown out when the foundations of the palace were being dug – and he could find no indication of its age. At Arpachiyah it was for the first time found both accurately stratified and associated with contemporary architecture.

More will need to be said later about this beautiful Halaf pottery, *43–4* on which the elaborate designs are executed in glossy paint with an overall burnish. Its character is sufficiently distinctive to have provided an invaluable dating criterion when found at the further extremities of its distribution in northern Syria and southern Anatolia. In the same sense, it is important to notice that it has no exact equivalent anywhere in southern Mesopotamia. At Arpachiyah also, the first examples were found of small objects in other categories – stylized cult-figurines of terracotta, stamp-seals with figured designs of men or animals and a variety of beads and amulets – all of which came soon to be considered representative of the 'Halaf period'. Yet the feature by which this site has been primarily remembered are the circular buildings, found in its deeper levels and known at the time by the Greek word 'tholoi'. Built of *36* *pisé* on stone foundations and apparently domed, they were sometimes approached through a rectangular ante-room or 'dromos', thus increasing their resemblance to the 'bee-hive' tombs of a much later age at Mycenae.

TEPE GAWRA

While Mallowan was excavating Arpachiyah, an American expedition had begun work on a much larger mound called Tepe Gawra, some miles to the northeast.[53] As was usual in those days, the Americans were more liberally financed than the British, and their leader, E. A. Speiser, was consequently able to plan an excavation covering the whole summit of the Gawra mound. During the years that followed, therefore, its silhouette was dramatically changed, from an initial height of over 18 m to rather less than 9 m. The shortcomings till then associated with the restricted area of stratigraphical soundings were thus eliminated and the exposure of the entire settlement made possible. During their earlier years, Speiser and his successors were engaged in clearing levels of habitation contemporary with the Sumerian cities in the south, or corresponding with the Protoliterate phase of the pre-dynastic period. The latter proved to represent a culture so distinctive in character that, for the time being it was referred to as the 'Gawra period' of northern Iraq. There were rich graves with gold jewellery; temples with curious, unfamiliar planning; strikingly carved amulets and everywhere evidence of the large-scale use of copper. These were some of the characteristics of Gawra, levels VIII to XI (down), which will presently be referred to at greater length, since Gawra serves as a key-site to the stratigraphy of northern Mesopotamia.

It was not until the Arpachiyah excavations were over that the workers at Gawra began themselves to encounter Mallowan's

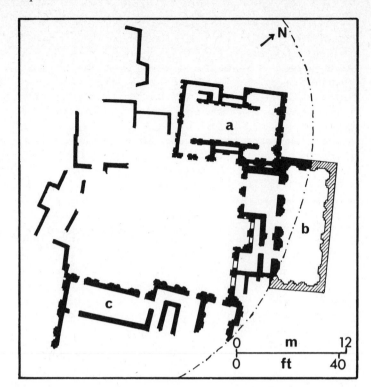

32 Tepe Gawra, plan of the 'acropolis' at level XIII (*c.* 3600 BC), with its ʿUbaidian temples facing an open courtyard. The fragile wall construction is reminiscent of the ʿʿUbaid 3' temples at Eridu, levels XI–IX (cf. ill. 10). There are no ritual installations in this case. *a*, northern temple; *b*, central temple; *c*, eastern shrine; dotted line indicates edge of mound. (S. Ebrahim after Tobler, 1950)

'northern ʿUbaid' painted pottery. Here they were able to study its development over a period represented by no less than eight building-levels (XII to XIX), and to learn a great deal more about

32 it. It was in level XIII that the culture seemed to have reached its state of maximum sophistication. At this time, the greater part of the mound's summit was occupied by what amounted to a religious acropolis; an open space surrounded by a trio of large and elaborately built mud-brick temples, satisfactorily corresponding in many respects to those in the ʿUbaid levels at Eridu, with which they were later shown to be contemporary.

All through the deeper ʿUbaid levels at Gawra, traces were found of pottery shapes and forms of ornament surviving from the previous Tell Halaf period. When level XX was reached, the transition between the two cultures was found to have been passed. Polychrome pottery predominated and all other finds could be seen to be characteristic of the Tell Halaf period. There was even an interesting circular building which could, not quite conclusively, be identified as a temple. But at this point the Gawra sounding ended and no further clue was found to an earlier occupation.

It remains to be added that, already known at this time, was one other form of painted pottery, which seemed to have been contemporary with or to have preceded the manufacture of Tell Halaf ware. This had first been found before 1914 by Ernst Herzfeld, when he was excavating the huge, 9th-century AD city of Samarra, on the Tigris, halfway between Mosul and Baghdad,[54]

41–2 and came to be known as 'Samarra ware'. Among the foundation of Islamic buildings, Herzfeld came upon traces of a prehistoric settlement or cemetery, where this beautiful and unusual pottery had been in general use. Herzfeld being at that time unable to detect any architectural remains or stratigraphical indications, the age of the settlement temporarily remained a mystery, and it is only in much more recent times that the date of its first appearance – a little before that of the earliest Halaf pottery – has been ascertained. This too will later be explained.

KÜYÜNJIK

The combined results of excavations so far mentioned constituted our total knowledge of northern Mesopotamian stratigraphy up to the outbreak of the Second World War. It remains only to discuss an immensely deep sounding made by Mallowan beneath the Assyrian Ishtar Temple in the Küyünjik mound at Nineveh.[55] This operation had a number of extremely important results. First, in an upper level, Mallowan had the good fortune to discover the life-size bronze head of an Akkadian king, now considered one of the great masterpieces of Mesopotamian art (see chapter 7); secondly, he found textual proof that in Sumerian times Nineveh had been a city with temples. Thirdly, he was able to confirm the sequence of prehistoric phases so far known and, more significantly, to prove the existence of an earlier, pre-Halaf culture. Directly above virgin soil, at a depth of 27 m beneath the summit of the mound, he found an unknown type of pottery with finely scratched incisions which he provisionally labelled 'Ninevite I'. For ten years after Mallowan had left Iraq to excavate in Syria, a small bag of these curious potsherds remained in the Iraq Museum, to represent the earliest form of pottery as yet found in Mesopotamia.

HASSUNA

The next development came in 1943, when inspectors of the Iraq Antiquities Directorate located a small mound called Hassuna, on the fringe of the cultivated upland 20 miles due south of Mosul, whose surface was littered with Ninevite I pottery. The excavation of Hassuna involved a renewal of the 'Uqair partnership between the present writer and Fuad Safar: its result far exceeded our expectations.[56] A new and earliest chapter was added to the history of Chalcolithic settlements in northern Iraq, beginning with the arrival of a still-nomadic people, whose camp-sites were almost immediately overlaid by the primitive houses of a small farming community. An excavation covering an area about 20 m square enabled us to follow the development of this village through six successive building-levels, and to associate its final occupation with the arrival of new inhabitants at the site, using an early form of Tell Halaf painted pottery.

Counting from the bottom upwards, levels III to V represented what we considered to be the 'Standard' Hassuna culture. The pottery was all unburnished; some incised with pin-scratched designs, some painted and some combining both forms of ornament. In the three levels below (II, Ic and Ib), a so-called 'Archaic ware' appeared, burnished or decorated with glossy paint.

40

Throughout these six sub-phases, the general features of the village remained fairly consistent; small houses of *pisé* clay were grouped around courtyards resembling farmyards. There were reasons to think that they had pitched roofs of wood and thatch, exactly as are found in neighbouring villages today. There were also ample indications of primitive agriculture, sickles with flint teeth set in bitumen on a wooden haft, showing that at least these people were reaping the wild grain which still grows in the vicinity. But there were also elaborate grain-stores, protected with gypsum and bitumen, which proved that seed-grain was kept for re-sowing. Curious oval 'husking-trays' of baked clay were used for the process of winnowing. Bones of domestic animals were plentiful, while obsidian arrowheads and javelins indicated that hunting was still practised. Some sort of religious belief was already suggested by a damaged 'goddess' figurine of a now well-known type.

In levels Ib and Ic, plain burnished pottery was mostly of a sort associated elsewhere with the late stages of the Neolithic; and then finally, directly above virgin soil in level Ia, there was a complete change. Shelters, if any, must have been of a perishable material, for all we found were several widely separated domestic hearths, each with an identical assemblage of primitive artifacts around it. There was crudely made pottery, always including a peculiar, tall-sided storage-jar, apparently for milk, and implements such as heavy chert hoes or handaxes. In one case a skeleton still lay crouched beside the ashes of a fire. Here then, as it seemed to us, were the symbols of a transition from the nomadic life of herdsmen and hunters to the economy of a settled farming community.

OTHER HASSUNA SITES

During more recent years, two major attempts have been made to amplify our knowledge of the Hassuna culture and if possible to trace its immediate antecedents. One was the work of a Soviet expedition at a site called Yarim Tepe, to the southwest of Tell ʿAfar in the Sinjar district, northwest of Mosul.[57] Here, one of several mounds was excavated from 1969, with exemplary attention to method, and the results recorded with almost exaggerated precision. They served both to amplify and to supplement those of our own excavations at Hassuna. Many small houses – over 100 rooms in all – were examined, at thirteen successive occupation-levels, covering the whole sequence of developments originally recognized by ourselves at the name-site, and some features previously lacking made welcome additions to our knowledge. These included bracelets of lead, a new and interesting category of human figurines and also prototypes of the stamp-seals familiar in later periods.

Meanwhile, in the early 1970s, a second investigation with a similar purpose was undertaken by British excavators led by Diana Kirkbride in the Jazirah steppe country to the west of Hatra. In this area, now totally desiccated, 87 sites were found, of which no less than 40 showed signs of occupation in the Hassuna/Samarra period. One of them, named Umm Dabaghiyah, was selected for excavation down to virgin soil, and for the excavators the deeper

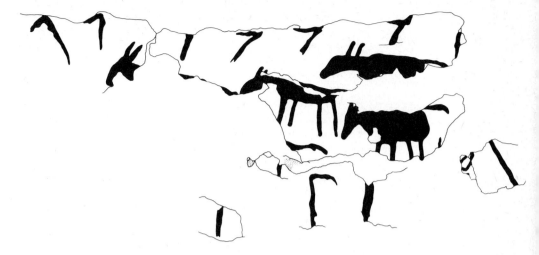

33 Onagers (wild asses) depicted in a primitive wall-painting from the pre-Hassuna settlement at Umm Dabaghiyah in the Jazirah (*c.* 5700 BC). These animals were hunted for their skins. (After Kirkbride, 1975)

34

33

levels had a surprise in store.[58] Here they were faced with abundant parallels to the earliest occupation (level Ia) at Hassuna, but, in contrast to the nomadic camp-sites of the first arrivals at that site, substantial buildings appeared of a sort already observed at Yarim Tepe (level I) and clearly designed for some purpose other than domestic habitation. Rows of rectangular compartments, too small for habitation, were grouped in a grid-shaped plan, as though for storing some commodity suitable for trade. The evidence of animal bones found in profusion nearby, of which onager and gazelle accounted for 68% and 16% respectively, led the excavators to consider some sort of commerce in skins – possibly those of the onager, which survived in that region until late in the 19th century AD. This theory was rather dramatically confirmed in the final season of excavation when, on the walls of dwelling-houses in the deeper levels, rudimentary mural paintings were found, clearly representing onagers in flight, apparently towards a line of netting staked to the ground.[59]

Diana Kirkbride proposed a date for the Umm Dabaghiyah settlement in the early 6th millennium BC, contemporary with the deepest level at Hassuna, thus attributing it to the phase which we have elsewhere labelled 'Pottery Neolithic'. She could recognize no relationship between these skin-trading hunters and the hill-people of Jarmo in the northeast, though the two cannot have been widely separated chronologically.

SAMARRA AND SAWWAN

During the years following the finds at Hassuna, a secondary problem which occupied Mesopotamian prehistorians concerned the status of the distinctive and finely painted Samarra pottery, which appeared side-by-side with the fully developed 'standard' Hassuna wares, appearing to be an extraneous product, perhaps imported from elsewhere. At Matarrah, south of Kirkuk, where Braidwood excavated soon after the publication of Hassuna, this pottery seemed to be preponderant; he therefore concluded that he was dealing with a basically 'Samarran' culture.[60] Few distinctive criteria of such a culture were, however, there apparent and its final revelation in an authentic setting had to await the discovery in 1964, by an Iraqi scholar, B. Abu-al-Soof, of a new and extremely productive site in the immediate vicinity of Samarra itself.[61] This was the settlement now known as Tell-es-Sawwan, where five occupation-levels were subsequently excavated, all but the earliest exclusively associated with the intriguing painted wares, originally found unstratified in this area by Herzfeld. Like Kirkbride's site in the Jazirah, Tell-es-Sawwan held many surprises. In addition to dwelling-houses of sun-dried brick, there were strange, T-shaped buildings with many rooms, identified by the excavators as granaries. One of them showed evidence of religious installations.

35

During the third occupation, the whole area of habitation had been enclosed by an outer wall, irregularly buttressed and protected by a formidable ditch – the earliest defensive system yet found in Mesopotamia. Other discoveries at Tell-es-Sawwan included more than 100 burials, mostly beneath the floors of houses. Grave-goods from this source were indeed remarkable: quantities of fine alabaster vessels, and, of the same material, a striking collection of human figurines, almost totally dissimilar from those of baked clay, found elsewhere in a Chalcolithic setting.[62] In another sphere, food-grains and other vegetable remains together with a plentiful variety of fish and animal bones, have made it possible to envisage the life of the settlement: a mixed economy based on agriculture, aided by rudimentary irrigation, hunting and herdsmanship.

45

Here then was an indigenous manifestation of the hitherto elusive Samarran culture, centred apparently upon the Tigris at the northern extremity of the alluvial plain. Excavations at related sites have indicated its geographical extension, in the east to the frontiers of Iran (Choga Mami, near Mandali) and westward to the Euphrates (Baghouz, near Abu Kemal).[63] The fact that at Tell-es-Sawwan hardly a single sherd of Hassuna ware was found emphasizes the disparity between the two cultures.

Architecture

THE PRE-HALAF PERIOD

At the earliest village sites in northern Iraq, house walls are most commonly built of *pisé*, and rendered in mud plaster. In rarer cases (e.g. Umm Dabaghiyah), gypsum plaster was preferred for wall-faces and pavements alike. Sun-dried bricks, shaped in a wooden mould, do not appear until the end of the Hassuna period. Stone foundations occur only at Jarmo, where stream-beds could have provided the material. At Jarmo also, pavements were of 'clean mud packed over beds of reeds'. From the beginning, multi-roomed dwelling-houses seem to have been planned on a rectilinear principle. At Umm Dabaghiyah each consisted of one main room, often measuring no more than 2 × 1.5 m, and others even smaller, reached through archways less than 1 m high. Here, unexpected features were fireplaces with hooded chimney-flues, connected through the base of the walls with external bread ovens. A single example of a similar contrivance was found at Jarmo. A built-up step and toe-holes in the walls apparently made access to these rooms possible through an opening in the roof. At Yarim Tepe, the

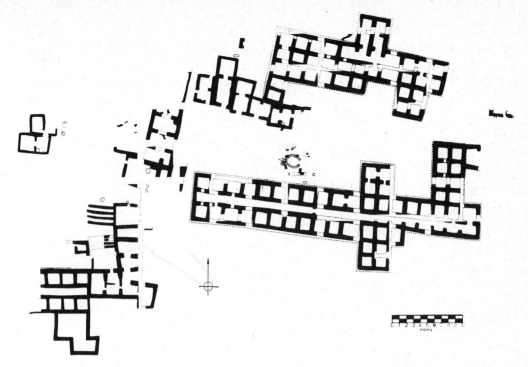

size and number of the rooms was considerably greater, one single house measuring 14 × 6 m. Houses were built in contiguous groups (Umm Dabaghiyah), lining narrow alleys (Yarim Tepe) or facing their own open courtyards (Hassuna). In addition to the usual domed bread ovens, many houses were provided with large circular grain-bins, partly buried in the ground and lined with gypsum or protected by a coat of bitumen.

In the village at Umm Dabaghiyah, domestic quarters were subordinated to the two great cellular blocks of storage chambers, whose hypothetical association with a trade in hides has already been mentioned. Their walls were of 'strongly tempered clay', 50 cm thick and unplastered. The individual cells, of which over seventy were excavated, had an average dimension of 1.50 × 1.75 m and no communicating doorways.

THE SAMARRAN PERIOD
Architecture of this period is represented at two sites on the periphery of the southern Mesopotamian alluvium: Choga Mami[63] on the Iranian frontier and Tell-es-Sawwan on the Tigris.[61] The former was a large, agricultural village (350 × 150 m), apparently profiting from some primitive system of artificial irrigation. Houses had up to twelve rooms, with walls built of 'cigar-shaped mud-bricks' and plastered with clay. In the more sophisticated settlement at Tell-es-Sawwan, building methods had improved and a wooden mould had been used to make prismatic bricks (Arabic, *libn*), with average dimensions of 80 × 30 × 8 cm. The large T-shaped buildings at this site, built to a standard plan with up to fourteen rooms, are not yet fully explained. Doorways between rooms showed that they were for habitation and some of their contents suggested normal domestic occupation; yet they were first identified as granaries, and for one

34 Plan of the Umm Dabaghiyah settlement at level IV, with storage buildings, perhaps for drying onager skins. (After Kirkbride, 1975)

34

35

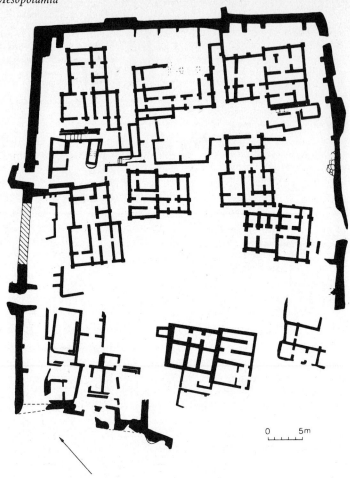

35 Tell-es-Sawwan, layout of the Samarra period settlement at level III (*c.* 5350 BC), with distinctively planned buildings in a walled enclosure. (After Abu al-Soof, 1968)

of them a religious purpose was suggested by a room with some sort of ritual installation, a niche with an alabaster statuette.

THE HALAF PERIOD

In the Halaf levels at Arpachiyah, an architectural innovation takes the form of circular buildings, called by the excavators 'tholoi'. At various levels in the mound itself or in outlying parts of the site as many as ten of these were found, though no more than two seem to have existed simultaneously. The earliest are isolated circular structures, 4 m or so across; but later their diameter increases to over 6 m, and the thickness of their walls to 1.65 m. They are now approached through a rectangular 'dromos', like the 'bee-hive tombs' at Mycenae, and in one case there is a transverse antechamber. As a rule only their stone foundations had survived; but one provided evidence of a *pisé* superstructure – probably a low dome. Owing to the number of graves and cult-figurines found in their immediate vicinity, Mallowan was inclined to attribute a religious purpose to these buildings. But more recent discoveries in Syria and Iran of settlements where dwelling-houses were predominantly circular, have made this interpretation less convincing.[64] Within the frontiers of Iraq, a contemporary parallel

36

to the Arpachiyah 'tholoi' occurs at Tepe Gawra (level XX) and there are earlier examples at Yarim Tepe.

THE 'UBAID PERIOD

The earliest building in northern Iraq to be confidently identified as a temple occurs in level XIX numbering downwards at Tepe Gawra, and coincides with the beginning of the 'Ubaid period at that site. It has a rectilinear plan, with flimsily built mud-brick walls, but is reconstructed on a more impressive scale in level XVIII, with no less than twenty rooms arranged around a central sanctuary (?). This has a podium in the middle but no recognizable altar. Circular buildings reappear in level XVII, but they show no evidence of cult-practices and temples are not again found until level XIII, when, as has already been mentioned, the summit of the mound was cleared to create an emplacement for a group of three obviously religious buildings, with distinctive plans and wall-treatment. They were built around an open courtyard, almost 20 m wide, overlooked on three sides by their façades, which were ornamented with a complicated system of multiple recessing and painted in different colours. Of the so-called 'Northern Temple' the entire plan was recovered: a rectangular sanctuary running the whole length of the building, with two lateral chambers on either side, separated by deeply recessed niches whose purpose is not apparent. As is usual in a pre-literate setting, there is no evidence to associate the building with a particular cult. The mud-brick walls are surprisingly thin, but strengthened at regular intervals by stouter piers, upon which the ceiling beams must be presumed to have rested. This system of building is one which we have already seen in temples XI–IX at Eridu in the south, though the sub-period which they represent would appear to antedate the 'acropolis' at Gawra. In the north, Gawra XIII seems to represent the culmination of the 'Ubaidian period. In level XII there were signs of a great conflagration which had destroyed the entire settlement.

THE 'GAWRA' PERIOD

It is from a sequence of four later occupations at Gawra (levels XI–VIII), that most is to be learnt about developments in northern Iraq during the phase which in the south has been called the Uruk period. Here, the cultural transformation following the end of the 'Ubaidian epoch can be seen as clearly in the architectural remains as in the character of the pottery and the increasing profusion of metal objects. Rather surprisingly, the most conspicuous building in level XI was a circular affair known to the excavators as the 'Round House'. Its metre-thick outer wall has a diameter of over 18 m and internally the plan can be seen to comprise no less than seventeen rooms. Their arrangement has no ritual significance and there is no justification for attributing to the building any religious purpose. In this connection we are reminded by D. and J. Oates (1976) that

round houses are found in some of the earliest settlements in the Levant from the Natufian period onwards and represent, with rectangular houses, one of the two simple forms of permanent structure that might have evolved from different traditions of construction in the temporary dwellings of a mobile population.

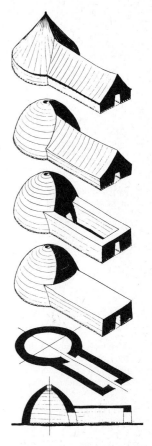

36 Alternative reconstructions of the 'tholoi' at Arpachiyah: circular buildings, entered through a rectangular 'dromos' (Tell Halaf period, *c.* 4800 BC). They may, or may not be religious shrines. (After Mallowan and Rose, 1935)

37

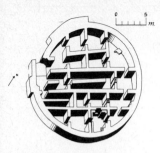

37 The heavily built 'Round House, in level XI at Tepe Gawra: a building of unknown purpose, corresponding in date to the Protoliterate period in southern Mesopotamia. (M. E. Weaver after Tobler, 1950)

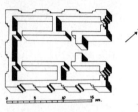

38 Projected reconstruction of a 'Gawra period' temple in level VIII. Several examples were found of temples built to this plan, which is peculiar to the site and period. A comparison with the pre-Greek 'megaron' plan has been tentatively suggested. (P. P. Pratt after Speiser, 1935)

There accordingly seems to be little reason for attributing to the 'Round House' in level XI any non-secular function. Indeed, it is during this same occupation that elsewhere the first example appears of an actual temple, planned in a manner which was to persist throughout the remainder of the Uruk period. These peculiar buildings, of a type found until now only at Gawra, have aroused a good deal of interest.[65] They consist of a rectangular sanctuary, approached through an open portico, with two lateral chambers on either side. One example in level VIII has a free-standing altar or offering-table at one end of the cella, while another has façades ornamented all round with doubly recessed vertical panels. It is notable that more than one such building was often found in the same level and that burials seemed to be concentrated around them.

TELL BRAK

The only other temple building of the Uruk period in this northern area of Mesopotamia was found by M. E. L. Mallowan in 1938 at Tell Brak, a site on the River Khabur beyond the present Syrian frontier.[66] This large building (30 × 25 m) differed completely from those at Tepe Gawra described above, having many features in common with the Uruk temples in the south. The central sanctuary extended from one side of the building to the other and had small transepts at one end, similar to those mentioned earlier in level IV at Uruk itself. A row of lateral chambers on one side was balanced by a more complicated arrangement of chambers on the other, and the whole enclosed in a stout mud-brick wall on stone foundations. Its decoration, with coloured clay cones and inlaid-stone rosettes, provided another parallel with the southern temples. But most surprising of all was the elaborate ornament in the

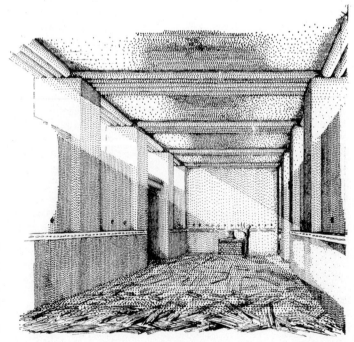

39 An artist's reconstruction of the main shrine-room in the 'Eye Temple' at Tell Brak (Jemdet Nasr period). The altar and wall-faces were ornamented with rich mosaic and inlay, partly of gold. The floor was littered with many thousands of beads and small amulets. (Cf. ill. 46). (P. P. Pratt)

sanctuary itself. Its whitewashed walls were 'decorated with coloured stone rosettes, strips of red limestone inlay and copper panelling'. There was an altar at one end, bordered at top and bottom with sheet-gold between bands of coloured stone, attached by gold-headed silver nails. The temple was raised upon the ruins of two other similar buildings and it was named by the excavators the 'Eye Temple', on account of the 'eye' or 'spectacle' motif appearing *39* everywhere in the ornament and in the form of innumerable votive *46* images of alabaster, buried beneath the floor in a medley of beads, amulets and stamp-seals. Since these had clearly survived from the lifetime of earlier temples Mallowan attributed the Eye Temple itself to a late stage in the Uruk–Jemdet Nasr period. Regarding the significance of the 'eye' symbol, the excavators could reach no definite conclusion.

Pottery

PRE-HALAF

In northern Iraq, the task of correlating the finds from a dozen important excavations and of analysing the interplay of successive cultural changes which they imply has now been prolonged for almost half a century. It has involved a long process of meticulous recording, while the patient consideration of logical inferences has moved from one stage to another. In this milieu, the study of pottery and small finds has assumed an even greater importance than was the case in the south, where other forms of evidence were available and the influence of intrusive cultures from beyond the frontiers of Mesopotamia less evident. As a result, and particularly in the realm of pottery, the field of study has assumed a high degree of complexity and may well appear intimidating to the student or layman who must approach it through a labyrinth of technical description and diagrammatic illustration. In the present context, therefore, a simplified commentary on variants in ceramic practices and some other artifactual peculiarities may be sufficient to convey an impression of the varied evidence which has contributed to an orderly interpretation of prehistoric developments.

At the earliest sites hitherto discussed in this chapter, we have been largely concerned with the transition from what has been called Pre-Pottery Neolithic to Chalcolithic cultures. Conveniently, this has been found to coincide with the first use of painted ornament on pottery. The initiative in this respect must be attributed to the first settlers in the Jazirah and Sinjar districts. At Umm Dabaghiyah the painted patterns are primitive – spots, stripes and chevrons – but there are also crude figures of men and animals in plastic relief. At Hassuna burnished and coarse, straw-tempered pottery in level Ia gives way to 'archaic' painted wares (levels Ib–III), with parallel lines of glossy paint or a burnished finish. The remainder of the pre-Halaf occupations produced the so-called 'Hassuna standard' wares, with pin-scratched or painted *40* ornament, used together or separately on an unburnished slip to decorate a very limited range of characteristically shaped bowls and jars. Side-by-side with these from level III upwards, Samarra pottery appears, distinctive in itself and clearly a luxury *41* commodity imported from elsewhere.

40 Painted and/or incised 'standard wares' and a 'husking-tray': all characteristic of levels III–VI at Hassuna. A few sherds of this pottery were collected from the deepest level in Mallowan's sounding in the Küyünjik mound at Nineveh (over 30 m beneath the surface). (After Lloyd)

41, 42 (*Below right*) Typical Samarra painted wares from Hassuna, including (bottom left) a crude local imitation and (above) a so-called 'face-urn' similar to those found in the deepest levels at Troy. (After Lloyd and Safar, 1945). (*Below left*) A photograph of one of the bowls, with a design showing stylized ibexes

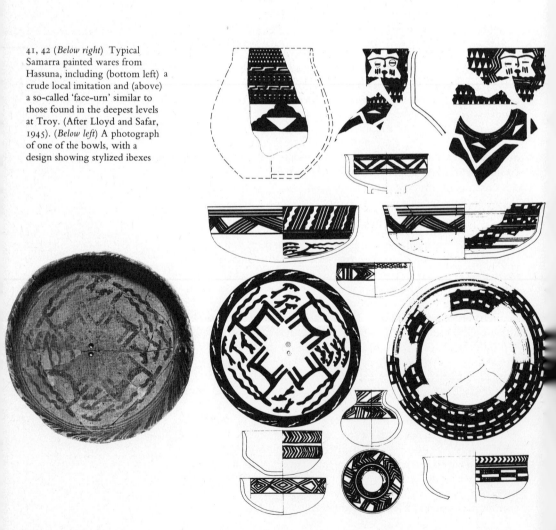

The repertory of Samarran designs has been exhaustively studied   *41–2*
at Baghouz and elsewhere.[67] Perhaps the most characteristic form
is an open dish with internal border ornament and a centripetal
design, often incorporating human or animal figures. Samarran
designs are painted in black or reddish brown on a thick cream or
pinkish slip, with multiple chevrons and other geometric devices,
in which the painted lines are wider than the spaces between them.
At Hassuna and the main Samarran sites there are also 'face–urns',
like those found at Troy, with the principal features modelled in
relief. The skill and good taste of the Samarran potters is
emphasized by the ineptitude of crude imitations occasionally
made locally at sites like Hassuna.

TELL HALAF

The elaboration of painted designs on pottery reaches its peak in the
polychrome wares of the Tell Halaf period.[68] The colours used are   *43–4*
in fact mainly restricted to red, reddish or purplish brown and
black; but when applied for instance to an apricot-coloured slip,

43 Polychrome and other
painted wares of the Tell Halaf
period (*c.* 4800 BC). Patterns in
this 'fully developed' style
include (bottom left) the stylized
'bucranium' motif. The Halafian
culture extended northward into
Anatolia and westward through
Syria to the Mediterranean.
(After Mallowan)

44 A polychrome dish from
Arpachiyah, of the Tell Halaf
period

the tones vary greatly and their contrasts are emphasized by the
sparing use of white paint. Where the Samarra patterns contrived
to give an impression of movement, those of the Halaf pottery have
been described as 'static' or 'architectonic'. They cover a larger
proportion of the vessel's surface than is the case with most other
styles, and there is a good deal of rectilinear panelling, checker
patterns with alternating detail like tile-work, dotted areas and fish-
scale ornament. The development of these designs can be traced
through successive stages, of which only the last is truly
characteristic. One individual motif may be taken to illustrate this
process, namely the bull's head or 'bucranium'. In its earliest,
naturalistic form, it appears isolated and empanelled. Later it is
simplified, turned sideways and repeated to make a running
pattern, which is finally stylized to a point at which its original
significance is forgotten. Among the various forms of Halaf pottery
there are also characteristic shapes, of which the most popular is
perhaps the shallow open dish, decorated inside with border
ornament and a central panel. But there are also flat-bottomed
bowls, carinated bowls with flaring rims and distinctive squat jars.

The distribution of Halaf-type pottery is again interesting. It has
been found as far north as Diyarbakir in Anatolia, and westward
from the Euphrates crossings to the ʿAmuq and the Mediterranean
coast at Ras Shamra. Its southern limits seem to correspond
approximately to the latitude of Baghdad. It has no relationship
with contemporary ceramic developments in Iran, except with the
Kermanshah area, and must be considered indigenous in northern
Mesopotamia.

NORTHERN ʿUBAID
The formative stages of the ʿUbaid culture are still something of a

mystery; but its attainment of a mature form seems to have coincided with the earliest unification of upper and lower Mesopotamia. Whether it evolved in the two areas simultaneously or (which appears more probable), spread northward from the direction of the Arabian Gulf, the characteristics by which it can be recognized archaeologically are as easily distinguishable at Gawra or Arpachiyah as they were at Ur and Eridu. The earliest 'Ubaid levels at Gawra suggest that the transition from one culture to another was a gradual one. The pottery at first retains some characteristics of the Halaf period or combines them with new conventions. Yet, when the new culture has reached its full maturity, in Gawra XIII, the differences between northern and southern 'Ubaid pottery are no more than could be occasioned by local disparities in the raw materials available or an improved understanding of technical processes, such as the firing of clay and the handling of paint. One particular type of vessel, found in both settings, is of so eccentric a shape that it must be assumed to symbolize some short-lived but universal convention. Variously described as a 'lenticular' or 'tortoise' jar, it is a flat hole-mouthed affair with a single trumpet-shaped spout rising almost vertically from its shoulder. Its stratigraphical contexts in the north and south respectively are of some significance, since they link the first two 'Ubaid levels at Gawra (XIX–XVIII) with the post-Hajji Muhammad phases (3 and 4) at Eridu. This could perhaps be taken to equate Samarra in the north with the 'Eridu' phases in the south.

Post-'Ubaid

Less need perhaps be said about the pottery of the post-'Ubaid phase, which has logically been taken to correspond with the Uruk period in the south. Its outstanding characteristics are, first, the total absence of painted ornament, and secondly the fact that, unlike the 'hand-made' pottery of earlier periods, most vessels now showed traces of having been turned on a fast-moving wheel. At levels XI–VIII at Gawra, pottery of brown or buff clay with straw tempering replaces the fine, greenish-grey fabric of the 'Ubaid period. The burnished or polished monochrome wares, so common in the south at this time, are rarer here, though lightly burnished grey pottery actually predominates at the contemporary site called Grai Resh, in the Sinjar district west of the Tigris. [69] As in the south, however, one of the most distinctive forms of pottery at these and other northern sites during this period is the 'bevelled-rim bowl' or *glockentopf*, a small, very coarsely made vessel, produced in great numbers and easily broken. In the present writer's opinion, it was given away free with the food which it contained or was used for votive offerings.

As a symptom of the great cultural change which can be detected in these levels at Tepe Gawra, ceramic innovations are hardly less conspicuous than the evidence of a sudden interest in metallurgy. A principal source from which the metal was derived seems to have been the frequent groupings of richly furnished graves, to which we must now refer.

Burials

Where burials are concerned, we have till now mentioned only in passing those for instance at Tell-es-Sawwan, with their votive treasure of alabaster vessels or figurines and the 'Ubaid cemetery at Arpachiyah which was the source of so much painted pottery. At other northern sites, the few simple shaft-graves and urn burials dating from the early periods were of less interest. At Gawra, however, the sudden multiplication of interments during the final 'Ubaidian occupation (level XII) seemed to anticipate the more sophisticated funerary practices of the Uruk period. In levels XI–VIII, burials were of two sorts.

There were no less than 200 simple interments, of which about 80% were infants, buried indiscriminately beneath the floors of houses or in the vicinity of religious buildings. Some adults were perhaps buried in a cemetery beyond the limits of the village; but the more distinguished members of the community were provided with carefully built tombs, among the buildings on the mound itself. There were as many as 80 of these structures: rectangular chambers of stone or mud-brick, roofed with timber or stone slabs. Each as a rule contained a single body in a contracted position, apparently fully dressed, though sometimes also covered or wrapped in reed matting.

Apart from the structure of these tombs, their interest centred on the wide variety of personal ornaments which they contained. Beads, in particular, had been used to decorate every part of the body, so that over 25,000 could be recovered from a single burial. Listed among the materials of which they were made are turquoise, jadite, cornelian, hematite, marble, limestone, quartz, obsidian, lapis lazuli and diorite, as well as shell and ivory, implying trade with countries as remote as Afghanistan. Perhaps most surprising of all was the profusion of ornaments in gold. Most of these were rings, rosettes, small 'studs' and crescentic decorations, cut from sheet metal and applied to the cloth of garments or diadems; but there was one small object, a finial ornament of electrum in the form of a wolf's head, composed of separate elements skilfully welded together.

The main significance of these tombs in levels XI to VIII lies first in the implication they suggest that the mound at Gawra was now occupied by a people with new skills and increasing sophistication. Above all, the advance in the practice of metallurgy is most remarkable. In the 'Ubaid levels beneath, a mere half-dozen metal objects were found, hammered or cast from pure copper without the addition of tin. In the post-'Ubaidian levels, metals generally, including bronze, seem suddenly to be in general use. For the excavators were able at one point to record that 'the whole ground seemed to be tinged green with decaying copper or glinting with gold'. If the Gawra settlement at this period may be thought of as an unpretentious rural community, the discovery of a site at which the metropolitan aspect of the same culture could be examined and compared with the contemporary achievement of Protoliterate peoples in the south would teach us much about the chronological and other relationships between them.

45 *Below*: a male figurine in terracotta from level I at Tell-es-Sawwan. In later (Samarra) levels at this site, upright alabaster figurines of a quite different type were found in large quantities, with many bowls of the same material. Ht 6.7 cm. *Above*: a Samarra-period terracotta head from Choga Mami. Ht 4.8 cm

Small Objects

FIGURINES

Cult objects are comparatively rare among the small finds at Chalcolithic sites in northern Iraq. An interesting exception is the class of female figurines, loosely associated with the term 'mother-goddess'.[70] Unlike the 'lizard-headed', standing figures of the 'Ubaid period in the south, these are usually steatopygous creatures, seated or squatting, with exaggerated breasts and thighs. In the earliest examples, for instance from Yarim Tepe, the surviving heads have pinched faces on thin necks and are prolonged in a form which suggests a conical headdress.[71] But here also there are already traces of the painted ornament characteristic of later times, when features such as 'trousers' with crossed braces or belts are represented, and some body ornament which may be tattooing. In several beautiful examples from Choga Mami of the Samarra

Overleaf
46 'Eye' or 'spectacle' idols, a great variety of which were found in the Jemdet-Nasr-period temple at Tell Brak. One particularly large one was thought by Mallowan to have stood upon the altar in the main sanctuary (cf. ill. 39). Examples were also found from the late 'Ubaid period onwards at Gawra. Their significance is unknown. Ht of tallest, 11 cm

period, heads are modelled and painted in much greater detail, showing, in addition to the conical hairdress, 'coffee-bean' eyes with painted eyelashes, and facial ornaments such as nose- or lip-plugs.[72] Figurines of this sort of the Halaf period are common to sites in Syria, such as Chagar Bazar and Tell Halaf itself,[73] but they are also found for instance at sites as far apart as Çatal Hüyük in Anatolia and Tepe Sarab in western Iran (Singh 1974, figs. 43 and 63), emphasizing the closer cultural contacts between northern Iraq and the neighbouring countries from the Neolithic period onwards. Their precise significance as cult objects has been variously interpreted. At Ur and Eridu they were found in graves, while at Arpachiyah and Tell-es-Sawwan a religious purpose was tentatively attributed to the buildings in which they were discovered.

Another class of figurine, important for dating purposes, is the 'spectacle' idol or 'eye' symbol, most notably associated with Tell Brak. Two dozen examples of these, in clay or stone, were found at Gawra, mostly in levels XI–IX, which should make them contemporary with the earlier building-levels of Mallowan's Eye Temple.

SEALS

Other significant objects, which make an early appearance in the painted-pottery levels, for instance at Gawra, are personal seals. Primitive 'seal-pendants' with geometric designs in the Halaf levels give way to hemispherical stamp-seals, whose pictorial designs attain an interesting degree of sophistication in the terminal phase of the 'Ubaidian occupation. A particular group of steatite or serpentine seals, attributed to the first post-'Ubaid period (level XI), show figured designs of great interest. Spidery engravings of horned animals and hunting-dogs alternate with ritual scenes in which masked men appear. Two figures are sometimes combined in an attitude of copulation.[74]

47 Stamp-seals and impressions from the 'Protoliterate' levels at Tepe Gawra. Other motifs include hunting dogs, masked men and human figures in an attitude of copulation. (From Speiser, 1935)

Foreign Relations

SUSIANA

It would be out of place, and even impracticable here, to follow or even summarize the parallel developments and interaction of Chalcolithic cultures in the neighbouring countries most closely associated with Mesopotamia.[75] In northern Syria, Anatolia and particularly in Iran – not to mention their remoter extension towards the Caucasus and Afghanistan – so much has been added to our knowledge of the period by recent excavations that they have in a sense usurped the priority of interest earlier accorded to the great river valleys. Nevertheless, there is one area, beyond the modern frontier of Iraq though adjacent to the ancient home of the Sumerians, which cannot escape our attention. This is the Iranian province known as Khuzistan, and named by archaeologists 'Susiana' after the great city which was its capital in Elamite times. Long before the beginnings of written history, this country was closely linked to southern Mesopotamia, of which it can be seen as a physiological extension. Here, due north of modern Basrah, the

48 Two examples of the finely painted pottery, called by de Morgan 'Susa I' (now known as 'Susa A'). It is dated to the transition between the 'Ubaid and Protoliterate periods, *c.* 4000 BC. Ht of pot above, 26.8 cm

line of the Zagros Mountains recedes eastward, leaving a wide area of seasonally fertile uplands, watered by the tangled courses of three rivers – Karkheh, Shaʿur, Ab-i-Diz – and connected by a fourth, the Karun, to the Shatt-al-Arab.

The first evidence of habitation here in prehistoric times was provided in 1897 by French excavations in the great city-mound at Susa itself. A huge cemetery, adjoining the later town-wall, produced much of the marvellous painted pottery now in the Louvre, which thus anticipated by almost twenty years Woolley's discovery of the 'Ubaidian culture in Mesopotamia. Most striking of all was a class of beakers and tall goblets, painted with stylized patterns of birds and animals, which the excavator, Jacques de Morgan, designated by the term 'Susa I' and which are still
48 considered by some to be the highest accomplishment of ceramic

craftsmanship in the Near East.[76] With no comparative material yet available, the age of this pottery was at first considerably overestimated. In fact, a further fifty years were to elapse before its correct placing in the sequence of prehistoric periods could be properly understood. During that time, many new discoveries in Iraq and a dozen excavations at smaller sites in Khuzistan itself (which have been more recently multiplied) furnished the material for a comparative study. This was undertaken by the late L. Le Breton and published in 1957.[77] It was now proved that de Morgan's 'Susa I' (in future to be called 'Susa A') belonged to the last of five phases into which the Iranian painted pottery cultures were divided ('Susiana a, b, c, d and e'), and that it corresponded chronologically with the transition from the ʿUbaid to the Uruk period in Mesopotamia. For the previous four periods ('Susiana a–d'), convincing parallels could be found with the whole sequence of developments in Iraq, from Hassuna and Eridu onwards. Le Breton was able to recognize three further phases ('Susa B, C and D') corresponding to the Mesopotamian Protoliterate. To 'Susa C' he was able to attribute the so-called 'Proto-Elamite' pictographic writing, found at Susa itself, where its use would have been a logical result of the close ties between Susiana and Iraq in the Uruk and Jemdet Nasr periods. Since it has now been found at such remote sites as Tepe Yahya, in the Soghum valley 140 miles south of Kirman, and at Sialk, Godin, Malyan and Choga Mish, it must have been widely employed in Iran at that time.[78]

Chapter Five

The Early Sumerian Dynasties

The Protoliterate period must be regarded, not as a prelude to Sumerian civilization, but as a first formative phase in its development, during which major contributions were made to the establishment of its identity. All that we know about it has been learnt from the results of excavations; but once it is ended, we find ourselves on the threshold of written history, and from now onwards must check our archaeological conclusions against the testimony of contemporary documents. The phase with which we shall next be dealing is generally referred to as the 'Early Dynastic' period: a title which is explained by the contents of a single, primarily important written document. This is the so-called 'king-list', in which the political anatomy of the Sumerian commonwealth and the succession of its rulers were at some time committed in writing to the memory of Mesopotamian posterity.[79] Several slightly varying versions of this text have survived, and among them is one which can be dated (partly by the point which it stops), to the beginning of the 18th century BC. The earlier part of the same list even reappears in Greek, among the writings of Berossus, an obscure historian of the Hellenistic age.

49

Before speaking further about this document, in which the concept of 'kingship' is at least implicit, it may be well to enlarge a little upon the titles variously attributed to the rulers of Sumerian city-states during successive phases of their political evolution. In the early inscriptions, a number of different terms are used to imply forms of state leadership which are not precisely defined. Among these are *ensi* ('lord'), *en* (perhaps 'overlord'), *lugal* ('great man' or 'king'), and the distinction between them has been the subject of much thought and some controversy. The fluctuating conclusions of authorities on the subject are usefully summarized by Saggs and Gadd, both writing in 1962. Saggs recollects the interesting proposal presented by Jacobsen in 1943. He reached the conclusion that 'Sumerian kingship was not primitive but evolutionary and that its action was, at least sometimes, controlled by an assembly of elders and community heads or even by the mass of free men'. This theory was based on a study of early literary sources: '. . . the myths, the tales of the behaviour and exploits of the gods, which are generally thought to reflect the sociology of the times at which Sumerian society crystallized in the city-state . . .', probably very early in the 3rd millennium BC. According to Jacobsen writing in 1943, one function of the 'general assembly' was to choose an official called *En*, who was 'primarily a cult-functionary, being the consort of the city's patron deity, and playing a vital role in the

Sacred Marriage upon which the fertility of the city state depended'. His secondary administrative functions, in connection with the temple lands, gave him great political importance, and at one stage he became virtually the ruler. Very early, there came about some division between the priestly and secular functions of the *En*, who no longer lived in the temple but in a pretentious palace of his own. Later, during the historical period, the actual ruler

49 Part of the 'king-list' document, found at Khorsabad by Loud. It is a late Assyrian copy of an earlier text

was no longer the *En*, but an official originally concerned in the agricultural operations, who bore the title *Ensi*. Cultic duties were delegated to a special priest or priestess. . . . In the event of an attack from the outside, the assembly had to choose a war-leader or king (*Lugal*). . . . The office of neither *En* nor *Lugal* was originally hereditary or permanent, that of the *Lugal* at least being granted only for the duration of the emergency.

The *En* or *Lugal* might attempt to perpetuate his position of authority and the two functions might then be vested in the same man. He could not be an absolute ruler, and could act only as authorized by the assembly.

Jacobsen's view of Sumerian society and its political structure, which aroused much interest when originally presented, is today less generally accepted, owing to a lack of further confirmation by new historical texts. The bare facts of what we are justified in concluding about the status of Sumerian rulers are that *lugal* remained the general designation of a 'king' and that an *ensi*, though a governor in his own right, might be subordinate to a *lugal* in another city.

The King-list

Here are some features of the king-list as we know it today. It presents us first with the names of eight semi-legendary rulers 'before the Flood', and of the cities with which they are believed to have been associated. 'After the Flood', we are told, 'Kingship was sent down from on high'. A more factual chronicle then follows, introducing us to a federation of city-states, only one of which at any given time held supremacy over all the others. A succession of dynasties is accordingly listed, each based upon an individual city, whose hereditary rulers on such occasions became 'Kings' of 'the Land' and accepted responsibility for its welfare. Occasionally genealogical information is given, or mention is made of some happening which explains the transfer of hegemony from one state to another. This secondary list, as has often been pointed out, 'was not composed for the benefit of modern scholars', and from their point of view has manifest defects. The stated lengths of individual reigns are, for instance, fanciful and it has long been realized that certain dynasties in fact ruled concurrently in their own cities. Yet it does serve to emphasize the Sumerians' overall conception of the Land as an entity. Also it embodies for the first time a catalogue of the principal Sumerian cities – Sippar, Shuruppak, Kish, Ur, Adab, Mari, Akshak, Lagash, Isin, Larsa and others about which less is known.

The king-list does not of course come under the heading of what we have called 'contemporary documents'. It is rather a retrospective record, assembled at a later date from traditional information. The same is true, for instance, of the great Sumerian epics, like the story of Gilgamesh, which have survived through repeated recopyings in the Akkadian and other languages of later ages.[80] We should now therefore glance at the actual historical information gleaned from the increasingly articulate writings of early Sumerian scribes, and note the extent to which their prolonged study in more recent times has served to authenticate some parts of these Mesopotamian classics.[81]

The Earliest Written Texts

The earliest pictographic writing found in the archaic levels at Uruk has been mentioned in a previous chapter, where it was noted that, even if the language of the 'Uruk 4' tablets could be considered as inconclusively identified, that of the 'Uruk 3' (Jemdet Nasr) texts was demonstrably Sumerian. Following these chronologically in the 'archaic' series were, first, a group of tablets found by Woolley during the 1920s, in a stratum preceding his 'Royal Tombs' at Ur, and secondly, inscriptions discovered by the German excavators, W. Andrae and R. Koldewey, at Farah (ancient Shuruppak), at the beginning of the present century.[82] At this point, however, we must recall that, practically without exception, the subject of all the writings so far mentioned are no more than lists and quantities of commodities or persons. The first instances of individuals (usually kings) adopting the use of writing for the purpose of recording such things as religious dedications or personal accomplishments are contemporary with or slightly later than the Farah group mentioned above, though they were found more recently, by Woolley at Ur. It is therefore true to say that, until late in the second decade of the present century, the royal names in the king-list, including even that of Gilgamesh himself, could have been considered creations of the Sumerian imagination. It is accordingly understandable that something of a sensation was caused by Woolley's discovery in 1919, among the ruins of an Early Dynastic temple at Al 'Ubaid, of a foundation tablet bearing the names of Mesannipadda, first king of the first Dynasty of Ur, and of his son, A'annipadda. [83]

By that time, methodical excavations by German, French and American archaeologists were in progress at the sites of other Sumerian cities mentioned in the king-list, including some from which large quantities of tablets had been unsystematically extracted by earlier excavators. In the decades which followed, therefore, many new Sumerian texts were discovered, not only by the diggers themselves but by philological scholars who were now at work studying museum collections. [84] In this way, further royal names were added to the list of kings who now proved to have been genuine historical characters. Before discussing these further, it will be necessary to anticipate the archaeological record, by citing briefly the broad conclusions which have come to be accepted regarding the chronology of the Early Dynastic period.

Archaeological Phases

This so-called Pre-Sargonid era (preceding the unification of Mesopotamia under Sargon of Akkad), has come conventionally to be divided into three phases. 'Early Dynastic I' (ED I), following directly upon the end of the Protoliterate, is approximately dated to the years between 2900 and 2750 BC; 'Early Dynastic II' (ED II) lasted until 2650 BC; while 'Early Dynastic III' (ED III), divided into two sub-phases, 'a' and 'b', is taken to account for the greater part of three further centuries. This system of chronology was constructed largely from evidence obtained in the 1930s during excavations by the Oriental Institute of the University of Chicago at sites in the Diyala region, east of Baghdad. [85] It was based, as we shall presently see, on progressive variations in the architecture, sculpture, pottery, seal-cylinders and other small objects associated with several temples, founded in most cases at the end of the Protoliterate period and repeatedly rebuilt in Early Dynastic times. Its validity has been confirmed, with only minor reservations, by subsequent soundings of the same sort at Nippur and elsewhere (see below).

The 'Flood'

The task of adapting this archaeological hypothesis to the chronological implications of the Sumerian texts has on the whole proved less difficult than one would have imagined. One initial problem concerned the date and significance of 'the Flood', which figures so prominently in Sumerian tradition and whose memory has indeed been bequeathed to ourselves through the medium of Hebrew scriptures. The archaeological evidence in this connection was unfortunately extremely equivocal. Great floods were a commonplace of Mesopotamian history until quite recent times; and it was therefore less than surprising to find that, in deep soundings at relevant Sumerian sites, clean strata of water-borne sand or clay appeared in stratigraphical contexts which varied in time from the 'Ubaid period at Ur to the end of the Early Dynastic phase at Kish.[86] At Farah (Shuruppak), however, a stratum of this sort occurs at the end of Early Dynastic I, and in this single case it could, as we shall now see, be cited (without much conviction) as supporting evidence for an inference from the Sumerian textual evidence.

Where the king-list is concerned, there can no longer be any doubt that the semi-historical epoch, represented by a succession of 'rulers before the Flood', must be equated with the archaeological series defined as 'Early Dynastic I'. The individual names of these 'rulers' are of little interest, since only the last to be listed has any historical significance. And here there is a connection of some importance with an episode in the Epic of Gilgamesh, when its hero made a journey to consult Utnapishtim, the Babylonian Noah, about the secret of eternal life. It had always been a matter of some surprise that this individual should receive no mention in the king-list, where the last name before 'the Flood' appeared as Ubartutu, a ruler of Shuruppak. In another version of the Deluge story, however, its hero is given the alternative name, Ziusudra, and a surviving fragment of the text makes it clear that he was the son of Ubartutu.[87] The implication here that Ziusudra and Gilgamesh were contemporaries is unfortunately refuted by the fact that the former was deified after the Flood, and was accordingly already a god when Gilgamesh met him.

On the subject of Gilgamesh himself, other sources of textual evidence were to prove more rewarding. One of these was an important text of which versions were found both at Ur and at Nippur, giving the names of kings who had piously repaired the structure of a shrine called 'Tummal', not yet located, at the latter city. These included the names of three kings, Agga, Gilgamesh and Mesannipadda, belonging respectively to the first dynasties of Kish, Erech (Uruk) and Ur.[88] The king-list, as we have said, would have us believe that these three dynasties followed one another in chronological succession. In this case, however, such a claim is clearly refuted by other evidence, which proves the three kings mentioned to have been much more nearly contemporary. We know for instance from a Sumerian epic that Gilgamesh of Erech fought against Agga of Kish, but also that it was Mesannipadda of Ur who put an end to the Kish dynasty. As for the latter king, his name appears not only on the foundation tablet from Al 'Ubaid, but on seal-impressions found in the Royal Cemetery at Ur. Armed with this and other evidence of the same sort, we are safe in dating all three kings to the third phase of the Early Dynastic period, perhaps between 2650 and 2550 BC.

Between the Flood and Gilgamesh, we are now left with a period of time (computed by Mallowan at about 100 years), corresponding archaeologically with Early Dynastic II. Many of the kings' names allotted to this period are either Semitic intrusions or recognizable divinities; but two of them have proved historical. The first of these is Enmebaragisi, father to Agga of Kish, whose name has been significantly found in an Early Dynastic II setting at one of the Diyala sites.[89] The other is Enmerkar of Erech,[90] subject of a very early Sumerian epic, who appears in the Greek version of the king-list as grandfather of Gilgamesh. With these two figures now authenticated, our line of enquiry is rapidly approaching its *terminus post quem* in the person of Ziusudra, the Babylonian Noah.

Early Dynastic Sites

KHAFAJE

We must now return to the archaeological record and enumerate some of the Sumerian sites which have contributed to our now very extensive knowledge of the Early Dynastic period. For this purpose, it may be well to start with the so-called 'Diyala' sites, if only because the finds there played so large a part in the establishment of a chronological structure on which subsequent calculations could be based. And in this area, priority should perhaps be accorded to the site called Khafaje (ancient Tutub), to which attention was drawn in the years preceding 1929 by the great quantity of fragmentary Sumerian sculpture which illicit digging was bringing into the hands of Baghdad dealers.[91] The source of these antiquities was a mound near the east bank of the River Diyala, some 15 miles north of its confluence with the Tigris, and a single season's excavation by a team from the Oriental Institute of the University of Chicago revealed the presence, directly beneath its summit, of at least two Sumerian temples, one of which, occupying a central position, was dedicated to the moon-god, Sin. During the years that followed, numerous rebuildings of the shrine were carefully traced, through levels representing every phase of the Early Dynastic period, down to an original foundation in Jemdet Nasr times.

The Sin Temple at Khafaje, like those of the Protoliterate levels in the Eanna Precinct at Warka, belongs to the category of 'ground-level' temples. That is to say, it was not at any time raised upon an artificial platform, but occupied a site whose shape, if not its size, was dictated by the layout of residential buildings around it. Following the already age-old tradition of temple building, its basic element took the form of a long rectangular sanctuary, with a podium altar at one end and an entrance on the cross-axis at the other. To this, in the case of the earliest Sin Temple, lateral chambers were added on either side, creating a conventional tripartite plan. Little was added to this simple structure until its fifth rebuilding at the beginning of the Early Dynastic period (Temple VI), when the shapeless forecourt through which its worshippers approached was extended and converted into a walled enclosure, with a formal gatehouse and various outbuildings. Four further

50 Projected plan of Sin Temple VIII at Khafaje dating from the Early Dynastic II period (*c.* 2750–2650 BC). Its plan is adapted to the irregular shape of the site originally available when Temple I was built in the Jemdet Nasr period. (After Delougaz)

93

rebuildings during later periods left the asymmetrical shape of the complex unaltered. Only in level IX was the outer entry given greater dignity and the courtyard provided with an open-air shrine.

P. Delougaz, who was in charge of the Khafaje excavations, found the whole summit of the mound honeycombed with the pits and tunnels of illicit diggers. One whole season had to be spent in removing the loose earth from them and in tracing the walls of which fragments had survived in undisturbed areas. In this way, his skill as an excavator enabled him to reconstruct the plans of the two latest Sin temples (IX and X) and to recover such objects as the looters had missed. The additional collection of votive statuary from this source, though impressive in itself, was overshadowed by the temple fittings, ritual vessels and small objects found undisturbed in the deeper levels. This valuable assemblage of finds was also supplemented by the contents of three smaller temples, found among the dwelling-houses to the west and south of the site, which had escaped the attention of the looters. One was a large shapeless enclosure containing two separate shrines, dedicated, as Delougaz understood from an inscription, to the mother-goddess, Nintu. There were also two smaller, single-shrine temples.

Since all these buildings appeared to be 'ground-level' temples, it was perhaps less surprising that, in the course of the first season's work, a wide area on the lower slope of the mound to the west was found to be covered by the scanty remains of a vast oval-shaped temenos which had once provided a setting for a typical 'high temple' raised on its artificial platform. The excavation of the 'Oval Temple' at Khafaje presented Delougaz with a technical problem which would have daunted many excavators. The area enclosed by its double line of outer walls had a maximum dimension of almost exactly 100 m; but neither the outer walls themselves nor those of the buildings which they enclosed remained standing more than a few brick-courses high. Delougaz was compelled to adopt a method of excavation earlier perfected by the Germans at Warka, which involved articulating every individual mud brick and thereby recreating the pattern of walls which they composed. After much labour in training Arab workmen to do this, the whole ground-plan of the complex was eventually recovered.

The plans and reconstructions show three stages of building in the second and third phases of the Early Dynastic period. First, there is an almost symmetrical oval enceinte, around which outbuildings are arranged to form a rectangular inner courtyard. Half filling this space, the outline only could be traced of the temple platform, with a single stairway leading to it. To the first enclosure wall a second is added, distorted somewhat in shape to allow room for an outer courtyard and a roomy dwelling-house, perhaps for a priest. In the second building phase (ED IIIa), the outer wall increased in thickness and was strengthened with external buttresses, while in ED IIIb a new and pretentious portal was added, occupying most of the outer courtyard. A section cut by Delougaz through the two enclosure walls showed their offset foundations beneath pavement level; but it also revealed a phenomenon which has rare parallels in other periods of temple building. Before the foundations were laid the entire area of the

51–3

53

51 Reconstruction of the Oval Temple at Khafaje, as rebuilt in the Early Dynastic III period (*c.* 2650–2350 BC). Only the foundations of the temple platform and its oval enclosure walls had survived; the appearance of the raised shrine itself is conjectural. (After Darby)

52 Air photograph of the Oval Temple, from the south, showing a later town wall and buildings in the background

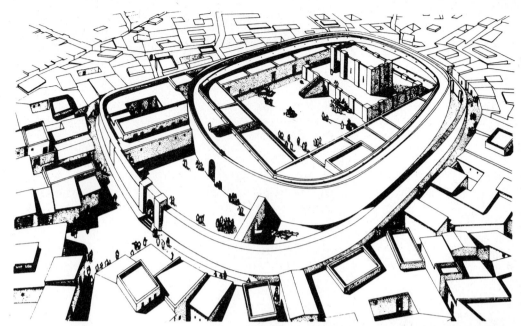

53 Excavating the foundations of the Oval Temple enclosure at Khafaje (looking northwest). The individual mud-bricks (of the 'plano-convex' type) had laboriously to be articulated. The excavators in the foreground have discovered the deposit of sand on which the foundations rested

temenos had been excavated to a depth of 4.6 m and then filled with clean sand, brought from some source outside the city. Delougaz estimated that 64,000 cubic metres of sand had been moved for the purpose, and assumed that ritual conventions could alone account for so great a labour.

Complementary to the finds from these temples at Khafaje were the contents of graves, almost 200 of which were found in the town area, mostly beneath the floors of dwelling-houses.[92] They varied from simple shaft burials to walled tombs, at least two of which were built of kiln-baked brick and covered with corbelled vaulting. The grave furniture consisted mainly of pottery vessels, whose great number and variety contributed effectively, as we shall later see, to the final analysis of Early Dynastic stratigraphy.

Tell Asmar

In post-Sumerian times, the city whose remains were found at Khafaje became part of a politically important state called Eshnunna, the capital of which was at Tell Asmar, 50 miles northeast of modern Baghdad. Here too there had been a city in Early Dynastic times, and a small temple was excavated by the Oriental Institute of the University of Chicago concurrently with those at Khafaje.[93] The 'Abu Temple' (as it came to be known after the discovery in it of a statue bearing the 'plant' insignia of that god, elsewhere described as 'Lord of Vegetation') was founded, like the Sin Temple, in the Jemdet Nasr period, and its architectural history could again be traced up to a final rebuilding early in Akkadian times. From a small and shapeless 'chapel', its plan developed first on conventional lines, into a building with a rectangular sanctuary and one row of lateral chambers. This 'Archaic Temple' corresponded in time to the first phase of the Early Dynastic period. In the second, it was replaced by a 'Square Temple', with rectangular chambers, three of which were miniature sanctuaries, arranged around a central court. In the third phase, the plan reverted to a 'Single Shrine Temple', similar to the smallest of the series at Khafaje.

54

The finds in these buildings at Tell Asmar were plentiful, and of a sort with which the Diyala excavators soon became familiar: beads, carved amulets, seals and even a bronze mirror, in addition to stone vessels and a wide variety of pottery. Where sculpture was concerned, a striking find was made in a sanctuary of the Square Temple. Carefully buried beneath the pavement beside the altar was a cache of twenty-one stone votive statues, remarkably well preserved. Furthermore, these were distinguished by a formalized style of carving, perhaps characteristic of the Early Dynastic II

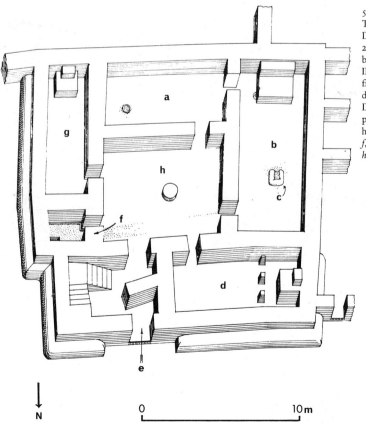

54 Projected plan of the Square Temple at Tell Asmar (Early Dynastic II period). A cache of 21 votive statues were found buried beside the altar in shrine II. The building differs little from plans of contemporary dwelling-houses. (After Delougaz and Lloyd, 1942). *a*, priests' room; *b*, Shrine I; *c*, hearth; *d*, Shrine II; *e*, entrance; *f*, ablution room; *g*, Shrine III; *h*, courtyard

N

0   10 m

55 A view of the Shara Temple (Early Dynastic II period) after excavation. The main sanctuary, with its altar and offering-tables, can be seen in the centre. Secular buildings of later times accumulated around the once consecrated site, when the temple itself had fallen into ruins at the end of the Early Dynastic period

phase, which contrasted interestingly with the more naturalistic Early Dynastic III sculpture from Khafaje.

TELL AGRAB

The third of the Diyala sites, and almost the last to be excavated, once more dramatically illustrated the capabilities of these Sumerian temple-builders. This was Tell Agrab, a large city-mound far out in the now-empty alluvial desert (*chôl*), 15 miles east of Tell Asmar.[94] The temple here, whose walls appeared directly beneath the surface, was again square in plan but measured no less than 60 m from side to side. Part of the building nearest to the city-wall had been denuded by rainwater, but the surviving half contained not only the impressive main sanctuary, but two subsidiary shrine-chambers and living accommodation for priests; their walls survived in some cases up to 2 m high. The most prolific source of removable objects was the sanctuary itself and a small 'sacristy' chamber adjoining its high altar. As had been the case in the Abu Temple at Tell Asmar, discarded or damaged cult-objects and votive offerings had been buried beneath pavement level, or even built into the structure of the altar itself. In the sacristy alone, many weeks were spent in recovering delicate products of Sumerian craftsmanship, deposited in layers and covered with hard earth. Among many thousands of beads and small objects, including carved amulets and seals, were unique art-works in sculptured stone or bronze and some hundreds of stone maceheads, perhaps used for processional purposes. More will be said later about these finds in dealing with the categories to which they belong. As for the stratigraphy of this temple, apparently dedicated to Shara, the patron god of Umma, the bulk of the surviving ruins could be dated to the second Early Dynastic phase; but small sections of an earlier building (Early Dynastic I) were excavated beneath it, while finds on the surface suggested a later occupation in Early Dynastic III.

UR-OF-THE-CHALDEES
In 1930, when work on the Diyala sites began, Woolley's excavation at Ur-of-the-Chaldees had already been in progress for more than ten years and his spectacular finds there had provided a great volume of comparative material for the benefit of other workers in the same field.[95] From prehistoric times onwards, Ur had been a great cultural and religious centre of the Sumerian people, and it continued to be so, long after its political importance had diminished.

At the site, whose modern name is Muqayyar, Woolley found himself dealing with a walled city, roughly oval in shape and having a maximum dimension of over $\frac{1}{2}$ mile.[96] It was surrounded on its north and west sides by an ancient bed of the Euphrates and had been served by two harbours for shipping. Near to the surface in the northwestern quarter were the walls of a very extensive religious precinct, built by Nebuchadnezzar in the 6th century BC to enclose its temples, temple-palaces and subsidiary buildings, most of which had been piously maintained and frequently rebuilt by a long succession of Mesopotamian kings. It is understandable, therefore, that little remained on the surface of their original foundations, which were by now for the most part deeply buried beneath the structural accretions of later times. This applied equally to the city's great ziggurat, built in part by kings of the Third Dynasty, late in the 2nd millennium BC. Woolley satisfied himself that, somewhere enclosed within its later fabric, were the remains of a much earlier tower – a modest ziggurat rather than a mere temple platform – and, deeply buried beneath the later pavements on either side of it, he found the denuded walls of other Early Dynastic buildings, clearly associated with it.

But it was in another part of the site that Woolley made the sequence of discoveries for which this Sumerian city became most famous. In the time of Nebuchadnezzar, the sacred temenos had been considerably extended at its southeastern end and the foundations of its new enclosure wall had penetrated into an important burial-ground of earlier times. It was here that Woolley made a deep sounding and was rewarded by the discovery of a cemetery, dating from the Early Dynastic period. Among many hundreds of more modest burials he encountered a group of 'Royal Tombs', whose accompanying display of contemporary riches astonished the world.

Woolley found altogether sixteen of these tombs, each distinguished by the construction in their shafts of stone-built chambers, sometimes with more than one compartment. They were roofed with corbelled vaulting of stone or brick and, in at least one case, the construction of a dome had been attempted. A more significant characteristic was the evidence which they provided of an elaborate funeral ritual, involving some sort of human sacrifice. The major tombs were approached from the surface by a sloping ramp, and it was at the foot of this, beside the tomb-chamber, that the bodies were found of soldiers and female attendants, as well as

56

57

99

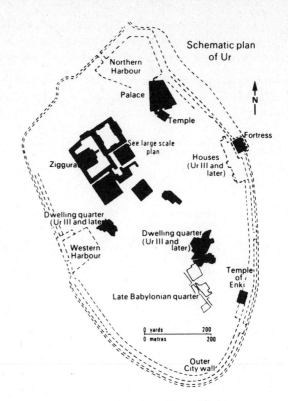

Schematic plan of Ur

Northern Harbour

Palace

Temple

See large scale plan

Fortress

Houses (Ur III and later)

Ziggurat

Dwelling quarter (Ur III and later)

Dwelling quarter (Ur III and later)

Western Harbour

Temple of Enki

Late Babylonian quarter

0 yards 200
0 metres 200

Outer City wall

56 The city of Ur at the time of its Third Dynasty and later. Ur-nammu's city-wall was destroyed by the Elamites in 2006 BC. Woolley found it to have been over 27 m in thickness and traced the remains of two harbours accessible from the Euphrates. The inner Temenos Wall was rebuilt by Nebuchadnezzar of Babylon fifteen hundred years later. (From Hawkes, 1974)

wheeled vehicles with their draft-animals, which had formed part of the funeral cortège. All these were disposed in an orderly manner in the shaft, while some privileged individuals shared the burial chamber itself with its principal occupant. The personnages whose deaths had been the occasion for so much ritual lay as a rule on a wooden bier, surrounded by a great wealth of personal possessions. The number and variety of these – ornaments, weapons, musical instruments and other treasures – create an inventory of beautiful objects, whose archaeological interest even exceeds their intrinsic value. Many of them have been made familiar to a wide public through the medium of book illustration and museum display; but the aptitude of their design and high standard of craftsmanship remain one of the great marvels of antiquity.

There is space here only to recollect some examples of the more characteristic burials, and for this purpose one must use the catalogue numbers by which Woolley distinguished them.

59   The burial whose contents are perhaps best known of all is that of 'Queen Shubad' (no. 800B), whose name, inscribed on her lapis-lazuli cylinder-seal, is now read as Pu-abi. Unlike some others, this grave had escaped the attention of tomb-robbers, so that both its stone chamber and shaft, with the retinue of attendants, remained intact. In the dromos (an extension of the shaft) were 5 soldiers, a wagon drawn by 2 oxen and 10 court ladies, one of whom was a harpist.[97] In the tomb-chamber, the queen was accompanied by two companions. She wore splendid jewellery, including the

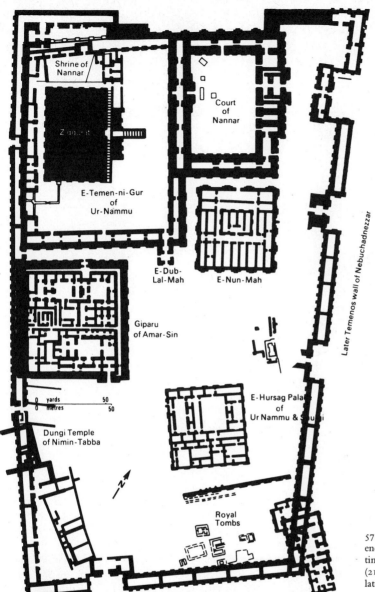

57 The great Temenos or sacred enclosure at Ur dating from the time of the Third Dynasty (2113–2006 BC), showing some later features. (From Hawkes, 1974)

elaborate headdress of gold and semi-precious stones of which reconstructions are to be seen in the British Museum and elsewhere. Around her were vessels of gold and silver, a harp decorated with a cow's head, an inlaid gaming-table, an electrum rein-ring surmounted by the figure of a wild ass, and 267 other objects of great value. A chest containing the queen's clothes concealed a hole in the floor, through which the workmen preparing her tomb had penetrated into and partially looted another chamber beneath. This Woolley assumed to have been the 'King's Tomb', since again its own shaft and dromos were occupied by appropriate sacrifices, formally disposed. There were in all 59 bodies, including 6 soldiers who had led the cortège, 2 chariots drawn by 6 oxen, 19 court ladies

58

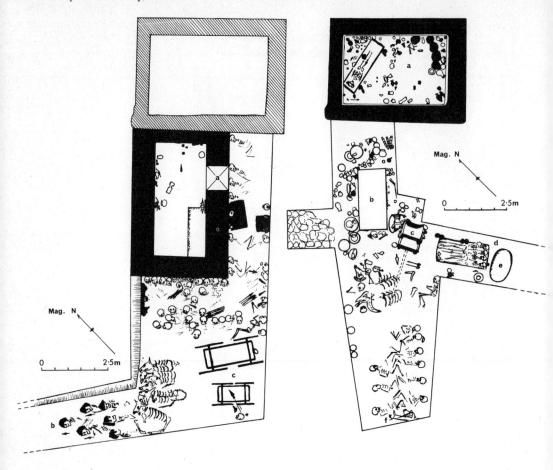

58 The so-called 'King's Tomb', no. 789, in the Early Dynastic cemetery at Ur, found by Woolley beneath tomb 800 (ill. 59). Against the tomb wall is a row of court ladies and near them guards with spears. (S. Ebrahim after Woolley, 1935). *a*, door; *b*, dromos; *c*, wagons

59 The tomb of 'Queen Shubad' (or 'Pu-abi' as she is now known), no. 800, built over the 'King's Tomb', no. 789 (ill. 58). (S. Ebrahim after Woolley, 1935), *a*, tomb 800B; *b*, chest; *c*, chariot; *d*, dromos; *e*, pit; *f*, lyre

in gold headdresses and, elsewhere in the shaft, a lyre with an inlaid sounding-box and the head of a bull in gold and lapis. Despite the hurried looting of the chamber itself, a silver model of a boat and a shell-inlaid gaming-table remained in place.

Another grave whose occupant was identified by his name on a cylinder-seal was that of Akalamdug (no. 1050). He was accompanied by the bodies of 40 attendants and from the shaft came two of the finest ceremonial daggers, one with a lapis-lazuli haft and granulated gold ornament. Another tomb was that of Meskalamdug (no. 755), owner of the famous golden 'wig-helmet', now in the Iraq Museum, whose name was also inscribed on a gold lamp. But the expenditure of human lives seemed to reach its climax in the great, anonymous shaft-grave (no. 1237), which contained 74 bodies – 68 of them women in full regalia, some with lyres. Mallowan, who was present when this burial was exposed, has described the impression which it created: '. . . the ghastly scene of human sacrifice, a crowd of skeletons so gorgeously bedecked that they seemed to be lying on a golden carpet'. Major treasures from this source included the two gold and lapis he-goats, rampant against bronze foliage, which reminded

Woolley of the biblical phrase, 'a ram caught by its horns'. Like the magnificent 'royal standard' with its inlaid scenes of 'war and peace', found in a plundered tomb elsewhere (no. 779), the purpose of these too was uncertain.

In the years since these discoveries were made, some authorities have questioned Woolley's use of the term 'Royal Tombs', suggesting an alternative identification of their occupants as participants in some fertility cult-practice.[98] Today, however, the evidence in favour of the excavator's own conclusion has come to be generally accepted. On the seal-cylinder of Akalamdug he is given the specific title, 'King of Ur', while that of Meskalamdug similarly designates him as *lugal* (king). As for the practice of human sacrifice, in a passage from the Epic of Gilgamesh a hero is 'accompanied in death by some of his retainers'. But Mallowan and others have also pointed out that at least half-a-dozen of these 'royalties' appear to be members of a single 'Kalam' family, and that they may well represent a 'dynasty', preceding that associated by the king-list with Mesannipadda and his successors. In the disturbed strata overlying Woolley's cemetery, inscriptions have been found, naming these kings of the canonical 'First Dynasty of Ur', and the circumstances suggest that their own tombs may have been more effectively plundered than those beneath. This being the case, the two dynasties have been respectively associated with the archaeological phases Early Dynastic IIIa and IIIb.

AL ʿUBAID

At this point something should be said about Woolley's earlier (1922) excavation at the small neighbouring site of Al ʿUbaid, where H. R. Hall had already discovered a rich deposit of Sumerian antiquities.[99] Here, the prehistoric settlement to which we have alluded in a previous chapter seems to have been abandoned at the beginning of the Protoliterate period. In Early Dynastic times, however, a temple had been built nearby, probably on the site of a much earlier religious shrine, and dedicated by King A'annipadda to the goddess Nin-khursag, mother and wife of Enlil. Its platform, whose façades were faced with kiln-baked brick, had survived almost intact, and it was in the angle between this and the stairway approaching its summit that Hall had made his most striking find. At some time the temple itself had been dismantled and destroyed, but much of its architectural ornament had been removed and was found still lying where it had fallen or been deposited. A great bronze lintel, with the projecting figure of a lion-headed eagle between two stags, may have decorated the main doorway and a pair of columns, encrusted with coloured inlay, perhaps helped to support it. The wall-faces nearby had also been ornamented with friezes of animals, modelled in high relief and sheathed in copper, while others, inlaid with limestone, depicted formal scenes similar to those on cylinder-seals. The actual form of the building to which these and other decorations had been applied unfortunately remains obscure.

In the mid-1930s, when the remnants of a contemporary temple platform were found at Khafaje, Delougaz suspected a close parallel with its counterpart at Al ʿUbaid. Further soundings which he was

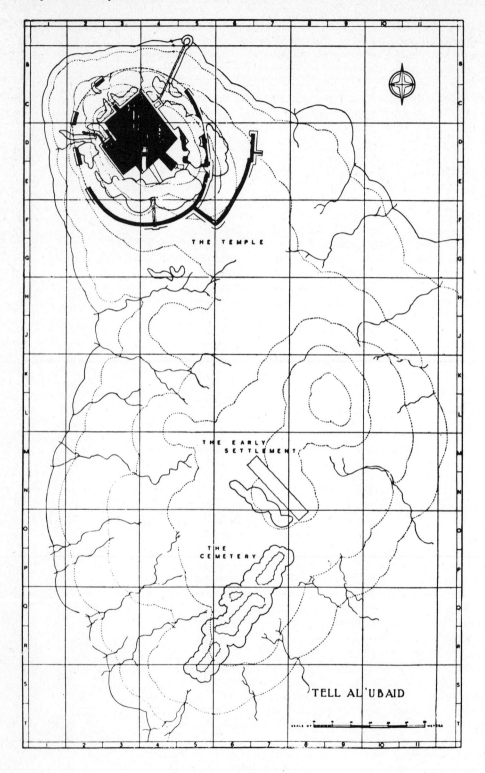

THE TEMPLE

THE EARLY
SETTLEMENT

THE
CEMETERY

TELL AL 'UBAID

SCALE OF .... METRES

then able to make in the vicinity of the Nin-khursag temple confirmed the fact that it too had once been surrounded by an oval-shaped enclosure wall.[100]

KISH

The only examples of temple platforms (described by their excavators as 'ziggurats'), dating from the Early Dynastic period, are those at the site of Kish. It will be remembered that this city, first in the series of dynastic capitals mentioned in the king-list, was held in great respect by the Sumerians; and indeed, the eponymous title 'King of Kish' was afterwards sometimes assumed by rulers of other cities which attained the hegemony of the Land (Sumer). Today, its site is represented by a wide grouping of mounds, once more bordering an ancient bed of the Euphrates, 9 miles east of Babylon. In the course of the city's history, its principal buildings were alternately concentrated in areas over 2 miles apart which are today known as Uhaimir and Ingharra (ancient Harsagkalama). Both were excavated in the 1920s and 1930s by English or French archaeologists.[101]

The earliest finds were made by E. Mackay in an outlying mound of the Ingharra group, afterwards known as Area 'A'. Here there was a cemetery, with graves mostly dating from the final phase of the Early Dynastic period; but, in clearing them, Mackay found that the earlier burials penetrated into the ruins of an extensive and important building belonging to a slightly earlier period. This was the so-called 'Palace A', the first example to be found of a monumental building devoted to other than religious purposes in the early days of the Sumerian dynasties. With its towered portico, buttressed outer walls and columned chambers, it once more emphasizes the dignity of contemporary architecture.

The excavation which was next undertaken in the main mound at Ingharra was in the end extremely productive, though it suffered from some deficiency in archaeological method, which served to detract from the clarity of its subsequent publication. Many years later, however, its stratigraphy was more effectively elucidated by a modern scholar, P. R. S. Moorey, after a painstaking re-

60 The site of Tell-Al 'Ubaid. Plan showing surviving platform of an Early Dynastic temple in an oval enclosure. It is built on the outskirts of a prehistoric settlement, dating from a thousand years earlier, which the Sumerians used as a graveyard. (From Delougaz, 1938)

61 The great lintel, now in the British Museum, from the Temple of Nin-khursag at Al 'Ubaid. Found with other architectural ornament, displaced and lying at the base of the platform, it is composed of copper sheeting over a wooden core and represents Imdugud, the lion-headed eagle with two stags (c. 2500 BC). Ht 107 cm

examination of the actual finds in relation to the contents of surviving field notebooks.[102] His conclusions were broadly as follows.

At the summit of the mound were two Early Dynastic ziggurats of different sizes. The smaller of these had been partly demolished to provide an emplacement for a Neo-Babylonian temple; but the excavators were able to trace the brick façade of an artificial terrace upon which it had stood. In doing so, they located its original foundation, at a level demonstrably contemporary with that of the palace in Area A (ED IIIa); but they could also distinguish a later building-level, separated from the first by a deep deposit of discarded brick debris, into which graves had been dug – some in the subsequent phase (ED IIIb) and others in Akkadian times. These burials could therefore be equated with the cemetery in Area A. The original ziggurat terrace was founded directly upon an easily recognizable 'flood stratum' which covered the whole site, and beneath this an important sounding was made. It revealed part of a residential area (Settlement Y), with dwelling-houses on either side of a narrow street.

Before reaching ground-water, the Y-sounding passed through three distinct occupation-levels, dated by pottery to Early Dynastic I and II, and at each of them there were further traces of flooding. In these levels also, there were many simple graves, dug beneath the floors of the houses; but there were also a number of so-called 'chariot burials', containing up to three wheeled vehicles, though the grave-goods which accompanied them – weapons, vases and even a rein-ring – were mostly of copper. It has been rightly argued that such burials would require deeper shafts than ordinary graves and that accordingly these must belong to an occupation above the main 'flood' level. This could make them contemporary with the Royal Graves at Ur, with which their contents are comparable.

LAGASH

The site called Telloh lies halfway between the Tigris and Euphrates, near the modern town of Shatra. Ever since the beginning of the present century, when E. de Sarzec brought from

101–2 it to the Louvre diorite statues of the governors (here called *ishakku*) of Lagash, it has been comfortably identified as the site of that city.[103] It was not until 1953 that a study by Thorkild Jacobsen drew attention to a neighbouring site called Tell Al-Hiba, 15 miles to the southeast, where excavators from the Metropolitan Museum and New York University have now located the true Lagash, capital of a state, one of whose religious centres was ancient Girsu,

103 now Telloh.[104] We have therefore to accept that 'Tell Al-Hiba (ancient Uruku) is Lagash city, of the state of Lagash, comparable to New York city of the State of New York'.[105]

Nevertheless, it is the finds made early in the present century by the French at Telloh which have provided us not only with important collections of tablets, but with treasures dating from the time of the great rulers of Lagash, mentioned in the king-list, and in some cases bearing their names.[106] Sculptured stone plaques,

68 weapons and seals are associated with Ur-Nanshe, who may have been approximately contemporary with Mesannipadda. There are

fragments of the famous 'Stela of the Vultures' which celebrated 69
the victory of Eannatum, ruler of Lagash, over the neighbouring
city of Umma, and on which he is depicted wearing a helmet
similar to that buried with Meskalamdug at Ur, and there is the
finely engraved silver vase of Entemena, Eannatum's successor.
Some of these objects are known to have contributed to the
endowment of a famous temple dedicated to Enlil at Girsu, but the
early excavations at Telloh were such that its ruins are unlikely to
have been recognized. More will now be learnt about the state
capital from the American excavations in progress there.

NIPPUR

This is another great city of the Sumerian epoch, first excavated by
Americans led by H. V. Hilprecht at the end of the last century.
The mounds, today known as Niffer, extend for almost half-a-mile
on either side of the old Shatt-al-Nil river-bed, northeast of
Diwaniyah. Beneath them on the northeast side are the remains of a
fortified religious quarter, with a ziggurat and temple dedicated to
Enlil at the highest point.[107] Renewed excavations during the
1960s under R. C. Haines partly centred on an area between the
ziggurat and the old water-course, where an Early Dynastic temple
was found, in this case associated with the name of Inanna, 'Queen
of Heaven'.[108] Like similar temples at the Diyala sites, it had been
maintained or rebuilt throughout all three phases of the Early
Dynastic period, and most effectively amplified the evidence
already available, regarding contemporary developments in
architecture, sculpture and the design of pottery.[109] Of great
interest in this respect are the exposures in two levels, VIII and VII
(numbered downwards), respectively representing Early Dynastic
II and the transition from that phase to Early Dynastic IIIa, the era
of the Royal Tombs at Ur.

The temple in level VII showed several remarkable features. Its 75
twin sanctuaries were sited at one end of the long, straggling plan
and were approached through a succession of courts and
antechambers, two of which had circular brick columns to support
the roof. Furthermore, contrary to the general practice at this time,
one of the sanctuaries was entered through a doorway at one end,
on the main axis of the building, thereby anticipating the
convention of later times. In these levels the Inanna temple also
produced a rich harvest of sculpture, partly in the form of votive
statues, whose clearly indicated stratigraphy provided new
evidence for the study of stylistic development. But relief carving
too was represented by an important series of square 'wall-plaques'
of the sort whose purpose is still disputed, though their figured
designs are common to almost all sites in these and later periods.[110]
Of pottery types a preliminary study has already been made, and
confirms to a large extent the chronological conclusions reached in
the publication of the Diyala sequence.

ASHUR AND MARI

Mention must now be made of two other sites, situated in the
rainfall zone beyond the limits of the alluvial plain, yet both clearly

to be considered as outposts of the cultural and political enclave which we call Sumerian. These are, first, Ashur (Qal'at Sharqat) on the Tigris, 188 miles north of Baghdad and Mari (Tell Hariri) on the Euphrates, 7.5 miles north of the present Syrian frontier.

Ashur was later to become the first capital of the state called Assyria. The city was founded on a high rocky promontory, overlooking the river at a point where its main stream was joined by a subsidiary waterway.[111] During the 2nd millennium B C it was surrounded by a powerful fortress wall, to which a second outer wall was later added, and extended to enclose a residential suburb, increasing the river frontage to a length of more than 1.8 miles. Among the public buildings, including three ziggurats, which occupied the northern heights of the old town in these later days, the German excavators under W. Andrae discovered a temple dedicated to the goddess Ishtar, whose earliest foundation dated back to Early Dynastic times. After recording and removing many later rebuildings, they were able to study this 'Archaic Ishtar Temple' and, in the best-preserved building-level, to expose its complete plan and to recover the greater part of its contents.[112]

126–7

Many years later, a very similar find was made by the French at Mari. Here it was to be expected that remains of the Early Dynastic period would be found, since in the king-list it is named as one of the cities from which a dynasty of kings ruled over Sumer. Sure enough, in a position adjoining one of the principal gates in the rampart surrounding the town, the excavator, A. Parrot, found a temple, again dedicated to Ishtar, of which the first three building-levels (a–c) dated from Pre-Sargonid times. In the years that followed, other temples of the same period were found nearer to the centre of the town, and these, like the Ishtar Temple, produced a rich harvest of sculpture and other objects. Meanwhile, Parrot and his team had become preoccupied with the clearance of an enormous palace, dating from the first quarter of the 2nd millennium B C, and this too was afterwards found to have replaced an earlier palace, contemporary with the Ishtar Temple. It was during clearances near this earlier building that they came upon a cache of valuable objects which included a seal-cylinder presented to a local ruler by 'Mesannipadda, King of Ur'.[113] The building was thus firmly dated to the third phase of the Early Dynastic period and the relations between the two Sumerian cities established.[114]

111

The shrines at these two northern sites can now be added to the category of small Sumerian temples at the Diyala sites and elsewhere, to whose architectural and other conventions they almost exactly conform. Each has one or more rectangular sanctuaries, with an altar at one end and an entry on the cross-axis. In each, well-preserved examples of votive statues had survived and, against the side walls of the sanctuary, clay benches could be seen upon which they had rested. At Ashur there were other sorts of votive objects and ritual fixtures in the form of miniature buildings in terracotta. Fragments of a small painted gypsum plaque, showing the recumbent figure of the goddess Ishtar in relief, were thought by the excavators to suggest the form which the cult statue might have taken.

62 A pseudo-Sumerian statue from Shuaira in northern Syria, a city whose inhabitants 'had adopted the garb and manners of the alien peoples dominant in their world at the time'

SHUAIRA

A final word should be said about this site, which is remotely placed in northern Syria, between the Khabur and Balikh rivers, eastern tributaries of the Euphrates. Excavated since 1958 by Anton Moortgat, it has revealed a curiously outlandish reflection of Sumerian civilization, much affected by environmental differences and alien influences.[115] Fully occupied, as the excavations appear to show, both in the Early Dynastic and Akkadian periods, its buildings are of undressed stone, sometimes surmounted by brickwork, and its craftsmanship much affected by the proximity of metal sources. The temples have open porticoes, reminiscent of those in the Protoliterate levels at Tepe Gawra, which have been compared with the 'megaron' dwelling-houses of Bronze Age Anatolia (see above) and there are strange, un-Sumerian burial chambers. Yet there are also many votive statues – albeit small in   62 size and rather crudely made – and pottery vessels with figures in relief and other objects which are unmistakeably Early Dynastic. Of the inhabitants themselves Mallowan says: 'They need not have been Sumerians; they need not even have had any Semitic affinities. It may be assumed that they were wealthy natives, who, like many before them and many after, had adopted the garb and the manners of the alien peoples dominant in their world at the time.'[116]

Variants in Terminology

Readers of Moortgat's reports on this excavation[117] should be warned that some German scholars adopt a different terminology for the chronological sub-divisions of the Early Dynastic period, substituting names with a more epigraphic flavour. The terms they use are approximately as follows:

1 There is a *Mesilim* period, called after a titular 'King of Kish' whose name has been found on a sculptured macehead. This is associated with a group of cylinder-seals in the 'Diyala linear style' (Frankfort), which Strommenger calls 'the early abstract style' of Early Dynastic II (ED II). It also corresponds to the level VIII Inanna Temple at Nippur.

2 Next comes a phase identified by Moortgat with 'cylinder-seals grouped around an inscription [formerly] read *Imdugud Sikurru*'. Strommenger calls this the *Farah* period, and sees in these seals the 'later more naturalistic style' of ED II, perhaps continuing into ED IIIa, like the level VII Inanna Temple at Nippur.

3 After this Moortgat couples together a *Meskalamdug* style with UR I (Mesannipadda) period, which Strommenger equates with ED IIIb.[118]

There have been criticisms both of these terms themselves and of the chronological conclusions which they imply. Mallowan, for instance, points out that Mesilim's name is not included in the king-list and that his macehead could be as late as ED III. (Rowton places him a little before Ur-Nanshe of Lagash, in ED IIIa). Mallowan also reminds us that the Royal Graves at Ur were dug into a layer containing tablets older than those from Farah. Generally, British and American scholars prefer the simpler system of numbered phases.

Chapter Six

Pre-Sargonid Art and Architecture

We have now summarized the main results of excavations at some of the principal ancient cities founded or occupied during the earliest historical periods in Mesopotamia. Our total knowledge of the civilization created during these centuries and of the way of life which it engendered has been acquired from two principal sources: first, from the study of material remains, exposed or recovered by archaeologists, and secondly from the contents of the written documents which their finds have made available to philologists. It is with the former source of information that we are here primarily concerned; so we must now consider the archaeological finds in greater detail. This may again be done under separate headings.

Sculpture

STATUES

It might today seem strange to us that sculpture in stone should feature so significantly in Mesopotamian art. Perhaps the very scarcity of the material and the remoteness of the sources from which it could be obtained themselves invested it with a rarity value, appropriate to the purposes for which it was generally used. For a fact that must initially be remembered is that all forms of Sumerian sculpture, whether statues in-the-round or relief carvings, were of a religious character and intended to perform some ritual function within the confines of a temple. In this respect, the commonest artform, and perhaps the most characteristic of the Early Dynastic period, is the category of votive or 'personal' statues, already frequently mentioned in describing the contents of early Sumerian temples. Fortunately the dedicatory inscriptions often found carved upon them leave little doubt as to their intention. The effigy of an individual worshipper, translated into stone and placed in the sanctuary of a religious building, could be expected to intercede on his behalf with an appropriate deity.[119]

In almost every one of the many temples mentioned in the previous chapter such statues were found. Whether lying displaced or broken beside the brick 'benches' on which they had stood, carefully buried beneath the floor of a sanctuary or even built into the structure of an altar, their recovery has contributed to the great volume of Sumerian sculpture now available for study. All that is now lacking in this field of discovery are the actual cult-statues themselves, which must have stood upon the altar-platform, creating a focal point for the liturgy of Sumerian religious ritual. Among the cache of discarded sculpture found in the Square Temple at Tell Asmar, a pair of male and female figures, almost half life-size, were tentatively identified by Henri Frankfort as god and goddess, by symbols carved on the base of the male figure. But the evidence of these and of the exaggerated size of their staring eyes have proved unconvincing to most other critics, who note in them an attitude of prayer common to all the smaller and less ostentatious votive figures: the folded hands, holding a cup from which a libation is about to be poured, and other features seeming more logically associated with a worshipper than with the object of his veneration. At Ashur too, in the 'Archaic' Ishtar Temple, W. Andrae imagined a gypsum figure of the deity, in high relief above the altar, since a miniature version of such a figure had been found among the debris of the sanctuary.[120] This proposal too did not prove wholly acceptable, since no imprint of it had been left upon the wall. It is in fact not improbable that cult-statues generally were too valuable and too easily removed to be likely to have survived.

It was Frankfort again who first attempted a stylistic analysis of these sculptures, using mainly as his study-material the 200-or-so complete or fragmentary statues recovered from temples at the Diyala sites.[121] Bearing in mind that their peculiarities might be slightly provincial, he was able to distinguish two separate stages in the development of their conventional design: an earlier and a later style of carving, corresponding as it proved, at least in the Diyala region, to the second and third phases of the Early Dynastic period.

Regarding the earlier of these two styles of carving, if we are to look first for its antecedents, they can be found only among the few surviving works of Protoliterate sculptors, to some of which we have already referred. Of these the only object comparable to our votive statues of later times is a rather crudely carved female figure from a Jemdet Nasr provenance at Khafaje, whose hands, folded around some missing object, already suggest an attitude of worship.[122] Chronologically, however, this object is separated from Frankfort's 'earlier' dynastic sculpture by a period of time corresponding to the entire Early Dynastic I period, to which no single work of sculpture has yet been firmly attributed. We shall therefore be justified in concluding that the Early Dynastic II style which we are about to consider, developed independently of any traditional influence. Its characteristics may perhaps best be seen in the group of statues from the Square Temple at Tell Asmar, all of which appear to be attributable to a single 'school' of sculptors.[123]

Of the 'worshippers' in this group, nine are men, dressed in the conventional garment of the period – a simple skirt of wool with a girdle and long fringe. One, who is bald and clean-shaven, can be recognized as a priest; the remainder have square beards and long hair, both neatly corrugated and painted black. Their eyes are inlaid with shell and lapis-lazuli. The twelfth sculpture is the kneeling figure of a priest carved in alabaster, ritually naked and wearing a toque-like headdress. The two female figures also wear a conventional garment, passing diagonally across the breast and draped over the left shoulder. As to their hairstyle, they show two variations of an arrangement common to both the second and third Early Dynastic phases: a 'halo-plait' passing vertically over the crown of the head with a 'chignon' behind. But many other devices are to be seen at this time. The stylistic peculiarity of these figures

63 Stone figure of a worshipper from Khafaje (Jemdet Nasr period): the earliest known prototype of votive statues found in great numbers among the sanctuaries of later Sumerian temples. The style of carving is still undeveloped. Ht 10 cm

64

64 Group of votive statues of the Early Dynastic II period, found in the 'Square Temple' at Tell Asmar. The tallest pair were at first thought to be cult statues of a god and goddess. They represent Frankfort's 'earlier style' of carving, with formalized geometric shapes. Ht of tallest figure, 76 cm

consists mainly in the distinctive rendering of the human body, by the reduction of its component shapes to abstract forms. Whatever the difference between individual statues, the formal principles are the same: the sculptor has somehow rationalized its combination of miscellaneous features into a manageable formula of semi-geometric equations. It can of course be contended that the general simplification of forms may have been dictated in part by lack of technical skill among these early stone-cutters; but the artistry with which it was achieved testifies rather to an interest in design, as opposed to actual representation. An interesting contrast is incidentally to be seen in the contemporary figures modelled for casting in metal. In the Early Dynastic II period metallurgy was already well understood and some striking works in copper were among the finds at Khafaje and Tell Agrab. But the designs are purely naturalistic and show no signs of deliberate formalization.

For the purpose of Frankfort's study, the Early Dynastic III style of sculpture was represented mostly by votive statuary from the later Sin Temples at Khafaje. But it is also abundantly illustrated by examples from other sites, both in Sumer itself and in the dependent provinces of upper Mesopotamia (where the distinction between the two stylistic phases is less clearly defined). The sculptors of this later period have gained in confidence. They have discarded the devices of formal simplification and are no longer afraid to interest themselves in the details of physical appearance. The subtler contours of the body are carefully modelled; mouths and cheeks are shaped to give the face expression; the corrugation

65 The seated statue of Ebih-il from Mari, representing the 'later style' of the Early Dynastic III period. He wears the characteristically Sumerian *kaunakes* garment with 'petals' of wool. His beard indicates the use of a drill: a hallmark of Mari sculpture. The figure is dedicated to the goddess Ishtar. Ht 52.5 cm

66 Seated statue of an individual called Ur-Nanshe, from the Ishtar Temple at Mari. According to an inscription, she (or he?) was a singer at the court of King Iblulil, which may account for the unconventional hairstyle. (Early Dynastic III period). Ht 26 cm

of hair and beards are replaced by a pattern of curls, sometimes separated by drill-holes. An even more conspicuous change has taken place in the design and portrayal of clothing. Now for the first time the so-called *kaunakes* appears: a system of weaving which covers the whole garment with petal-shaped tufts of wool in an overlapping pattern, thought of by some as an attempt to simulate sheep-skin.[124] Certainly it transforms the appearance of these statues and is freely represented in other forms of pictorial art at this time.

There is now in fact a striking uniformity of style and artistic convention throughout Mesopotamia. Fashions in dress and personal appearance are governed by a rigid convention which ignores any regional difference of race or tradition. The idiosyncrasy, for instance, of shaving the head while growing a luxurious beard, which is seen in statues from Khafaje or Warka, is equally common at Mari on the upper Euphrates, where the population is predominantly un-Sumerian. It is in fact from the Ishtar Temple and other Early Dynastic shrines at this northern site that some of the finest and best-preserved Early Dynastic statues are derived, several of them inscribed with their names and occupations.[125] Some also, like the famous Ebih-il, superintendent of the temple, are shown seated upon a chair or stool: once more a convention which is to be seen at Khafaje and elsewhere. Only the women in some cases wear a 'polos' headdress, shaped like a biretta, and one of them has a *kaunakes* outer garment draped over the top of it. By contrast, the 'singer', Ur-Nanshe, is seated crosslegged on a cushion and has straight hair, parted in the middle.[126]

Equally rare are sculptured figures other than those of human beings, such as the bearded cow in alabaster from the Nintu Temple at Khafaje, which Delougaz suspected of being in fact a cult-statue.[127] We should accordingly now turn to the subject of relief carving, since it is plentiful and of great interest.

RELIEF CARVING

In Early Dynastic times this form of carving is at first best illustrated by a class of wall-plaques in stone or slate. They are square, perforated in the centre and decorated in relief with a variety of pictorial scenes. Their purpose has been widely discussed and a number of ingenious suggestions put forward.[128] The most obvious inference – that they were affixed to an interior wall-face by a central peg, perhaps with an ornamental head – is confirmed by some examples in which flanges of undressed stone at the sides of the square are clearly intended to be covered by the surrounding plaster. As for the scenes depicted, they are usually arranged in two or three registers, showing rows of figures engaged in religious ritual or ceremonies associated with royalty. Some are intended to commemorate a particular event; and in one well-known example, both the nature of the occasion and the names of the participants are recorded by inscriptions.[129] Ur-Nanshe, 'divine bailiff of Lagash', is seen carrying bricks for the construction of a temple, accompanied by his sons and attendants. But there were other, more standardized pictorial compositions, one of which had clearly at this time become so stereotyped among Sumerian craftsmen that a missing

67 Sumerian wall-plaque from Khafaje (Early Dynastic III), showing servants attendant upon a king, with his chariot in readiness below. A missing fragment (bottom left), has been replaced by part of a similar plaque from Ur, proving that the design was standardized at this time. The plaque is 51.5 cm square

68 Wall-plaque carved in relief, from Telloh. Ur-Nanshe of Lagash is seen carrying a basket of bricks for the building of a temple – and again, seated among his children. The archaic inscriptions are an unusual feature of this plaque. Ht 40 cm

fragment of a plaque from Khafaje could be restored by reference
to a replica found at Ur, some 100 miles away.[130] This was the
well-known 'banqueting scene', where a royal person in the top
register is being served with food and drink, while below his empty
chariot is being prepared. Musicians and domestic animals
complete the pattern.

As we have mentioned earlier, an important sequence of these
plaques was found at Nippur in levels VIII and VIIB of the Inanna
Temple. They have been very carefully studied by D. P.
Hansen,[131] who points out that, in the earliest examples of all, the
figures are merely drawn with incised lines, whereas they are later
made to project from a recessed background. The designs at this
stage are restricted to simple motifs, reminiscent of cylinder-seals. It
is not until the second phase that they are improved by detailed
modelling and that subjects like those mentioned above begin to be
depicted. One may mention in passing that a musician depicted in a
banqueting scene from level IIIB at Nippur carries an eight-
stringed lyre with a bull-headed sounding-box, precisely similar to
those found in the Royal Tombs at Ur (Early Dynastic IIIa).[132]

Sumerian relief carving reaches a high degree of proficiency in
the final phase of the Early Dynastic period (ED IIIb). Unfortunately few examples of major works from this period have
survived, and our judgment must be based primarily on the
monument known as the 'Stela of the Vultures', fragments of
which were recovered by the French excavators of Telloh and are
now in the Louvre. The scenes, which are carved in horizontal
registers on both sides of the stone, commemorate the victory of
Eannatum, ruler of Lagash, over the neighbouring state of Umma.
The king, wearing a helmet resembling that found in the Tomb of

69

69 Part of the so-called 'Stela of
the Vultures' from Telloh,
showing Eannatum, 'Divine
Bailiff of Lagash', at the head of
the Sumerian phalanx, and
(below) driving his chariot. He
wears a helmet similar to that of
Meskalamdug, found in his tomb
at Ur. Ht 182 cm

70

70 Part of a complicated pot-stand from Tell Agrab (Early Dynastic II), carved in high relief with a scene familiar in cylinder-seals of a 'hero' figure holding spotted lions by their tails. Ht 20 cm

Meskalamdug at Ur, leads a phalanx of his spearmen into battle, drives a chariot at the head of his light infantry and afterwards presides over the ceremonial burial of the dead. On the reverse side, the victory is symbolically attributed to his god, Ningirsu, the warrior-god, son of Enlil, who gathers his victims in a net, sealed with the image of Imdugud, the lion-headed eagle. The objective record of a tumultuous event thus culminates in the expression of a religious abstraction. This monument, with its individual style of carving and ingenious pictorial composition, may well be considered one of the great documents of human history.

Returning for a moment to the Early Dynastic II phase, there are other forms of stone sculpture found in temples: vases, for instance, or vase-holders, with figures partly carved in-the-round. An elaborately ornamental example from Tell Agrab depicts the naked and bearded 'hero', familiar on cylinder-seals, grasping two lions by their tails. In another, a kneeling priest, also naked, bears a vase on his head. But there is another category of vessels which have long remained an enigma on account of their wide distribution in countries other than Mesopotamia. These are flat-bottomed bowls with almost vertical sides, made of a soft greenstone, formerly referred to as 'steatite' (now more accurately identified as chlorite). Their carved designs are unique. To take a typical example from Khafaje, now in the British Museum, standing or seated human figures, Sumerian in appearance, hold spotted snakes or stylized streams of water, which undulate around the face of the vase, above and between mythical beasts and symbols.[133] These include lions, leopards and small bears, with birds of prey and occasional scorpions. But also prominent and more unusual are humped bulls

71

71 A 'steatite' vase, imported from Baluchistan, showing a seated Sumerian figure, a spotted snake and a humped bull (zebu), which is not native to Mesopotamia. These vases have a wide distribution throughout Mesopotamia and Persia. Ht 11.4 cm

of the zebu breed, which is not native to Mesopotamia. Some of these figures are sparingly enriched with inlays of paste or coloured stone. Most remarkable of all, however, is their wide geographical distribution. Almost identical examples have been found as far north as Mari, south of Sumer itself at sites in the Arabian Gulf and, finally, as far away as Mohenjo-daro in the Indus Valley.

Some light has at last been thrown, at least on the subject of local manufacture, by finds at the extraordinary site called Tepe Yahya in Baluchistan, which lies on a main route from Sumer to northern India. Here, in a level appropriately dated to the Early Dynastic II period, C. C. Lamberg-Karlovsky recovered over 1,000 fragments of these 'steatite vases', including some unfinished vessels and 'wasters', together with large pieces of the raw material from which they were being carved. He later located the nearby source from which the chlorite was obtained.[134] The excavator was also able to confirm that in the Early Dynastic III period the designs deteriorated into more simple representations of reed architecture.[135] But their symbolic significance and the talismanic(?) properties which made them so internationally popular at present remain a mystery.

Architecture

BUILDING METHODS
The Sumerians, like other inhabitants of Mesopotamia, constructed their buildings of mud bricks, shaped in a four-sided mould and dried in the sun. Up to the end of the Protoliterate period small rectangular bricks laid flat in horizontal courses (German, *riemchen*) seem to have been the rule; but, after a transitional period, covering the Early Dynastic I period, these disappeared completely and a new method of building was adopted. Bricks were now slightly

72

larger and 'plano-convex' in shape, having one rounded face often marked with the impression of a finger or thumb.[136] They were laid 'on-edge' like books on a shelf, successive courses leaning sideways in opposite directions to create a herring-bone pattern (easily recognizable as a criterion of the second and third Early Dynastic phases). Kiln-baked bricks of the same shape proved more suitable for pavements and wall-faces in parts of a building where water was in use, or for the revetment of an external façade. At a few sites, such as Eridu, Ur, and Mari, some poor-quality stone was locally available and could be used for foundations or powdered to make gypsum plaster. For the rest, buildings of the Early Dynastic period are assumed to have had flat roofs, constructed of palm-trunks, brushwood and clay. Doors pivoted on an indented stone, while windows – generally small and high up in the walls – could be protected by perforated terracotta grilles. In the absence of suitable wood, columns for supporting the roof were rare; but circular pillars, composed of segmentally shaped bricks, were not uncommon in major buildings.[137]

73

TEMPLES

A good deal has already been said about the planning of temples at this period. We have seen how they can apparently be divided into two classes: first, the 'high' temples, raised on brick platforms or actual ziggurats, and secondly those at ground-level, sometimes enclosed by private dwelling-houses. Unfortunately, for reasons which have been explained, very little is known about the planning and appearance of the former, and we are able only to assume some similarity to their prehistoric prototypes. In the second category, however, we are now provided with a dozen examples, so widely distributed among the Sumerian cities and sharing so many characteristics in common that a general analysis can be made of their design and function.

72 In the modern villages of Iraq bricks are made of mud, tempered with chaff and cast in a bottomless wooden mould, smoothed on top and dried in the sun

73 Method of laying the 'plano-convex' bricks, used exclusively in the Early Dynastic II and III periods.

The nuclear element in these temples, then, is a rectangular sanctuary with a door in one of the long sides ('bent-axis approach'). At one end there is a raised brick altar and behind it a wall-niche marking the position in which the cult-statue must have stood. Elsewhere in mid-sanctuary are smaller brick platforms or pedestals usually referred to as 'offering-tables', while brick benches along the bases of the walls served, as we know, as emplacements for votive statues (Ashur). More portable forms of furniture included tall pottery stands, in which some sort of foliage was placed; figures of carved stone or copper, supporting vases or bowls of incense (Khafaje, Agrab, Ur, etc.); 'rush-lights' of copper (Kish) and larger offering-stands of stone or terracotta, sometimes simulating buildings (Ashur). Explicit indications of actual ritual are to be found only in the actual structure of the altar. Its upper surface was sometimes protected by an inlaid slab of stone or slate (Asmar), from which ran a small terracotta drain, discharging into a concealed pottery jar (Agrab). These provisions could suggest either animal sacrifices or the pouring of libations, both of which are portrayed on cylinder-seals and elsewhere.

In its simplest form, this sanctuary chamber needed only a buttressed outer façade, small towers flanking the entrance and a modest annexe containing a bread-oven (Asmar, Single Shrine Temple) to fulfil the requirements of a religious building.[138] As larger and more elaborate temples developed, a main sanctuary as described above continued to be the nuclear element of the plan, around which extensions of various sorts could be added in ways varying according to the shape and other limitations of the site. The first addition (reflecting traditional precedents), would be rows of lateral chambers on either side, including one with a stairway giving access to the flat roof. Next, a forecourt could be contrived by enclosing the open space which usually existed at the approach to the main entrance. In due course this would itself be surrounded by subsidiary chambers, forming a small precinct, itself entered through an outer gateway with flanking towers.

This process of growth is well illustrated by the Sin Temple at Khafaje which, in the final stages of its development, still occupied an irregular-shaped site, surrounded by private dwellings.[139] A complete contrast is presented by other temples for which an open site was available, making it possible for the building to be pre-planned and symmetrically composed. An unpretentious example is the Square Temple at Tell Asmar, which is neatly arranged around a central court in such a way that two minor shrines can be added to the main sanctuary. This more formal type of design, unhampered by site restrictions, reaches perfection in the great 74 Shara Temple at Tell Agrab, whose massive outer walls enclose a number of self-contained units, each with chambers grouped around a separate courtyard.[140] In addition to the generously proportioned main sanctuary, with its two-tiered altar and ranges of offering-tables, two minor shrines are again added, together with elaborate accommodation for resident priests.

A comparative study of all these buildings and the characteristics which they share has now made it possible to visualize rather clearly the appearance and function of a typical place of worship in early

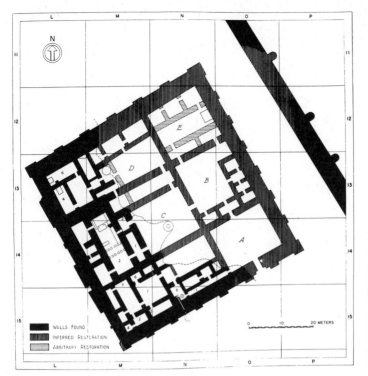

74 Plan of the 'Shara Temple' at Tell Agrab and adjoining city-wall, partly reconstructed by reasoned conjecture. The surviving part comprises (*top left*) a unit with two minor shrines; (*centre*) the main sanctuary, with dependent chambers; and (*below*) a priests' residence. The high altar was built in two tiers, with a miniature stairway. (From Delougaz and Lloyd, 1942)

Sumerian times. One example only seems to deviate from the architectural formula most generally accepted. In the Inanna Temple complex at Nippur, in addition to a sanctuary of the conventional 'bent-axis' type there is a second, free-standing shrine, isolated in its own courtyard and entered by a doorway centrally placed at the end opposite the altar.[141] This arrangement was to become the basic principle of all Mesopotamian temple planning from the end of the Early Dynastic period onwards.

Before leaving the subject of Sumerian temples, something may well be said about the apparent discrepancy between the modest scale of their architectural remains and the magnitude of the purpose which they served. Quite apart from their function as a

75

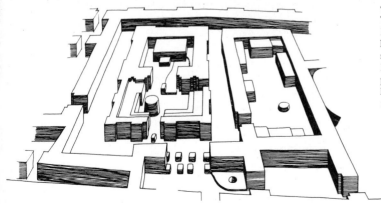

75 Two sanctuaries of the 'Ishtar Temple' at Nippur (level VII, Early Dynastic II). That on the left has the long-axis approach, more common in later times. Elsewhere in this complex were pairs of brick columns. (From Hansen and Dales, *Archaeology*, 1962)

setting for seasonal ceremonial and religious ritual, their paramount function as centres for the economic and political administration of the state would surely lead one to expect far larger and more pretentious buildings than those which we have till now been describing. Let us, for instance, glance at a brief account given by H. W. F. Saggs of their status in this respect and the part which they played in the life of a Sumerian city. He says:

> The government of the Sumerian city-states at this time [mid-3rd millennium BC], was hieratic. ... The city and its lands, with all its inhabitants, was the estate of the city-god, with the ruler or priest-king (of whom Gilgamesh was a prototype) as his steward. The gods created Man to do their service, wherefore the free citizens were the servants of the god.

Their primary function was thus,

> that they should serve the temple estates, or (what was the same thing in ancient eyes) the human who acted as the god's steward, namely the *Ensi* (governor or prince) of the city. In return, each free citizen received an allotment from the god's estates, that is from the temple lands.

It is clear that, in early days, the greater part of the land – or perhaps all of it – belonged to the temple, and it was let out to the people on a share-cropping basis. The *Ensi* was the bailiff of the city-deity and administered the temple estates with a hierarchy of officials to serve him. Private ownership of property in land continued to be very rare until the final years of the Early Dynasties, when the more powerful *Ensis* tended to divert public funds for the aggrandisement of their own families. This led to the rise of a secular power, distinct from the religious authority (and perhaps to the kind of confrontation which took place under certain 'governors' of Lagash). By that time, state rulers had begun to acquire, as we shall see, large palaces of their own; and these perhaps relieved the pressure of space in the temples themselves. But one must also remember that, through the whole of the Early Dynastic period, the service of scribes was still at a premium and the actual bulk of written documents accumulated in the process of state administration still on a very modest scale. Let us now therefore consider what is known about such buildings from excavations.

PALACES

Where secular buildings are concerned, those loosely described as 'palaces' form the most obviously important group. And here we find that any commentary on their architecture is hampered by our imperfect understanding of their function and practical requirements. In the earliest phase of the historical period, the concept of a 'temple' seems to have implied a seat of royalty, as well as the administrative centre for the ruling hierarchy. Later, however, a more effective separation must have taken place between church and state; for the king now had a residence of his own, presumably of a sort which could meet the requirements of political activity and ceremonial. It is these characteristics therefore that we should expect to find in our so-called 'palaces'. There are in fact four notable examples, of which three only – at Kish, Eridu and Mari – have sufficient features in common to suggest a conventional formula for such buildings. The fourth is the Northern Palace at Tell

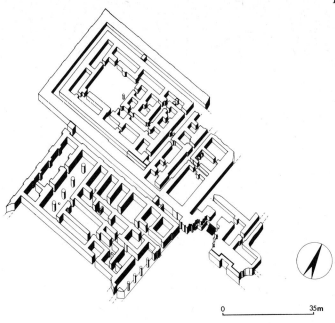

76 Twin palace buildings of the Early Dynastic IIIa period and a monumental gateway at Kish. Here again, circular brick columns are an unusual feature. (After Mackay)

Asmar, which seems at this period to be composed merely of domestic units, each grouped around its own courtyard.[142]

The palace complex at Kish (Early Dynastic IIIa) is composed of two buildings separated by a narrow alleyway.[143] The larger of them, approached through a towered gateway, is protected by duplicate outer walls and has a single interior courtyard, around which it is formally planned. Of the less heavily-walled building annexed to it, the only distinct features are at one end a long hallway with four central columns and at the other some sort of columned 'loggia'. Beyond this, neither plan is in any way self-explanatory. Equally enigmatic in most respects are the twin palaces of the Early Dynastic period, located outside the raised temple-precinct at Eridu.[144] Once more these are protected by

76

77

77 Outside the raised temenos at Eridu, one of two palaces dating from the Early Dynastic period. The unit consisting of a main reception room and square court, sets a precedent for palaces of later times. (After Safar, 1950)

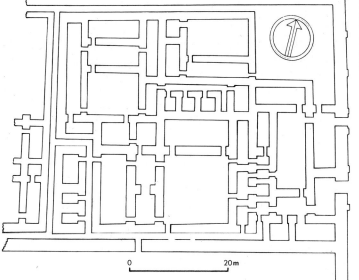

double walls, buttressed like those at Kish in a manner normally considered more appropriate to a temple. Yet here also we see the earliest known example of an 'audience-hall' or 'throne-room', opening off a square central courtyard: an arangement which we shall find adopted from now onwards as the basis of the main 'reception-suite' in all Mesopotamian palaces.

This combination of square courtyard and rectangular throne-room is even more strikingly illustrated in the 'Palais Pré-sargonique', which French archaeologists have partially excavated beneath the southeast corner of the huge 18th-century BC palace of Zimrilim at Mari.[145] Whether or not this will prove to be a single element of a much larger building, its importance as an independent unit is emphasized by the duplication of its outer walls on all four sides. It is also confirmed by another aspect of the building, which has led the French to speak of it as a *zone sacré*. The rectangular hall has a small sanctuary at one end; the square court has ornamentally recessed wall-faces and is provided with ritual installations of various sorts; foundation deposits had been laid beneath the pavement of corridors separating the outer walls. If such discoveries seem strange in a building apparently dedicated to a secular purpose, it should be mentioned in advance that similar features occur in the main reception suite of the great palace built on the same site by Zimrilim some seven centuries later. As we shall see, they have been subject to diverse interpretations.

Cylinder-Seals

The transition from one phase of the Early Dynastic period to another is clearly reflected in the changing designs of cylinder-seals.[146] We have already observed a certain deterioration in the artistic quality of seal-cutters' work towards the end of the Protoliterate epoch, and little improvement is to be seen during the century-or-so which followed. All interest in mythology and religious symbolism seems to have been abandoned, in favour of decorative compositions based on the shapes of animals and plants, supplemented by meaningless ornament curiously reminiscent of textile designs. This 'brocade style', as it has been called, is the hallmark of the first Early Dynastic phase. A reversion to more interesting and imaginative subjects begins to take place early in phase II. One subject which is revived and soon gains in popularity is that of 'animal contests': attacks by lions on cattle and their defence by human or half-human 'guardian' figures. In this role the bearded

78   'hero' reappears and the 'bull-man', now wearing a girdle and ornamental side-locks beneath his horns.[147] Intricate patterns are made from these figures, which are sometimes interlaced or inverted; but there is little attempt at plastic rendering and the linear designing is undisciplined. At a later stage experiments are made with pictorial subjects such as the well-known 'banqueting

79   scene', but the results are hardly more successful. A notable innovation, however, is the occasional introduction of a pictographic inscription.

In the third Early Dynastic phase, seal-making finally attains its full status as miniature relief carving. The figures become more

78 Cylinder-seal of the Early Dynastic II period. Familiar figures of the naked 'hero' and the 'bull-man' protect horned animals from attacking lions

79 A 'banqueting scene' of the Early Dynastic III period. The seated female figure in the top register is identified by an empanelled inscription as Pu-abi (previously known as 'Shubad'), a queen whose body occupied one of the richest tombs in the Royal Cemetery at Ur. Opposite her is presumably her husband Abargi

80 Improved carving in the Early Dynastic III period. Bulls, now shown full-face, are protected from lions by the usual mythical figures

81 A seated figure, identified as Shamash, the sun god, in his boat, with other deities and appropriate animal symbols

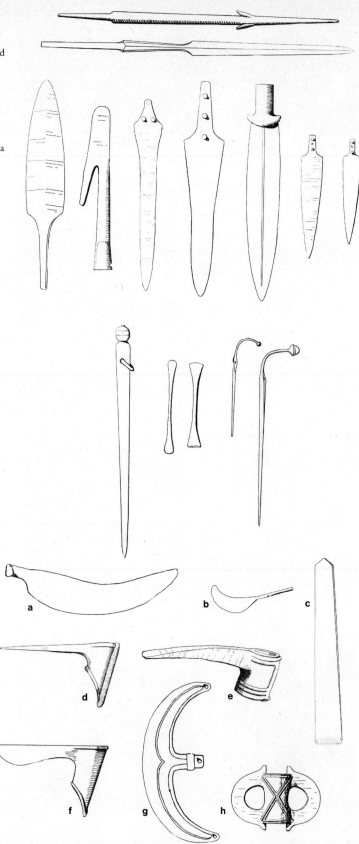

82 Metal tools and weapons from Ur tombs. *Top row*: tanged and ribbed spearheads; *second row*: leaf-shaped spearhead, harpoon, knives and daggers; *third row*: drill-bits, straight and curved pins with eyeleted shanks; *bottom row*: a and b, scrapers; c, chisel; d and e, socketed adzes and f, axe cast in a two-piece mould; g and h, crescentic battle-axes

massive and are skilfully modelled; lions and 'guardians' alike are often depicted full-face and more ornamental species of ruminants *80* are introduced; scenes of combat are punctuated by empanelled inscriptions; designs are occasionally divided horizontally into two registers. Perhaps the most intriguing subjects chosen for these Early Dynastic III seals are the mythological or ceremonial scenes in which men and gods take part. Their interpretation has always depended largely on the evidence provided by Sumerian literature, and since more of this became available, many themes have been reliably identified. One sees for instance the sun-god, Shamash, *81* voyaging in his boat through the cycle of night and day, surrounded by symbols which the texts explain. Then there is the fertility god on a throne, before which priests pour libations or pile offerings on an ornamental stand. More rarely portrayed is the ritual 'marriage', which took place between a god (Ningirsu) and goddess (Bau) at the New Year's Festival. But secular 'banquet' scenes make an alternative to religious subjects, sometimes attended by a burlesque 'orchestra' of animals. Many of these motifs now appear in other forms of ornament, especially on objects from the Royal Tombs at Ur.

As for the materials from which the seals are made, many varieties of semi-precious stone are now in use. The cylinder could even be capped with silver at either end or, in rare cases, made of solid gold.

Metallurgy and Composite Craftsmanship

Treasures recovered from Early Dynastic levels at Sumerian sites testify to the ability of specialists in several different fields of craftsmanship and, in some of the most strikingly beautiful objects, one sees how their skills have been combined.[148] In a class by themselves are the metalsmiths, whose services must at this time have been so greatly in demand at all levels of society. Their products, in the form of weapons, implements and utensils, have survived in great numbers, side-by-side with pictorial representations of the purposes for which they were used. In a well-known relief, spears, shields and helmets of copper are to be seen; in another battle-axes; 'guardian' figures in seal designs wield daggers with crescent-shaped handles; 'rein-rings' with their animal mascots appear on chariots in battle-scenes; and at a 'banquet' copper 'drinking-tubes' are used.

For votive and ceremonial purposes, replicas of such objects were made in precious metals and delicately ornamented. The work of Sumerian goldsmiths ranks with that of the best craftsmen in any later age and there were few technical processes with which they were still unfamiliar. In fine hammered work, for instance, as well as *repoussé*, chasing, engraving, granulation and filigree, they were entirely proficient. The perfection of their skill is seen in an object like the wig-helmet of Meskalamdug, which Woolley has described as '. . . a veritable *tour-de-force*; beaten up from the flat, with locks of hair hammered in relief and individual hairs represented by fine chased lines'. At the same time, some more simple objects, like the fluted cups and vases from the same tombs,

83 Copper stand for an incense-bowl representing a naked priest. Ht 55.5 cm. Three were found in the Oval Temple at Khafaje (Early Dynastic III), smaller ones at Tell Agrab

84 A reconstructed figure in the Iraq Museum of Meskalamdug, wearing the ceremonial wig-helmet, found in his tomb at Ur. Beaten from a single sheet of gold and delicately chased, its perforations are for attachment to a leather lining. (*c.* 2500 BC)

85 Reconstructed figure in the Iraq Museum of a court lady from a royal tomb at Ur, wearing an elaborate headdress and jewellery of gold, lapis-lazuli and carnelian. There were 68 similarly dressed women in the 'dromos' of a single tomb (no. 1237), known to the excavators as the 'Death Pit'

83

show something more than mere technical competence. In their combination of shape and ornament one recognizes a real talent for elegant design. The work of craftsmen in gold and silver is again to be seen in the ornaments of female attendants in the Ur tombs: 'the gorgeous beech-leaf headdresses, the gold and silver florally decorated combs; the wreaths composed of little amulets in the shape of bulls, rams, birds and fish' and the huge boat-shaped earrings.[149]

In another sphere, the most remarkable accomplishments in casting must be attributed to the coppersmiths of the Early Dynastic period. Examples of their work are already in evidence at Tell Agrab during its second phase and they include the remarkable group in miniature of a chariot drawn by four onagers and driven by a bearded 'king'.[150] Technologically this work is of special interest because it shows evidence of casting by the so-called *cire perdue* or 'lost-wax' process which now appears for the first time. More common finds in the Diyala temples were copper statues in the form of naked priests (or 'heroes'), with attachments enabling them to be used as offering-stands. One of these, from a group of three found at Khafaje, measured 76 cm high, while fragments of another from an Early Dynastic III provenance at Tell Agrab showed it to have been life-size.

INLAID ORNAMENT

Another realm in which Early Dynastic craftsmen excelled was that of inlaid ornament in coloured stone and other materials. Its uses, perhaps developing from the cone-mosaic technique of an earlier period, varied from pictorial friezes decorating the façades of buildings to the miniscule enrichment of precious objects. In the former case, carved figures of white limestone were set against a background of grey slate. For small-scale ornament a wide variety of coloured materials were used to form a surface incrustation, laid in bitumen over a wooden core. Of figurative designs executed in this technique, individual features could be carved in shell, bone or mother-of-pearl, to be fitted into a coloured background. A few detached figures of this sort were first found in Palace A at Kish. But the full possibilities of the medium were revealed by the abundant and often undamaged examples surviving among the treasures of the Ur tombs. Gaming-boards, toilet boxes and the sounding-boards of harps were some of the objects decorated in this way, often with spirited scenes recalling those on cylinder-seals. Individual figures cut from shell or nacre could be engraved with additional detail and the incisions filled with red or black paste. Flakes of lapis-lazuli would then be fitted together to form a background, and the design enclosed in a formally patterned

86 Miniature group in copper of a chariot drawn by four onagers and driven by a bearded Sumerian king. It was found in the 'sacristy' room near the high altar in the 'Shara Temple' at Tell Agrab and is the earliest known example of the *cire perdue* ('lost wax') process. Details of the chariot and harness have been reconstructed after careful study. Ht 7 cm

87 The so-called 'royal standard' from a tomb at Ur: a mosaic of shell figures on a background of lapis-lazuli, depicting on this side a 'peace' scene of banqueting and agricultural activity. Ht 20 cm

88 Reverse side of the 'royal standard', showing a 'war' scene, with the king (*primus inter pares*), his helmeted infantry and chariots in action. This object may have been the sounding-box of a musical instrument

border of other colours. At Ur, the *tour-de-force* in this category of ornament was the famous 'royal standard' with its scores of busy figures on either side, representing scenes of 'war and peace', and thought by some to be the sounding-box of some musical contrivance.[151]

Less well-known than the Ur 'standard', owing partly to the incomplete state in which it was found, is a similar and equally magnificent mosaic panel from Mari, composed of elements in ivory, shell, schist, lapis and gold.[152] In the uppermost of its three registers, a procession of conventionally dressed male figures attends a libation ceremony, carrying appropriate vessels; but the scenes beneath them are composed entirely of women, whose dress and occupation are of unique interest. Above, two figures face each other at either end of a couch supported by legs resembling those of a bull, and bend forward to arrange its *kaunakes* draperies. Approaching them from behind are other women, wearing the 'polos' headdress and carrying votive vessels. Below them are pairs of women with unfamiliar coiffures, one of each pair seated on a three-legged stool while the other assists her in a task for which a 'distaff' appears to be changing hands. Without exception, these female figures wear, over their usual lower garment, a fringed shawl, conspicuously fastened by a long metal pin with its head bent at rightangles (a commonly found object, whose purpose has till now remained obscure). From a perforation at the head of the pin hangs a string of curiously shaped amulets or charms. Supplementary details add to the interest of this intriguing composition.

COMPOSITE OBJECTS

It remains for us to consider some examples of the composite objects which figure so conspicuously among Early Dynastic art treasures. In a category of their own are musical instruments found in the Ur tombs, which Woolley extracted from the earth with such meticulous care. In referring to these the word 'harp' is sometimes used rather loosely, since in fact only two answered to this description. The most common instrument was a lyre, with rectangular wooden sound-box inlaid in coloured ornament, upright members at either end and a cross-piece to which the strings were attached with wooden pegs for tuning. Usually the body of the lyre had a frontal ornament of metal in the form of a bull's head; but there was also a 'boat-shaped' lyre, with the copper figure of a stag set against the foremost upright. As we know from pictorial inlays found both here and at Mari, these instruments could be held at chest-level by a standing player, or themselves stand upright on the ground between the player's knees.[153] There was also a so-called 'harp-lyre', with twelve strings attached to a single upright and a bull's head, reconstructed by Woolley for the British Museum. But R. D. Barnett has now shown how a study of its actual remains in Woolley's photographs and notebooks

89 Shell inlay warrior with a battle-axe from the Ishtar Temple at Mari (Early Dynastic III)

90 A lyre from the tomb of Meskalamdug at Ur, with the head of a bearded bull in gold and ornament of other materials. An instrument of this sort appears in the 'peace' scene on the 'royal standard' (ill. 87 top right). It is held at waist height by a standing man, accompanied by a singer. Ht 122 cm

revealed the components of two separate instruments: the sounding box of a conventional lyre and the single upright member of a harp.[154] Combined with the figured inlay of their frontal panels and the gold or silver sheathing of their framework, the bull's head ornaments with their luxurious beards of gold or lapis-lazuli add a final element of grandeur to a characteristic Sumerian design.

91　　If one more example is required, we should remember the so-called 'ram caught by its horns', which is in fact not a ram but a he-goat, symbolizing the generative vitality of the animal kingdom.[155] Its head and legs are of gold, its belly of silver, its fleece part lapis and part shell. The stylized plant against which it stands is also sheathed in gold. This object is one of a pair which were taken to be ornamental supports for some sort of vessel or cult-object.

Pottery

Painted pottery with geometric and figured designs reappears for the last time during the first Early Dynastic phase, especially at the Diyala sites. This is the so-called 'scarlet ware', which retained some *92* characteristics of the fine polychrome pottery that preceded it in the Jemdet Nasr period.[156] Technically, however, the decoration is less competently applied. The designs are in bright red paint, outlined in black over a buff or yellowish slip; but the paint is friable, lacking the 'soapy' burnish of its earlier prototype. The commonest form of vessel is a broad-shouldered jar, with a shallow neck and one or more triangular 'lugs' beneath the rim. The painted designs are in many ways unique. Filling the panels into which the surface of the vase is divided are groups of human and animal figures. In one example from Tell Agrab, three naked women are shown beating tambourines for the benefit of a tethered animal which appears to be a sacred bull. Other animals, conspicuously male, are of the antelope type with twisted horns. A fine example from Khafaje, now in the British Museum, has a more ambitious design, in which a wheeled chariot is with difficulty represented.

After the brief appearance of these attractive vessels in the Early Dynastic I and II phases, painted decoration on pottery seems to have been completely abandoned, nor does it appear again at any period in southern Mesopotamia. In the second and third Early Dynastic phases, painting is replaced by incised ornament in a wide variety of forms which, in combination with the changing shapes of the vessels themselves, provide useful criteria for dating purposes.

In southern Iraq, the production of 'scarlet ware' seems to have been confined to the Sumerian provinces east of the Tigris, extending to the present frontiers of Iran. It is of some interest to remember that to the north also, in an area reaching from Nineveh to the confines of Syria, the final phase of the 'painted pottery era' was marked by the appearance of a new and remarkable form of design. This was the elaborately decorated ware first found by Mallowan in his deep sounding beneath the greatest of all Assyrian mounds, and since known as 'Ninevite Five'.[157] He has described

91 He-goat in composite materials: gold, silver, lapis-lazuli etc., on a wooden core. One of a pair found in a royal tomb at Ur, it symbolizes the fertility of plant and animal life and was used as a support for some other object. Ht 50 cm

these vessels as 'tall fruit-stands with pedestal bases, high-necked vases with angular shoulders and ring- or pedestal-bases, carinated bowls and other types'. He adds: 'Many of these vessels are overcrowded with designs, especially the bigger ones which depict long-necked giraffe-like goats, waterfowl, fish and many monotonous geometric patterns'. With its deep purple designs on a neutrally coloured ground, this pottery seems unrelated to the 'scarlet ware' of the south, with which it is now known to be contemporary.[158] Here in the north also, in the phase which followed, it was gradually replaced by unpainted pottery whose quality depended upon the use of fine clay and the elaboration of incised ornament.

92 'Scarlet ware' of the Early Dynastic I period, developed from the polychrome pottery of Jemdet Nasr. The method of painting is here technically inferior, though ambitious figure designs are sometimes attempted

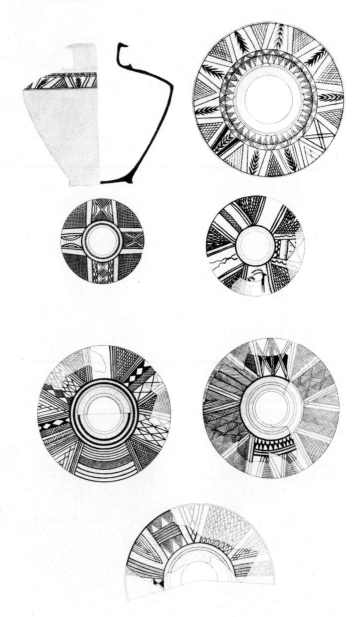

Chapter Seven

The Dynasty of Akkad and the Sumerian Revival

The term 'Pre-Sargonid', which is sometimes applied to the Early Dynastic period, serves in itself to emphasize the importance of the event which brought that period to an end. Sargon-of-Akkad's accession to power in about 2370 BC, and his rapid subjection of the old Sumerian city-states, resulted for the first time in the temporary supremacy of a Semitic element in the population of Mesopotamia.

The transition from Sumerian to Akkadian rule must itself have portended a revolution in political ideas. Its magnitude will become apparent if we recollect for a moment the unchanging pattern of Sumerian history during the preceding centuries and the peculiar conventions by which it was dictated. These latter are indeed implicit even in the formal statements of which the king-list is composed, and they can be spelt out in a few words. The primary assumption here is that the land of Sumer was an entity made up of a number of city-states and that only one of them at any one time was supreme over the others. The overall kingship remained in this one city until, by force of arms it was removed to another. Also, each city had its own patron god, who *owned* the state; but these tutelary deities remained unaffected by inter-state conflicts. They were not held responsible for the rivalry of kings who were their 'agents', though disputes among themselves were equally frequent. Finally, although the cities were continually fighting, either for supremacy or for adjustments of their frontiers, there remained among their rulers a strong sense of pride in the solidarity of 'the land' itself. And here one must remember that Sumer was regarded as a finite entity. The dozen-or-so city-states of which it was composed occupied a restricted territory (hardly larger than the modern Irish Republic), with northward extensions reaching no further than cities like Mari or Ashur, which shared the same culture. Sumerian ambitions did not reach beyond these limits, remoter lands being of little interest except where trading was concerned.

With the foundation of an Akkadian kingdom in the north, all this was changed. In the dynamic authority and statesmanship of its first ruler a new factor became apparent. Unhampered by Sumerian tradition and the limitations which it had imposed on earlier kings, Sargon's own conception of monarchy was absolute and his ambition pointed beyond the bounds of an united Sumer and Akkad. It may be well, therefore, before returning to the archaeological record, to summarize such facts as are known regarding the origin and history of the Akkadian dynasty.

93 Life-size head in bronze of an
Akkadian king, perhaps Sargon
himself (2370–2316 BC), found
out of context in ruins of the
Ishtar Temple at Nineveh by
Campbell-Thompson and
Mallowan. Note the refinement
of modelling characteristic of this
period. Ht 30 cm

Semites in Mesopotamia

First, then, a word must be said about the Semites, whose presence
in Sumer at a much earlier date has already been inferred from the
linguistic peculiarities of certain traditional names of Mesopotamian cities.[159] Regarding their country of origin, the one-time
conception of the Syrian desert as a centre of diffusion for nomadic
peoples has first to be discarded – if only because the greater part of
it almost certainly remained uninhabited from the end of the
Palaeolithic period until late in the 2nd millennium BC, when the
camel first came into use for desert transport. Lacking the mobility
of the modern Bedouin, nomadic herdsmen of those early days
must have confined their movements to the peripheral grasslands,
adjoining the territories of more settled agricultural peoples, whose
society they gradually infiltrated. Certainly this was the case on the
Mesopotamian side of the Syrian desert, and here there is some
evidence to indicate the direction from which the infiltration took
place. Semitic personal names appear in written texts throughout

the Early Dynastic period, and their geographic distribution suggests that, whereas Semites were in a minority in the most southerly Sumerian cities, their numbers increased as one moved northward. In Mari and Ashur they already accounted for the greater part of the population.

In the case of the Akkadians, their nomadic origin (if any) seems to have been quickly forgotten, and in the early texts there is no suggestion of the Sumerians having either opposed their intrusion into the country or later resented their presence. Certainly, by the time of Sargon's accession, the central part of Mesopotamia, from the region of Nippur northward to the Hit-Samarra Line, including the Diyala district, had long been known as the 'Country of Akkad'. For this reason the name Akkadian came to be applied to the non-Sumerian peoples of Mesopotamia generally. Culturally the most conspicuous distinction between the two ethnic groups was a linguistic one. The Akkadians had retained their own Semitic form of speech and, for purposes of writing, were compelled to use an awkward adaptation of the old cuneiform script. Nevertheless, once it was perfected, this written form of Akkadian was destined to become the *lingua franca* of the Near East where commercial and diplomatic correspondence was concerned. For the rest, Sargon's subjects continued to share the religious beliefs and social practices of the Sumerians.

Sargon and his Successors

The legend of Sargon's humble origin became a familiar theme in the literature of later times: the upbringing of an orphan boy by benevolent peasants and his employment as cup-bearer to a king of Kish whom he eventually replaced upon the throne. These were preliminaries to a spectacular military career, which started with his defeat of Lugal-zaggesi of Uruk, temporarily the paramount ruler of all Sumer. Having then subdued the cities individually and 'washed his weapons in the Lower Sea', Sargon founded a new capital at a place called Agade. Unfortunately this city is one of the few important political centres of Mesopotamia whose site has not yet been located. It seems in any case to have been well to the north of the main Sumerian enclave, though still accessible by river to sea-going vessels. One notices that at this point there is some evidence of discrimination in favour of the Akkadian element among Sargon's supporters. Akkadian governors were installed in the other Sumerian cities and the Sumerian language ceased to be used for administrative purposes. On the other hand, much time and energy was devoted to the restoration or rebuilding of old Sumerian religious monuments, and one remembers for instance that Sargon's own daughter became priestess of Nannar, the moon-god of Ur.

For Sargon, as we have said, the domination of Sumer was no more than a preface to the extension of his conquests beyond the natural frontiers of Mesopotamia. His first venture of this sort carried him eastward into Elam, where he defeated the combined forces of four rulers, led by the King of Awan, and established a viceroyalty in the city of Susa, which from now onwards acquired

93

a new political status. His second expedition followed the course of the Euphrates into northern Syria where, according to his own account, 'the God Dagan gave him the Upper Region'. This would imply that he gained access to the cedar forests of the Amanus Mountains and to the silver mines of the Taurus. Later expeditions assured the allegiance of settlements around or beyond Nineveh, and there is a famous text, known as the epic of 'The King of Battle', which shows the king advancing deep into the heart of Anatolia, to protect his own 'merchants' from the exactions of a local ruler, described as the King of Burushanda, somewhere in the region south of modern Kayseri. Also, accepted with some reserve, is an account of an expedition by sea, which carried him as far as the southernmost extremity of the Arabian Gulf, and some credit is given to his claim to have crossed the 'Sea of the West', to reach Cyprus and Crete.

It is at least clear that successive enterprises of this sort led eventually to the creation, for the first time in history, of a Mesopotamian empire and to the exploitation for commercial purposes of countries hitherto almost unknown. Apart from the new sources of timber and essential metals which the opening of northern routes made accessible, and the many commodities obtainable from the east, by way of Elam, the possibilities of seaborne trade in the Arabian Gulf became increasingly apparent. We are told for instance that, in Sargon's time, 'the ships of Dilmun, Magan and Meluhha were moored at the quayside in front of Agade'.[160] The first of these names, identified with the island of Bahrein, is already mentioned in texts of the Early Dynastic period as a centre of commerce; but if Magan can be recognized as Oman or the Makran coast, Meluhha must be taken to be further afield and may well have served as a link with the contemporary civilization of the Indus Valley. By trade, at least, the Akkadian empire had reached the limits of the known world.

Sargon's reign lasted for fifty-five years, but before he died, he found it necessary to repress the first of a series of revolts, which also darkened the reigns of his successors. Of his sons, Rimush was killed in a palace revolution, but Manishtusu and to a greater extent his grandson, Naram-Sin, were able to continue the aggrandisement of the Akkadian empire. Naram-Sin seems to have been a ruler of the same calibre as Sargon and like him became a hero of legend. His long reign (2291–2255 BC) was occupied by a series of military operations, some of which are reflected in his own surviving monuments. In the north, for example, a campaign against a Hurrian king was commemorated by a royal relief, carved on a rock-face at Pir Hussein, near Diyarbakir (now in the Istanbul Museum). Another rock-sculpture at Darband-i-Gawr in northwest Iran (now dated to the Third Dynasty of Ur) records a victory over the Lullubi, one of the tribal peoples of Luristan, who presented a continual threat to the Mesopotamian frontier;[161] and another similar victory is celebrated in the design of the famous 'Stela of Naram-Sin', discovered at Susa and now in the Louvre. Monuments such as these are, as we shall see, of special interest since they contribute to the regrettably meagre remnants of Akkadian sculpture.

But, in the end, it was the Guti or Gutians, neighbours of the Lullubi in the north, who effectively overran the homeland of the Akkadians. This happened in the reign of Naram-Sin's successor, Shar-gali-sharri and, since their onslaught coincided with a concerted uprising of the old Sumerian states, the centre of government in Agade was destroyed and the empire disintegrated. The political chaos which ensued must have been considerable; for the compilers of the king-list content themselves with the rhetorical question, 'Who was king? Who was not king?' The fact remains that for the greater part of a century, Mesopotamia was ruled by semi-anonymous barbarians, who have left few monuments or comprehensible inscriptions.

Archaeology

We have mentioned earlier in the present chapter the energy which the Akkadian kings devoted to the rebuilding of temples and sanctuaries in the old Sumerian cities. With this in mind, it is curious to observe how few traces of their work have actually been revealed by excavations at the sites themselves. One explanation to be considered is that, in almost every case, the process of rebuilding had in fact to be repeated a couple of hundred years later by the Third Dynasty kings of Ur who, perhaps intentionally, concealed all evidence of their predecessors' accomplishments. At the same time, it has to be remembered that these sites were some of the first to be excavated, at a period when the recovery of written texts and other removable antiquities took precedence over the study of architectural remains. The shortcomings of these early systems of excavating no longer need to be emphasized. Their relevance in the present context may however be illustrated by some selected examples.

BUILDINGS

H. V. Hilprecht, excavating at Nippur in 1899–1900, discovered that the great Third Dynasty ziggurat covered the remains of an earlier one, founded by Naram-Sin of Akkad, but its investigation he considered to be impracticable.[162] Vincent Scheil, at Sippar (Abu Habba) in 1893, encountered a great religious temenos, originally founded by Sargon of Akkad, but could trace and record only part of the buildings which replaced it a thousand years later.[163] E. H. Banks, at Bismaya (Adab) in 1903–4, during his search for tablets or statues, noted the existence of a palace, private houses and a cemetery, all of the Akkadian period, but made no records of them.[164] By 1923–33, things were a little better, when Ch. Watelin, working in the Ingharra mound at Kish, could distinguish repairs and additions made to an older ziggurat in Akkadian times, and record contemporary graves in the 'A' Cemetery.[165] At Ur, any traces of buildings dating from the Sargonid period were deeply buried beneath the ruins of later times; but Woolley was at least able to study and minutely to record as many as 400 Akkadian graves.[166] It remained for other British and American excavators in the 1930s to throw light on some peculiarities of Akkadian architecture.

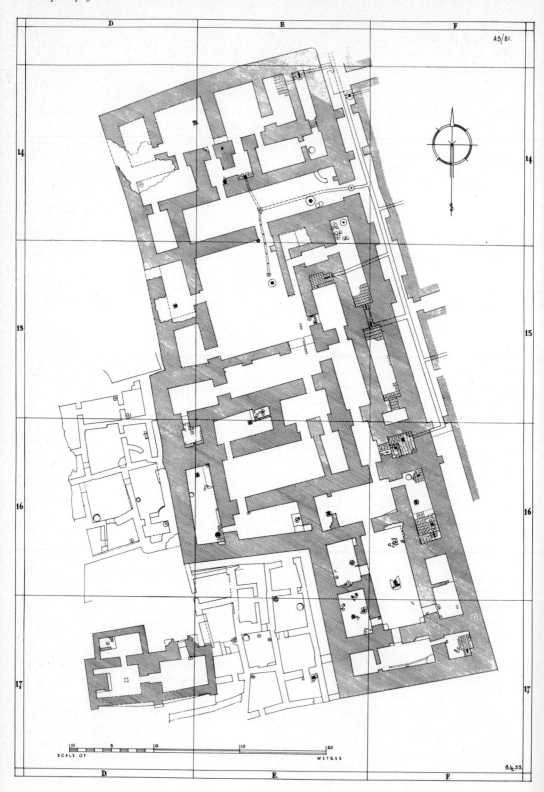

TELL ASMAR

Reference has already been made to the discovery at Tell Asmar in the Diyala region of a large and well-planned residential building dating from the Early Dynastic III period. At a slightly later date it had been rebuilt on a much more pretentious scale, with walls over 2 m thick and an overall dimension of 73 m.[167] This so-called 'Northern Palace' was adapted, like its predecessors, to an irregular shaped site, and an analysis of its plan suggests its division into three distinct units. Centrally placed, one sees a suite of major residential and reception rooms, whose function is easy to infer. Annexed to this in the south, and accessible from it by a narrow doorway, is a self-contained unit with its own courtyard; and one may recollect that the contents of its surrounding rooms (mirrors, ornaments and toilet accessories), implied its occupation by women. Lastly to the north, and separated from the central suite by a system of courtyards leading to the main entrance, there was a third unit with service accommodation. But perhaps the most curious feature of this building was a range of variously shaped rooms on the east side, with built-in installations of kiln-baked bricks. These appear to have served some purpose involving the use of water, since each of them had a drain leading to a brick-vaulted sewer in the narrow alleyway outside the building. One notices that there are indeed small lustral places or toilets annexed to larger rooms at other points in the plan; but these longer chambers to the east seem to have had some other function, which has led one authority even to suggest that the building has been wrongly identified as a 'palace'.[168] Chronologically it is dated by brick-shapes and other evidence to the earlier years of the Akkadian epoch.

KHAFAJE AND BRAK

There was other evidence at the Diyala sites of extensive occupation during the Akkadian period. Near the Northern Palace at Tell Asmar, private houses covering a wide area were exposed

94 Plan of the 'Akkadian Palace' at Tell Asmar, with its royal apartments, elaborate drainage and separate wing for women. The adjoining Abu Temple (bottom left) was also rebuilt at this time (c. 2350 BC) with a double sanctuary. (Lloyd 1933)

95 Foundation plan of the 'Palace of Naram-Sin' at Tell Brak, a military stronghold on the northern frontier of Mesopotamia. (P. P. Pratt after Mallowan)

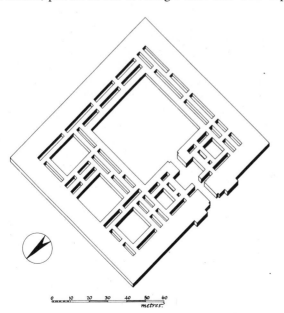

0 10 20 30 40 50 60
metres

and carefully studied.[169] At Khafaje, in an outlying part of the site, an enclosure wall had been built around a group of Akkadian buildings, of which only the foundations survived;[170] and there were traces of an Akkadian occupation directly beneath the surface at Tell Agrab. But one of the most impressive and historically significant buildings dating from this period was discovered by Mallowan at Tell Brak,[171] a little beyond the modern Syrian frontier in northern Mesopotamia. This again has been called a 'palace', but would rather seem to have been a military outpost or fortified entrepôt, occupying a strategic position on the trade-route to southern Anatolia in the time of Naram-Sin. Built upon a site adjoining the prehistoric 'Eye Temple', referred to in an earlier chapter, only its foundations had in part survived; but from these the plan could be restored of an approximately square building, with immensely thick outer walls and a maximum dimension of over 100 m. The plan itself, as one would expect, consisted largely of long storage chambers, grouped around a system of open courts. Plundered after the fall of the Akkadian empire, and destroyed by fire, it had been replaced by a less substantial building in the time of Ur-nammu (2113–2096 BC).

95

SCULPTURE

Well-preserved examples of Akkadian sculpture are hardly more plentiful than surviving buildings of the period, a fact which must be deplored if one considers the remarkably high quality of their achievement. Outstanding in this respect are two conspicuous monuments which chance circumstances have preserved for us. One is the life-size head in bronze of an Akkadian king, discovered out of context in the Assyrian ruins of the Ishtar Temple at Küyünjik (Nineveh) and now in the Iraq Museum.[172] Mallowan, who had the good fortune to find it, provisionally identified it as a portrait of Sargon-of-Akkad, perhaps dedicated by his son Manishtusu, whose name is recorded as founder of the temple. The king is depicted wearing an ornamental coiffure, whose style resembles the wig-helmet of Meskalamdug or that worn by Eannatum in the 'Stela of the Vultures'. On the other hand, his moustache and divided beard have a new air of sophistication and the modelling of his face shows a notable improvement on the work of Sumerian sculptors. One of his eyes has been damaged by the forcible removal of its valuable inlay.

The second most important monument of the Akkadian period is the 'Stela of Naram-Sin', found by de Morgan at Susa, whither it had been brought by the Elamite king Shutruk-nakhkhunte as part of 'the booty of Sippar'.[173] The purpose of this relief is to commemorate an Akkadian victory over the Lullubi tribesmen. In a composition skilfully suggesting a campaign among wooded mountains, one's eye is drawn to the dominant figure of the king, standing high above his troops and protected by the symbols of his gods. Wearing a horned headdress to signify his own divinity and carrying a bow, he tramples the enemy beneath his feet. Aesthetically, this is a magnificent design, and would alone serve to emphasize the creative ability of Akkadian artists. If further testimony is needed in this respect, it must be sought among more

96 The Stela of Naram-Sin, King of Agade (2291–2255 BC), celebrating a victory over the Lullubi and carried as booty to Susa by an Elamite ruler. In mountainous and wooded country the Akkadian monarch is depicted at the head of his troops protected by the symbols of his deities. The expressive freedom of the design and its fine carving shows a notable improvement on early Sumerian relief sculpture. Ht 198 cm

fragmentary remains from Susa and elsewhere. Pieces for instance survive in the Louvre of other diorite stelae, depicting scenes from the triumphant aftermath of Sargon's victories over anonymous enemies.[174] Had these been less firmly dated, one would still have attributed them to an earlier phase in the stylistic development of Akkadian carving. With figures arranged in horizontal registers, these reliefs retain many characteristics of their Sumerian prototypes, though the *kaunakes* garment is less in evidence and the nude bodies of defeated enemies show an improved understanding of musculature. A striking advance in the mastery of such designs does however appear to have taken place in the time of Sargon's successors. For there are fragments of a similar stela in the Iraq
97 Museum, dating almost certainly from the reign of Naram-Sin, in which one sees an ultimate refinement of relief carving, comparable with that of contemporary Egyptian sculptors.[175]

CYLINDER-SEALS

Some compensation for the paucity of Akkadian sculpture is provided by the rich harvest of contemporary cylinder-seals, recovered from graves and private houses at some of the sites to which we have referred. The skill of Akkadian seal-cutters and their talent for design set a new standard for glyptic art in Mesopotamia.[176] In the first place, some innovations are to be noticed in their choice of subjects; but more important than these is an overall change in the principle of their designs and style of carving. The aim of earlier artists had been to link their action-related figures together in a continuous frieze. This is now abandoned, and the new designs are contrived in such a way that the seal's rotation produces a succession of self-contained *tableaux*, often isolated from each other by empanelled inscriptions. The figures themselves are also much changed. Generally larger and more widely separated, the depth of carving gives higher relief to the impression and much attention is paid to ornamental detail. Unfilled spaces between them enhance the purity of their outline, while emphasizing by contrast the elaboration of their modelling and the felicity of the patterns which together they compose.

Amongst the mythical figures of earlier times, the 'naked hero' and his companion the 'man-headed bull' are still to be seen in
99 combat with horned animals or lions; but the contestants are separated and the animals often arranged antithetically, like the 'supporters' in a heraldic design, with a central motif in between. Mythical and religious scenes are also again popular, but must now be integrated into the framework of a static design. They are widely varied and of considerable interest. Apart from the more conventional subjects of worship and ritual, reference can easily be detected to the familiar myths of Sumerian literature. Once more the sun-god appears in his boat, or the water-god with streams flowing from his body. There is the bird-man, Zu, who stole the 'tablets of destiny', Etana, who attempted to reach heaven on the back of an eagle, and many other figures of legend, which have been identified in the course of long studies devoted to the subject of these seals.[177] Unique among them is an example dating from the Akkadian occupation of the Abu Temple at Tell Asmar, whose

97 Unprovenanced fragment of an Akkadian relief, showing naked prisoners after a victory: a rare example emphasizing the high attainments of Mesopotamian sculptors at this period

imagery, characteristic of the Indus Valley civilization, established one of the first chronological links with the contemporary cities of Mohenjo-daro and Harappa.[178]

GASUR

Mention should be made finally of one further site from which important material of the Akkadian period was recovered by an American expedition in the late 1920s. This was Nuzi, in the neighbourhood of Kirkuk, which became a city of some importance under its Hurrian rulers in the 15th century BC. Excavations beneath the Hurrian palace area produced evidence of continuous occupation throughout the 3rd and early 2nd millennia, during which time the place seems to have been known as Gasur. Already in the Early Dynastic period a temple had existed here, dedicated to Ishtar like the contemporary shrine at Ashur which it closely resembled. Important finds in the vicinity of this building included a large collection of tablets, throwing much light on commerce and trade connections in the Akkadian period. Among the texts also, were found references to mercantile establishments in Anatolia, which lent new substance to the Sargonid legends associated with this subject. Other finds contributed to the hitherto unfamiliar typology of domestic and military equipment in the Akkadian period. Metal objects, seal-cylinders and pottery were plentiful, and could afterwards be compared with those from contemporary levels at Tell Brak, with which they had more in common than with their counterparts in the south.[179]

98 Akkadian cylinder-seal. The ornamental 'combat' motif is isolated between vertical reeds and an empanelled inscription. Both design and modelling here reach a high standard

99 'Bull-man' and 'hero', each in combat with wild bulls, are arranged antethetically, with a mountain/tree symbol between

100 Mythical scene showing a 'fertility' god being raised from 'beneath the mountain' by Ishtar and a water-god, with other deities in attendance

Gutians and Lagash

The situation in Mesopotamia during the long interregnum which resulted from the Gutian occupation is veiled in obscurity by the absence of written texts. But it seems at least unlikely that any systematic control was maintained over the whole country. The interlude was, as we know, finally brought to an end early in the 22nd century BC by a military insurrection, led by a ruler of Ur; yet, some sixty years before this occurred, our attention is already drawn to the survival in the city of Lagash of a Sumerian ruler, who had attained sufficient independence and wealth to restore its temples and reorganize the irrigation of its territory. This was Ur-Baba, whose successor, Gudea, has been ensured a prominent place in Mesopotamian history, first, by the great number of inscriptions dealing with his accomplishments which have survived and, secondly, by his patronage of a school of sculptors in hard stone, who have bequeathed to posterity some of the most striking masterpieces of Mesopotamian sculpture. From Gudea's records, we even learn of a successful military campaign against Elam and the dedication of its spoils to his god Ningirsu, the embellishment of whose temple, E-ninnu, is described in much detail.[180]

DE SARZEC

The modern 'spoils' of Lagash, installed in the Louvre, are the results of excavations at the site called Telloh, conducted by the French scholar-explorer Ernest de Sarzec during the final quarter of

101 Fragments of a diorite statue, now in the British Museum, probably from Telloh. The style of carving is well adapted to the quality of the material. The bald head is not unusual in this setting. Ht *c.* 73 cm

the last century.[181] To understand the sensation created by the arrival of his finds in Paris, one must recall that they provided the first substantial evidence of a civilization in Mesopotamia antecedent to that of the Assyrians, and that they remained unique in this respect until the resumption of excavations in southern Iraq after the First World War. A brief summary of de Sarzec's discoveries may not therefore be out of place.[182]

TELLOH

Telloh is a very large site, near the Shatt-al-Hai canal, with a maximum diameter of about 0.9 miles. Of the principal mounds grouped near its centre (identified by the French alphabetically), the most productive were Tell A ('Palais'), Tell K ('Maison des Fruits') and Tell V ('Tell des Tablettes'). Attracted to the site by the finds of illicit diggers, de Sarzec's first two seasons of excavation (1877–8) amply confirmed the importance of Tells A and K, where he reported the discovery of a 'superb fragment de statue', foundation deposits with stone tablets and bronze figurines, two large inscribed clay cylinders, a fragment of the 'Vultures' stela and a 'statue colossale' which he left in place. Early in 1879, during his absence on leave, H. Rassam, representing the British Museum, slipped in and made some soundings of his own, but was frustrated by labour difficulties. A year later de Sarzec was back again and began a third campaign, resuming his excavation in Tell A. This time his success was phenomenal ('... toute la collection des grandes statues de Gudea et Ur-Baba, plusieurs morceaux de la stèle des Vautours, des statuettes en pierre, des figurines de bronze des vases et un grand nombre d'inscriptions. Butin énorme, qui arriva en France en mai 1881').

Up till now and during his fourth season, de Sarzec had been dealing with relics of the post-Akkadian phase in the history of Lagash. In his fifth and sixth campaigns, having transferred his activities to Tell K, he became involved with the remains of an earlier period. Inscriptions were found mentioning the names of governors of Lagash – Ur-Nanshe, Eannatum, Entemena, Urukagina – who had ruled the state in the Early Dynastic period, and an outstanding find at this time, bearing the name of Entemena, was the now-famous 'silver vase', with its finely engraved symbolic design. Four further campaigns were to follow before de Sarzec's death in 1901; but, after the discovery in 1893 of the source (Tell V) from which illicit diggers had been obtaining large quantities of cuneiform tablets, the French excavators became primarily occupied in attempts to prevent the total pillage of their site. Unfortunately, owing to de Sarzec's failing health and other circumstances, there were long periods when it remained unguarded and the robbers were consequently given free rein. The number of tablets which found their way into the markets of Baghdad during those years have been computed at between 35,000 and 40,000, as compared with the 3,800 which were recovered by the French from their excavations.

GUDEA

The statues of Gudea and his son Ur-ningirsu, seated or standing and sometimes more than half life-size, are all identified by inscriptions. They are carved from boulders of hard diorite, brought by ship from Magan at the southern end of the Arabian Gulf. The exposed parts of the body show a refinement of modelling well suited to this material and the sculptor's treatment of his subject conveys an impression of strength in repose. Beardless and sometimes bald, the heads are set low in the shoulders, while the eyes profit from the absence of coloured inlay.[183] While admiring the masterly design of these sculptures, one is compelled to regret the loss of the temple in which they stood, and of other rich furnishings which Gudea records having dedicated to his god Ningirsu. During his excavations, de Sarzec paid little attention to architectural remains. After his death, however, the work at Telloh was resumed and continued intermittently until 1909 under the direction of Gaston Cros, who seems rapidly to have acquired the rudiments of the wall-tracing technique. One gathers from A.

102 Diorite statue found near Telloh, probably depicting Gudea himself, to judge by the characteristic headdress. The quality of these sculptures is partly dictated by the hardness of the stone, which will take a high polish. Ht 105 cm

101–2

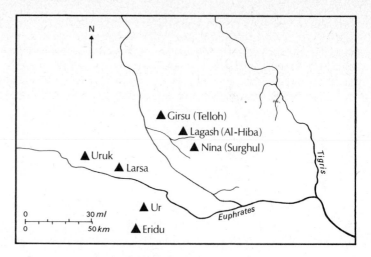

103 Map showing the relative positions of Telloh and Al-Hiba in the ancient state of Lagash. (S. Ebrahim after W. S. Thomas)

Parrot's summary of his reports that he did much to clarify the topography of the site. In Tell A, beneath the ruins of a palace built by an Aramaean ruler in the 2nd century B C, he located what he considered to be some remains of the Ningirsu temple and, in Tell K, a fortification built by Gudea. Among his finds elsewhere was a headless statue, subsequently re-united in the Louvre with the fragment till then known as the 'Tête-au-Turban'.

Al-Hiba

More than seventy years after de Sarzec's death, in 1972 extraordinary discoveries were made during a survey undertaken by Th. Jacobsen and F. Safar, which led to an excavation sponsored by the Metropolitan Museum and University of New York, under the leadership of V. E. Crawford, at a site called Al-Hiba, 15 miles southeast of Telloh. A variety of Sumerian inscriptions were found on tablets, stamped bricks and other objects (some of them associated with a temple building). Their content provided *103* indisputable proof that Al-Hiba was in fact the site of the ancient city of Lagash. Further excavations may throw new light on this paradoxical situation; but for the present it is only possible to conclude that the city discovered by de Sarzec at Telloh and now identified by its ancient name, Girsu,[184] was a secondary political or religious centre in the state of Lagash.

The Third Dynasty of Ur

The Sumerian revival itself must be thought of as having begun in about 2120 B C, when Utu-hegal, King of Uruk, initiated the first large-scale revolt against the tribal rulers. He was supported by the Sumerian governors of several other cities, and one of these, Ur-nammu, seems to have replaced him after his first military successes. It was he who completed the liberation of Sumer and founded the great Third Dynasty of Ur, thereby inaugurating what is sometimes called the Neo-Sumerian period. For a little over a century, under this king and his four successors, Ur, like Agade, was the capital of an empire; here as elsewhere much time was devoted to ambitious building programmes, which have left their mark on the cities in the form of ziggurats, temples and palaces. For our present purpose therefore, it may be well to concentrate on Ur itself, whose site (Tell Muqayyar) was so thoroughly excavated by Woolley between the years 1922 and 1934.[185]

BUILDINGS AT UR

Woolley published an overall plan of the city of Ur as he found it, with details of the fortifications partly restored.[186] Represented here are of course the city-walls as rebuilt by the Neo-Babylonian kings in the 6th century BC; but there is no reason to suppose that their outline differs greatly from those built in the time of Ur-nammu fifteen centuries earlier. The town which they enclose takes the form of an irregular oval with a maximum dimension of almost exactly 1200 m, and in Ur-nammu's time was already surrounded by a wall and a rampart. Woolley describes it as follows:

The rampart was of mud brick with a steeply sloping outer face; the lower part was in fact a revetment against the side of the mound formed by the older town, but the upper part of it extended inwards over the top of the ruins to make a solid platform. . . . Along the top of this ran the wall proper built of baked bricks. . . . This massive fortification was further strengthened by the fact that the river Euphrates (as can be seen from the line of its old bed), washed the foot of the western rampart, while fifty yards from the foot of the eastern rampart had been dug a broad canal, which left the river immediately above the north end of the town. On three sides therefore Ur was ringed by a moat and only from the south could it be approached by dry land.

It was presumably from this side that the walls were assaulted by an Elamite army in 2006 BC when the city was destroyed. For Woolley adds:

. . . of Ur-Nammu's wall not a trace remained. We would come on examples of very large bricks specially moulded with the king's name and titles, reused in some later building, but none of them were *in situ*. Just because the defences of Ur had been so strong, the victorious enemy had dismantled them with special care.

THE ZIGGURAT

A second heavily buttressed enclosure wall surrounded the sacred temenos in the northwest part of the town. In Woolley's plan of this precinct one sees that it was considerably enlarged in the time of Nebuchadnezzar, whose new wall passed across the ruins of the Third Dynasty mausoleum, which had been sited just outside the old temenos, near the earlier Royal Tombs. Of the buildings inside the original enclosure, by far the most conspicuous was the colossal ziggurat, built by Ur-nammu and completed by his son Shulgi.[187] *104* This remarkable monument, which is better preserved than any other of its sort in Mesopotamia, was studied and recorded with great care by Woolley, whose well-known perspective reconstruction of its original appearance has recently facilitated the partial restoration of its ruins by the Iraq Government. It is a solid structure, built in three 'stages'. The core is of mud brick, probably laid around and over the ruins of an earlier tower, and it was faced

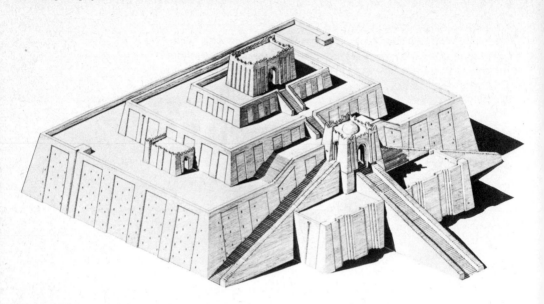

104 The Third Dynasty ziggurat of Ur-nammu at Ur, convincingly reconstructed by Woolley except for the form of the summit temple, which is hypothetical. The overall dimension at ground level is 61 × 45.7 m

with a skin of baked brick, set in bitumen, about 2.4 m thick. The lowest stage, which is best preserved, measures 61 × 45.7 m at ground level and is about 15 m high. The initial approach to the summit was by a triple stairway, with three converging flights and squat tower-buttresses in the angles between them. Where they met, at the first terrace level, the remnants of four brick piers suggested some sort of portico, which Woolley hypothetically provided with a domed roof. The height and dimensions of the two upper stages were ascertainable, but they were also much denuded.

Woolley observed three peculiar aspects of the ziggurat structure, for which he has offered tentative explanations. The fabric of the tower consisted of sun-dried brickwork, reinforced with thick layers of woven reeds at intervals of six or eight courses. Penetrating into its core, he found that bricks and mortar alike were hardened and discoloured by fire, a phenomenon which he attributed to the saturation of the structure by damp (perhaps while temporarily in ruins), and the consequent occurrence of internal combustion in the decaying vegetable matter. Conversely he was surprised by the multiplication of 'weeper-holes' penetrating the baked-brick outer shell of the lowest stage; and he wondered whether the terrace above could have been planted with trees which would have required irrigation. He had in fact found carbonized tree-trunks near the base of the tower.[188] Finally he discovered a slight outward deviation in the line of the main façades at pavement level. This he was tempted to compare with the subtle distortion of perspective contrived by the builders of Greek temples fifteen centuries later. Remembering the great weight of the tower and the pliable quality of mud brick, others have mistrusted this explanation.

THE TERRACE
With the exception of the mausoleum which we have mentioned, all the major buildings originally founded by the kings of the Third

Dynasty fell within the area of the old temenos as it existed at that time. For the most part, they had been so frequently rebuilt, with adjustments to their planning and arrangements, that the analysis of their ruins required much skill and patience. Indeed, had it not been for the convention by which, from Akkadian times onwards, baked bricks were stamped with royal inscriptions, the task would have been impossible. Ur-nammu built his ziggurat on a raised terrace, surrounded by double walls with intramural chambers ('E-temen-ni-gur'). To this he added a second courtyard, with a monumental gateway at temenos level, which he dedicated to Nannar, patron god of Ur. Southeast of the ziggurat terrace was a huge and heavily fortified building called 'Gi-par-u', dedicated to Ningal, the consort of Nannar but also containing several minor shrines, incorporated during its long and complicated architectural history. This is probably to be regarded as the *tieftempel* or ground-level sanctuary. A smaller, square building ('E-nun-makh'), in the angle between the two ziggurat courtyards, has been variously identified as a palace, a temple or a 'treasury'.

The main entrance to the ziggurat terrace in Ur-nammu's time was by a rather inconspicuous gateway in the eastern corner, known as 'E-dub-lal-makh'. Its outer portico, looking southward over the more public part of the precinct, contained a statue of Nannar and was used by the king as a 'Seat of Judgment'. Later rulers separated it from the terrace and made it into a court-of-law, with its own subsidiary chambers grouped around it. Yet, almost seven centuries later, the Kassite king Kurigalzu still referred to it as 'The Great Gate, the Ancient One'. Of the remaining Third Dynasty buildings, two only survived in their original form. One of these, in the southeast angle of the old precinct, was 'E-kharsag', clearly the residential palace of Ur-nammu and his successors. The other was the mausoleum, about which there is more to say.[189] This formidable conglomeration of buildings comprised Ur-nammu's own tomb and those of his two immediate successors. Below the contemporary ground-level were the burial-chambers themselves with their corbelled brick vaults and long flights of steps leading down to them. Above these were the remains of elaborate and formally planned funerary chapels.

THE MAUSOLEUM

One should say at once that the looting of these tombs in antiquity has to be regarded as a major tragedy. Judging from the astonishing wealth of the older dynastic tombs, which were otherwise conceived on a much more modest scale, these first great imperial monarchs must have been provided with immeasurably richer grave-deposits and buried with even more elaborate ceremony. All that is now left is the shell of the buildings with their vaulting partially intact; and Woolley found no more than fragments of gold leaf, testifying to treasure which was removed from them. Almost without exception, the tombs of subsequent rulers in Mesopotamia have remained unlocated.

Regarding the vaulted chambers themselves, they had long *105* flights of stairs leading down into them and were roofed with corbel-type vaulting composed of baked bricks. In estimating the

105 Entrance to the brick
vaulted tomb-chamber of Ur-
nammu in the royal mausoleum
at Ur

height of the chambers, Woolley became aware of a curious
circumstance. It was evident that, in the case of Ur-nammu's tomb,
the pavement on which the burial was actually laid out seemed a
somewhat shoddy affair and left a space between itself and the
vault, in which there was only just room for a man to stand. He
then found that the stairway went down several metres beneath
this, to a proper pavement laid with several courses of baked bricks
set in bitumen. What had apparently happened was that, when the
tomb was actually constructed, the builders had not taken into
account the flood-level of sub-surface water; so that, when the king
died and the time came for the tomb to be used, it was found to be
filled with water to a considerable depth. The only remedy
therefore was to fill it up to above water-level with rubble and then
repave it. Evidently, since that time, the water-level had receded,
because Woolley was able to excavate all the tomb chambers down
to the original pavement level, and, after shoring up the vaults with
timber, it became possible for visitors to walk about in them.
Today, a more permanent reconstruction of the vaults has been
achieved and they have become a tourist attraction.

Where the Ur mausoleum was concerned, Woolley as usual made an extremely thorough study of the surviving remains. He was even able to record details of a temporary superstructure, connected solely with the ritual ceremony of inhumation, which was later replaced by permanent memorial chapels.

TEMPLES AND SCULPTURE

The period of Sumerian revival seems to have coincided with a notable change in the planning of ordinary temples. The 'bent-axis' approach of earlier times was now abandoned in favour of a more obvious symmetry. The new plan, which was to survive with only minor variations throughout the remaining history of Babylonia, is to be seen in its simplest form at Tell Asmar (Eshnunna), where a subject prince dedicated a temple to Gimil-Sin, the deified King of Ur.[190] Tower-flanked portal and vestibule, ante-cella and inner sanctuary were now aligned on opposite sides of a central court, to create a single vista which terminated in the cult-statue itself. Ante-cellas could be duplicated and dependencies multiplied; but the cardinal sequence of features around which the plan developed remained constant from then onwards. As for the cult-statue itself, upon which the liturgy of Sumerian ritual was focused, some clue to its appearance may be sought in relief sculptures where deities are depicted. A rare example is to be seen in the so-called 'Stela of Ur-nammu', fragments of which were found by Woolley among the earliest remains of 'E-dub-lal-makh'. This was a monument 3 m high, divided horizontally to depict scenes connected with the building of a temple. In the only undamaged register, the king is

106 Tell Asmar (Eshnunna), cut-away plan and section of a temple (*A*) dedicated to Gimil-Sin, deified King of Ur, and the adjoining 'Palace of the Governors' with its private chapel, in the time of Illushuilia (2317–2283 BC). Vaulting over the 'Great Hall' is not impossible at this period. (Drawing by R. Leacroft) *1*, sanctuary; *2*, altar; *3*, great hall; *4*, throne-room; *5*, courtyard; *6*, private court; *7*, ablutions; *8*, palace chapel; *9*, ante-chamber; *10*, sanctuary; *11*, toilet

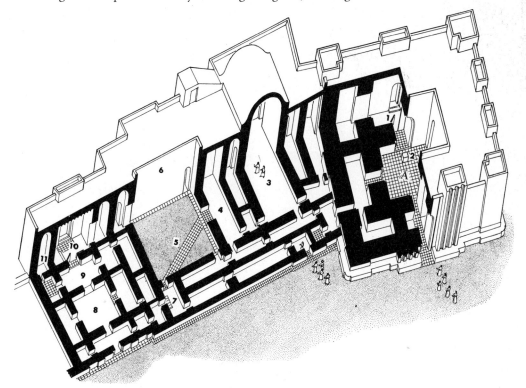

107 Detail of the Stela of Ur-nammu found at Ur, reconstructed from fragments. The King is instructed by seated gods to build a temple (perhaps the ziggurat). The 'Sumerian Revival' owed much to his initiative. Ht 304 cm

twice depicted in confrontation, first with a god and then a goddess (perhaps Nannar and Ningal), before whom he pours a libation over some sort of plant. Fragments of a terracotta vessel, similar to that in which the plant grows, were found beside the altar in the Gimil-Sin temple. In contrast to the secular dynamism of the Sargonid reliefs, the tranquility of this religious scene is once more characteristically Sumerian. Similar subjects depicted on the seal-cylinders of this period have a correspondingly static quality.

Chapter Eight

The 2nd Millennium BC

In the early years of the 2nd millennium, with the Sumerian empire disintegrating and a number of new states becoming actively independent, we are faced with an era of change in the political anatomy of Mesopotamia, which may once more justify a short historical digression.[191]

Conflicting States

Of the two peoples who were jointly responsible for the downfall of Ur's Third Dynasty, the Amorites from Syria settled in Babylon and other cities to the north, while the Elamites returned eastward across the Zagros, leaving a governor of their own choosing in the Diyala state, Eshnunna, to guard their interests in Mesopotamia. In Sumer itself, meanwhile, throughout the whole of the 20th century BC, one watches two states, Isin (modern Bahriyat) and Larsa (modern Sinkara), contending for control of the ancient cities and their sacred shrines. At first Isin is in the ascendancy, but its enemies are many, including not only Larsa but Eshnunna with its Elamite allies. Furthermore, by the end of the century, two formidable new states have emerged from their previous obscurity to become prominent in the political scene: Mari (modern Tell Hariri) and Ashur (Qal'at Sharqat), situated respectively on the middle courses of the Euphrates and Tigris. Also in about 1900 BC, when Larsa appeared to be gaining the upper hand, a new dynasty was founded in Babylon, whose sixth ruler, Hammurabi, was destined to reshape the whole political pattern.

Of the more northerly states which we have mentioned above, Mari is one at which we should take a closer look. Its ruins as we have said lie on the west bank of the Euphrates, a little to the north of the modern Syrian frontier. The Sumerian king-list attributes to it the status of a city with a dynasty of rulers; and sure enough, when a French expedition led by A. Parrot began excavating there in 1933, their first find was an Early Dynastic temple, dedicated like that at Ashur which it closely resembled, to the goddess Ishtar. By the beginning of the 2nd millennium BC, the place had acquired a special importance as a station on the great trade-route which brought timber and metal from Syria or from the mines of the Taurus Mountains. At the time when the First Dynasty of Babylon was founded, its rulers were consequently rich and prosperous. Their palace, which Parrot had the good fortune to find and the opportunity to excavate, was an enormous building which will presently be described, and it contained an archive of more than 20,000 tablets, revealing the city's history prior to its destruction by Hammurabi in about 1760 BC.[192]

The Mari tablets first introduce us to several obscure Semitic kings, and then to one more historical ruler, Iakhdunlim, early in whose reign the city temporarily lost its independence and was annexed to the state of Ashur. Mentioned in this connection is one of the first really notable Assyrian kings, Shamsi-Adad I, concerning whom a great deal is to be learnt from the Mari archive. The city of Ashur occupied a strategic position on a shoulder of rock, overlooking the Tigris at a point well beyond the limits of the alluvial plain.[193] Like Mari, it was an important trading centre, in contact both with the southern cities and with the sources of raw materials in Anatolia. Between about 1940 and 1800 BC it had even maintained a commercial colony or *karum* as far away as Kanesh (modern Kültepe) in Cappadocia. Under Shamsi-Adad its own territory extended northward to include the uplands around Nineveh; so its extension westward as far as the Euphrates now created a formidable kingdom. From the Mari archive one learns in great detail how this came to be administered by Shamsi-Adad and his two sons, one of whom, Ishme-Dagan, he established as governor of Mari. He himself preferred to be on the move from one minor city to another, and seems to have spent a good deal of his time at a place called Shubat-Enlil, probably on the River Khabur and now equated by some scholars with the site called Chagar Bazar, where Mallowan came upon tablets dealing with his financial affairs.[194] Other contemporary letters in which the Assyrian royal family is mentioned have been found more recently at Tell Rimah, the site of a provincial capital in the Sinjar area. The combined contents of all these texts have helped to create an extremely clear (and sometimes entertaining) picture, both of public administration and of personal relations between the ruling families. For this reason alone they are invaluable documents.

The end of Shamsi-Adad's reign is less easy to reconstruct. His southern garrisons seem to have been overrun by the armies of Eshnunna and Elam, which then drove westward to the Euphrates, and it may well have been in resisting this attack that the Assyrian king lost his life. When the situation again becomes clear, Ishme-Dagan has succeeded him as King of Ashur (1781 BC); but Mari has regained its independence and is ruled by Iakhdunlim's son, Zimrilim, who had been exiled to Aleppo. It was in Zimrilim's time that final improvements were made to the palace which Parrot excavated.

Zimrilim's political relations with the south, dependent on ephemeral alliances with Babylon and Eshnunna, were for the time being satisfactory. In the northwest, Syrian states such as Iamkhad, of which Aleppo was a principal city, Alalakh and even Qatnah in the plain of Homs, all remained friendly. Only to the east of the Euphrates at this time (*c.* 1800 BC), the country had begun to be disturbed by the arrival of new immigrants from the highlands of what is now Azarbaijan. These were the Hurrians: a people of unknown extraction, neither Semites nor Indo-Europeans. Ever since the Third Dynasty of Ur, there had been small centres in northern Mesopotamia whose rulers had Hurrian names. In Zimrilim's time they were already to be found at Carchemish, and later as far afield as Alalakh and the Orontes Valley. Nevertheless, it

108

108 Head of a basalt stela recording Hammurabi's code of laws, carried away to Susa during an Elamite invasion and now in the Louvre. The King is seen confronting the seated figure of Shamash, god of justice. Beneath are 16 columns of cuneiform inscription in which the traditional laws of Babylonia are definitively re-formulated. Ht of top of stela, 71 cm

is from the American excavations at Nuzi, near Kirkuk, that our rather scanty knowledge of them is mainly derived.

The Hurrians, in any case, were for the time being disunited and presented no serious threat to the cities of upper Mesopotamia. In the end it was the accession of a great statesman to the throne of Babylon which put an end to this peaceful interlude. In 1759 B C, the armies of Hammurabi defeated a coalition consisting of Larsa, Eshnunna, Elam and Mari. Two year's later Mari revolted, but was then completely destroyed, while Assyria, now much reduced in size, became a vassal of Babylon. As in the time of Sargon-of-Akkad, the whole country was now again united under a single ruler and an appropriate system of administration devised. Hammurabi's achievements in this respect are reflected in his famous law-code, inscribed on a basalt stela 3 m high, which is to be seen in the Louvre.

During the reigns of Hammurabi's successors, three unexpected developments foreshadowed the disintegration of his empire. In the south a people inhabiting the so-called 'Sea-Land' at the head of the Arabian Gulf, encroached upon the old Sumerian cities and created from them a new kingdom. Secondly, from the northeast came a host of Kassites, displaced from their homeland by the same movement of Indo-European peoples which brought the Hittites into Anatolia. And finally, in 1595 BC, the Hittites themselves under their king Mursilis I, after sacking in turn Carchemish and Mari, swept on down the Euphrates as far as Babylon itself, which they plundered and burnt, thereby putting an end to Hammurabi's dynasty.

The Hittite raid on Babylon was one of the stranger phenomena of Near Eastern history; for Mursilis was almost immediately summoned home, to deal with enemies who were threatening his own capital in Anatolia. It was accordingly the Kassites who profited most, because they were thus enabled peacefully to take over the government of Babylonia. They adopted the religion and culture of Mesopotamia so thoroughly and unquestionably that, for the next 360 years, one would hardly be aware that much of that country was now being ruled by a dynasty of completely alien kings. To the north, meanwhile, in the hilly country beyond Nineveh, and west to the Euphrates, much the same situation had arisen in regard to the Hurrians. Such rulers as they possessed had now been replaced by a new, Indo-European aristocracy, whose political acumen enabled them at last to acquire for their people a national identity. Between Assyria and the Hittites there emerged a powerful kingdom, thereafter known as Mitanni, with its capital at Washukkani (a site to the west of Nisibin which has not yet been located).[195] In the early years of the 14th century, one finds its kings corresponding almost on equal terms with Egyptian Pharaohs of the 18th Dynasty.

It was also during this century that Assyria, still with its capital at Ashur, began to reappear as a major power. As one able ruler followed another, its southern frontier was stabilized, while the Mitannians, under pressure from the Hittites, soon began to relax their hold on northern Mesopotamia. Finally, weakened by internal disputes, their royal family lost authority and its army ceased to be a match for that of Assyria. In 1250 BC, after several defeats, the last Mitannian king was slain by Shalmaneser I and his country became a province of the Assyrian state. Shalmaneser's successor Tukulti-Ninurta I (1244–1208) conquered Babylon and, during the remainder of the 2nd millennium one watches the earlier stages in the creation of an Assyrian empire.

With these historical events in mind, it may be easier to understand that the archaeology of the 2nd millennium can be divided into four principal phases, each of which is, as it happens, illustrated by the results of at least one major excavation. To begin with there is the 'Isin-Larsa' period (*c.* 2020–1763 BC), ending with Hammurabi's unification of Mesopotamia. This period is well represented at the Diyala sites: Tell Asmar (Eshnunna), Ischali (Neribtum), and Tell Harmal (Shaduppum). Next there are the reigns of Hammurabi and his successors, the Old Babylonian period, ending with the fall of Babylon in 1595 BC. For this we have Parrot's wonderfully comprehensive finds at Mari. Thirdly, in the south there is the time of the Kassite Dynasty (1595–1235 BC), documented primarily by the Iraq Government's excavations at Dur-Kurigalzu (ʿAqar Quf). In the north this partly coincides with a period of Hurrian-Mitannian domination, of which we shall find evidence at Nuzi and elsewhere. And finally, there is the growth of Assyrian power: the so-called 'Middle Assyrian' period, which will bring us to recall the excavations made by the Germans at Ashur itself.

Buildings of the Isin-Larsa Period

Eshnunna ceased to be a vassal of Ur in 2027 BC and some years later its first independent governor, Ilushuilia added a palace to the great temple which one of his predecessors had dedicated to Gimil-Sin, a deified king of Ur.[196] To the palace he annexed a smaller religious building, probably now dedicated to the local god, Tishpak. This 'Palace Chapel', like the older temple, adheres to the plan now uniformly adopted in Babylonia, with entry, courtyard, antecella and sanctuary all on the same axis. The palace itself is of greater interest, because it takes its place in a long line of secular buildings planned for the same purpose.[197] Facing the square court is a broad rectangular throne-room or audience chamber, with a staircase leading to the flat roof near one end. It is separated by smaller chambers from a 'great hall' (or *bitanu* court), perhaps used for assemblies. We shall see something of the same sort at Mari and, more than a thousand years on, in the standard 'reception suites' of the Late Assyrian palaces. In the Eshnunna palace, remnants of the state archive were found in the stair-well; but some of the most important historical evidence was derived from the stamped bricks, used during each successive reconstruction of the building, which provided a complete genealogy of local rulers.

We learn in this way that it was a later Governor, Ibiqadad II ('enlarger of Eshnunna'), who built an immensely greater palace, facing the earlier buildings across a broad street.[198] Of this only the foundations have survived; and it may well have remained unfinished. Yet here again one may recognize the standard arrangement of court, throne-room and 'great hall', now much enlarged and even duplicated. Elsewhere to the north, Ibiqadad's son (confusingly called Naram-Sin), built a separate audience hall – in this case differently planned, supposedly because he had 'assumed the prerogatives of divinity'.

Nearer to the River Diyala itself is Ischali (ancient Neribtum), where, 'in the year Rapiqu was sacked', Ibiqadad built a temple which is perhaps the finest monument of the Isin-Larsa period.[199] *109* The building is a precise rectangle, measuring approximately 100 × 60 m, and incorporates three separate shrines, the largest dedicated to Ishtar-Kititum, a local form of the great goddess. The whole complex is raised 3 m above ground-level on a platform or *kisu*, faced with kiln-baked bricks set in bitumen. Baked brick is again generously used elsewhere, for instance in the construction of a wide stairway, leading from the outer courtyard to that of the

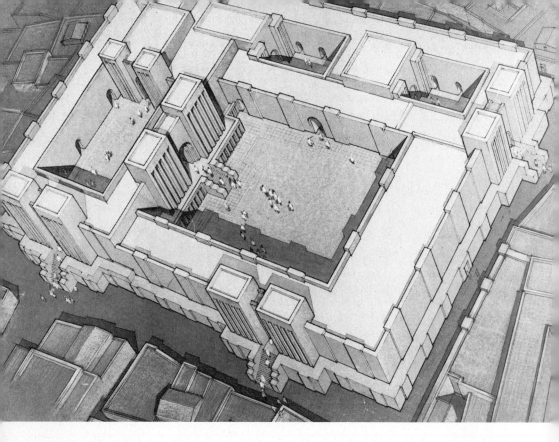

109 The Ishtar-Kititum Temple at Ischali (ancient Neribtum in the state of Eshnunna). Raised above its surrounding buildings on a terrace faced with baked brick, it comprised three separate shrines, of which the largest was raised even higher. A fine example of Mesopotamian architecture in the Isin-Larsa period (2017–1794 BC). (Watercolour by W. Suddaby)

major shrine which stands at an even higher level, and for the three towered gateways. An unusual feature is to be seen in one of the subsidiary shrines, whose sanctuary is set lengthwise on the main axis: a practice later adopted in Assyrian temples (German *langraum*). Elsewhere the *breitraum* arrangement is maintained. A striking reconstruction of the whole building is to be seen in a much-published drawing by the late Harold Hill. It makes an interesting contrast to Shaduppum (Tell Harmal), which is a small, outlying heavily fortified administrative station, on the outskirts of modern Baghdad.[200] But it too was provided with no less than four comparatively modest temples, the largest of which has outer and inner gateways, flanked by the almost life-size figures of lions in terracotta. Archives of tablets found in its administrative buildings included, among other important texts, a code of laws preceding that of Hammurabi.

Private Houses

Under this heading, a word should be said about ordinary dwelling-houses of the Larsa period. These are well represented in contemporary levels at the Diyala sites, but perhaps even better illustrated at Ur, by Woolley's excavation in a residential area to 110 the southeast of the temple precinct.[201] Here there was a tangle of narrow streets with modest houses on either side, and occasionally, at important cross-roads where several lanes met, small religious shrines occupying sites of their own. The houses themselves so closely resembled those of any small town in Iraq early in the

mag. N

present century, that they hardly merit description: blank walls facing the street, rooms in two storeys opening on to an unroofed central court, and in one, of which Woolley drew a well-known reconstruction, a sheltered wooden gallery at first-floor level, supported on posts.[202] Among their few distinctive features were the graves of their occupants, often buried beneath the ground-floor pavements.

110 A residential quarter of Ur in the 20th century BC. A tangle of narrow lanes lead off wider roads. The richer houses have two storeys of rooms, lighted by an open court, and closely resemble those in the older cities of modern Iraq. (After Woolley)

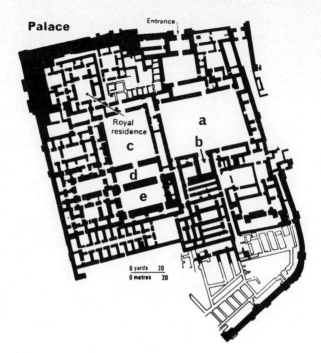

Palace

Entrance

Royal
residence

a

b

c

d

e

0 yards 20
0 metres 20

111 The great palace at Mari, as
completed by Zimrilim
(1779–1761 BC). The royal
archives were found in two
rooms near the approach to the
king's apartments, where there
was also accommodation (a
school?) for scribes. (After
Hawkes, 1974). *a*, outer
courtyard; *b*, audience hall (with
murals); *c*, ceremonial courtyard
(with murals); *d*, throne-room;
e, inner sanctuary and hall

The Palace at Mari

111   The Mari palace had doubtless been the residence of Zimrilim's
father, Iakhdunlim, and afterwards used by Shamsi-Adad's son
during the Assyrian interlude. But, as much of it was built of bricks
stamped with the name of Zimrilim himself, he must have
considerably enlarged and rebuilt it. It was, as we know, finally
destroyed when the city-walls were razed to the ground in the 35th
year of Hammurabi (1757 BC). Nevertheless, when Parrot found it,
its 4-m thick walls remained standing in some cases as much as 5 m
high and the lintels of some doorways were still intact.[203] The
whole building measures approximately 200 × 120 m – twice the
dimensions of the Ishtar-Kititum temple. Much of the plan consists
of a multiplication of what is really the Babylonian dwelling-house
unit – a number of chambers grouped around an open court; but
these are subsidiary to the great central system of reception rooms
and religious shrines.

From the main entrance with its guardrooms, one passes into a
huge outer courtyard (*a*), of which the main feature is a three-
sided audience chamber, approached by a flight of steps (*b*),
thought by some to be a surviving feature of an earlier building.
But it is the inner, and slightly smaller courtyard (*c*), on to which
the main suite of reception chambers faces. It is composed of the
now-traditional elements: first a throne-room (*d*) with a podium facing the central doorway, and then, separated from it by
vestibules, a larger element corresponding to the 'great hall' (*e*).
But the latter now has a clearly religious function; for, at one end,
steps lead up to a sanctuary and, facing it at the opposite end of the

hall, is a throne emplacement. As Parrot has observed, this gives the whole central suite a non-secular character, and we shall see that this is borne out by the relics of sculpture and mural paintings which are associated with it.

More simply decorated are the living apartments of the royal family in the northwest corner of the building, whose outer walls on both sides are enormously strengthened. The king's own chamber and that of the queen were recognizable, and in the court between, some sort of game had been marked out on the pavement. Closer than one would expect to this domestic unit were two chambers with rows of clay benches, identified as a school or offices for scribes. Accessible from these were two of the store-rooms in which archives were kept – originally arranged upon shelves. The third and most important archive room was conveniently placed between the inner and outer courts. Elsewhere, among the 200-or-more rooms clustering around the central unit, ranges of other store-rooms could be recognized, including one group centred upon a chamber known to the excavators as the *Cercle des officiers*, which was distinguished by its painted walls. Also near the southeast corner of the building were two rooms composing a minor shrine, connected by a 'processional way' to the main audience hall.

112

112 Palace of Zimrilim at Mari; toilet and terracotta baths in the royal apartments

Mural Paintings

113(*Top*) Mural painting on an outer wall of the throne-room in Zimrilim's palace at Mari ('*c*' in ill. 111). The 'Investiture' scene (above) shows the King before Ishtar, 'taking the oath' with his hand upon the divine emblem in the presence of other deities. Below, two figures of the 'goddess with flowing vase' are in attendance. On either side are 'sacred trees' and other symbolic figures. The Mari scene has been compared with the entrance to an Assyrian temple at Khorsabad (*above*), which again is flanked by 'flowing-vase' figures and artificial palm trees. (S. Ebrahim after Parrot, 1958)

More must now be said about the mural paintings, which have been the subject of much specialized study.[204] As Parrot himself has observed, they are of special significance, in that they clearly illustrate 'the spirit of synthesis which animated the artists of the middle Euphrates at this period': the curious combination of Sumerian heiraticism, surviving from an earlier age, with the distinctive naturalism of the Semitic approach to art. As he says, these influences seem to have contributed to creating a new school of decoration, which, had it been given time to mature, might have produced one of the high artistic epochs of Near Eastern history. The murals were painted directly upon a thin layer of mud plaster, in a manner which has been taken to suggest that the true 'fresco' technique was understood.

The largest and most ambitious composition, *L'Investiture du Roi de Mari*, was found, still in place, on an outer wall adjoining the central entrance to the throne-room, in a part of the courtyard (*c*) which was protected from the weather by a roof or awning supported on posts. The central design is composed of upper and lower panels. In the former, the king, draped in an elaborately fringed costume and *polos* headdress, receives or touches a divine emblem held by the goddess Ishtar, whose raised foot rests upon the back of a lion. Other gods and goddesses are in attendance. In the lower scene, facing each other, are two identical figures of the 'goddess with flowing vase', wearing a flounced dress and holding an *ariballos* vessel, from which streams of water, full of fish, undulate around the picture. Both scenes are framed on either side by tall panels with palm and other stylized trees, among which birds, mythical animals and divinities are to be seen. This composition has been ingeniously explained by one scholar as a ceremony taking place in the cella and antecella of a temple, of the sort which in later, Assyrian times was entered between 'flowing-vase' statues and artificial palms.[205] Whether or not this is so, the decorative effect of such a design, with its ornamental border and bright colours, must have been magnificent.

113

Another such painting adorned a wall of the audience chamber in the outer courtyard, like which it may be of slightly earlier date. Known to the excavators as *Le sacrifice de l'eau by du feu*, it is a scene of worship and libation, attended by monstrous figures of Sumerian mythology: Tiamat of the *Enuma Elish* epic and Shamash, 'rising behind his mountain to scatter the stars'. The king (Shamsi-Adad I?), again in his fringed garment, also appears in the surviving fragment of a 'sacrificial scene', whose original position in the building could not be positively determined.

We have noted above that, in the centre of the city at the southeast approach to the palace, a cluster of minor temples had already existed in Early Dynastic times, dedicated to such gods as Nin-khursag, or more local deities like Ishtarat and Ninni-Zaza.[206] Some of these still survived in the 18th century; but they were now dwarfed in size by the Temple of Dagan (a grain-god worshipped along the middle Euphrates), to whose sanctuary a small ziggurat was at some time annexed. Dedicatory tablets showed that this temple was in fact build by Ishtup-ilum, a governor of the city in the late Larsa period (*c.* 1890 BC), of whom a fine portrait statue was found, not in the temple but in the 'great sanctuary' of Zimrilim's palace. This and other Mari statues may therefore presently be discussed together with the combined products of the Isin-Larsa and Old Babylonian periods.

Tell Rimah

During the excavation of buildings to which we have so far referred, little information could be recovered regarding either their façade ornament or method of roofing. In the 1960s, a British expedition led by David Oates, and working at Tell Rimah, in the Sinjar district west of Mosul, was able to throw much new light on both these matters.[207] Here, where a largish mound already covered the remains of earlier settlements, a local ruler in the time of Shamsi-Adad I had built himself a city, surrounding it with fortifications and creating from the mound itself an emplacement for a remarkably fine temple. This building, as described by the excavator himself,

114

> was approached by a free-standing stair carried on vaults, and from its roof further stairs or ramps led to a high terrace, perhaps surmounted by a higher shrine. The whole, three- or four-tiered structure must have resembled a ziggurat. The temple itself on its platform high above the city, was laid out on the Babylonian plan and decorated in a style that also has southern parallels, although as a complete system of ornament it is unique. All the external and courtyard façades were adorned with engaged

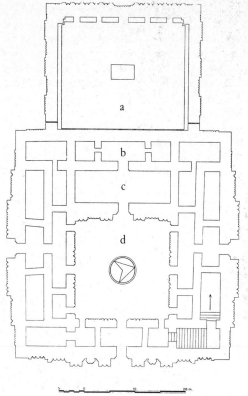

114 Plan of a temple at Tell Rimah in the Sinjar district, at the foot of a small ziggurat (late 3rd millennium BC). The façades are elaborately ornamented with half- and three-quarter-columns of mud-brick, some moulded spirally or to represent palm trunks. Remnants of complicated mud-brick vaulting had survived in this building. (After D. Oates, 1964).
a, ziggurat; *b*, shrine; *c*, antechamber; *d*, courtyard

115 Plan and section of 'pitched-brick' vaulting on pendentives at Tell Rimah. A simpler form of 'pitched-brick' vaulting was used 2000 years later in the great *iwân* behind the Arch of Ctesiphon. (After D. Oates, 1973)

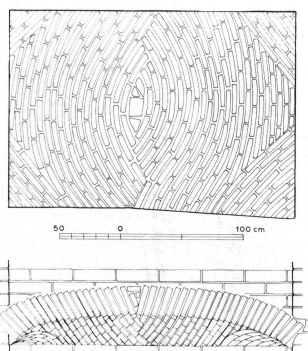

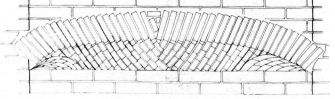

columns, set singly or in groups, 277 in all; the 50 large columns were built of carved bricks, laid in complicated patterns to represent spirals or palm-trunks.[208]

But perhaps the more extraordinary feature of this building was the prevailing use of mud-brick arches and vaulting, even for trivial purposes where wood could have been substituted.[209] Complicated vaulting systems, including the use of 'pitched-brick' construction and even pendentives, were contrived with such casual facility that a long and widespread tradition of building in this manner seemed to be implied.

115

Sculpture

Of the Mari statues, the only one undoubtedly contemporary with the palace is the 'flowing-vase' goddess, fragments of which were found both in the 'throne-room' and in the courtyard outside. (This must have been a fixture, since, by an arrangement of pipes, it actually dispensed water.) Stylistically however, it is of little significance, since its design in most respects suggests a traditional treatment of this particular subject. More characteristic are the several statues of local princes: Ishtup-ilum, found in the 'great sanctuary'; Idi-ilum from the southeast shrine and Pusur-Ishtar, which was part of a 'collection' of antiquities assembled by a Late Babylonian king (and now in the Istanbul

116

117

116 Statue in black stone of Ishtup-ilum, Governor of Mari, from the palace of Zimrilim (*c.* 2200 BC). Ht 152 cm

117 Statue of deified king dedicated to a temple by Pusur-Ishtar, Governor of Mari, found in the 6th-century 'Palace Museum' at Babylon. Like Ishtup-ilum, he wears a toga-like dress, also seen on contemporary statues from Eshnunna, found at Susa and now in the Louvre. Ht 175 cm

Museum). These compare interestingly with the statues of two Eshnunna governors, one of them seated, which were carried as booty to Susa. In a world where the crudity of the *kaunakes* was hardly remembered, these statues are dressed in a toga-like garment, whose fine texture and restrained modelling are effectively contrasted with the obtrusive detail of ornamental fringes and the pattern of formally dressed beards. They are by no means lacking in dignity.[210]

Other sculpture of the period is scarce and often of poor quality. Where relief carving is concerned, the scene depicted at the head of Hammurabi's 'law-code' stela is perhaps unique. The king, whose profile and headdress are familiar from fragmentary sculptures in-the-round, stands facing a seated god, with the emblem of divinity (justice?) in his hand, like Ishtar in the 'Investiture' painting. In the words of Henri Frankfort, the scene 'conveys, not only a sense of confrontation but of communication between the lord of justice and the law-giver'. But there is at this time another form of relief, modelled in terracotta. Of this, a fine example is the (privately owned) panel showing the naked goddess, Lilith, with her supporting lions and owls.[211] More common still are votive plaques of baked clay, cast in an open mould, which were probably sold to worshippers at a temple. Their subjects vary from the ubiquitous 'mother-goddess', now grotesquely conventionalized, to sensitively modelled figures of musicians, temple-women or more trivial motifs such as a bitch suckling her puppies. Corresponding to the fine terracotta lions from the temple gateways at Tell Harmal, similar beasts of bronze, with inlaid eyes, guarded the sanctuary of the Dagan temple at Mari.[212]

118 Painted terracotta plaque showing the goddess Lilith, 'Bringer of Death', winged and holding symbols of justice. Her name is associated with owls, both in the Gilgamesh epic and the Old Testament (*Isaiah*, XXXIV, 14). Ht 50 cm

119 Guardian lions in terracotta from temple gateways at Tell Harmal (ancient Shaduppum), a minor walled city in the state of Eshnunna. Reconstructed from some hundreds of fragments (*c.* 1900 BC). Ht *c.* 63 cm

118

119

The Kassites

120 Wall ornament from the
temple of Karaindash at Uruk: a
rare example of Kassite
architecture (14th century BC).
Ht of brickwork, 198 cm

121 The eroded ruin of a great
ziggurat at ʿAqar Quf, west of
modern Baghdad and site of the
Kassite capital called Dur-
Kurigalzu. The mud-brick core
is reinforced with layers of reeds
and heavy cables (Kassite
Dynasty, 15th–13th centuries BC)

In view of the fact that the Kassites ruled Babylonia for more than
four centuries, it is surprising to observe how little their national
characteristics are reflected in the material remains of their
occupation. These make it abundantly clear that, in religion,
administration and technical practices, they adopted and faithfully
maintained the age-old conventions of Mesopotamia, rebuilding
temples and honouring the shrines of Sumerian deities. An almost
unique exception in this respect is the temple of Karaindash at Uruk
which, with its exaggerated corner buttresses, seems at first to be
sharply differentiated from the buildings around it. Even so, its
elaborately decorated façade embodies one motif with which we
are already familiar. Tall niches between its projecting pilasters are
filled with the alternating figures of Babylonian gods and
120 goddesses, holding in both hands the traditional 'flowing vase'. For
the rest, they provide us with a very early example of the
'moulded-brick' ornament which was later perfected by Assyrian
and Neo-Babylonian craftsmen.[213]

121 The grandiose new capital, which was founded by the
Kassites themselves and called Dur-Kurigalzu, is distinguished
from other Babylonian cities only by the nature of its chosen site. It
was built upon a low outcrop of soft limestone, at the northern

extremity of the alluvial plain to the west of modern Baghdad, where the eroded core of its great ziggurat (now partially restored) still creates a conspicuous landmark. Iraq Government excavations in 1942–5 exposed a complex of temples at the foot of the tower and, further out on a peninsula extending into the neighbouring flood-basin, the remains of at least four palaces.[214] Peculiar features of the temple area were rectangular platforms faced with baked brick, supporting the principal shrines. Inscribed pivot-stones and tablets found in this area were mostly dated to the reign of a king called Kurigalzu; but the stratification of the palaces, which had been rebuilt at more frequent intervals, implied the existence of two earlier kings bearing the same name.

One of these palaces ('H'),[215] unfortunately in part denuded owing to the weathering of the mound, did show some signs of an architectural arrangement perhaps characteristically Kassite. The central courtyard was surrounded by multiple doorways, giving on to long galleries reminiscent of cloisters. The reveals of these doorways were decorated up to a height of about 1 m with mural paintings, depicting processions of court officials.[216] They wore a short-sleeved garment with a fringed girdle and a fez-shaped headdress over their long hair in the Assyrian manner. It has been suggested and is entirely possible that this figured ornament,

122 Kassite *kudurru* or boundary stone, assigning land to an official called Marduk-nasir. The armed figure of a king(?) is surmounted by religious symbols. Ht 53 cm

123 Head in terracotta of a bearded man from Dur-Kurigalzu. The style recalls that of the 18th Dynasty in Egypt. Ht 4 cm

forming a 'dado' at the base of the walls, foreshadowed the use of sculptured slabs for the same purpose in later Assyrian palaces. In Kassite times, relief sculpture was mainly restricted to boundary stones (*kudurru*), bearing the emblems of gods invoked as witnesses of a land-settlement, or of a king who had authorized it.[217]

Another palace ('A') of a much earlier period, had one long gallery, painted white, with triple rows of small plastered pedestals. The many fragments of gold leaf and other valuables lying on the pavement between these, strongly suggested its use as a treasure-chamber. Later it had been replaced by ranges of brick-vaulted repositories, probably intended for the same purpose.[218] It was here, and in the stair-wells leading to the roof, that other valuable objects had been scattered, perhaps at a time when the palace was looted. Among many damaged gold ornaments and beads, one intact gold bracelet was found, on which 'granular' ornament alternated with inlays of blue paste. Many fragments were also found of mosaic ornament in coloured glass. This would be contemporary with or older than the 18th-Dynasty Egyptian glass found at Tell-el-Amarnah. The craftsmanship of that period in Egypt was also recalled by the painted head of a man with a full beard in terracotta and the equally well-modelled figure of a lioness.[219]

123

124

124 Sensitively modelled head of a lioness from Dur-Kurigalzu. Our knowledge of Kassite art depends mainly on small objects of this sort. Ht *c.* 5 cm

NUZI

We have now to deal with the Mitannian occupation of northern Mesopotamia, which was in part contemporary with the Kassite dynasty in Babylonia. Mitannian kings reigned from their capital at Washukkani, near the headwaters of the River Khabur, from about 1500 BC until the mid-14th century, when their kingdom disintegrated. During that time, one of their southernmost strongholds was the city now known as Nuzi, 12½ miles to the southwest of modern Kirkuk (Arrapha), and its site was excavated by Americans from Pennsylvania, under R. F. S. Starr and others, during the late 1920s and early 1930s.[220] To anyone seeking the criteria of Mitannian culture, the results of this excavation are both rewarding and disappointing. A palace and temple were found, as well as a large number of important private dwellings. In the absence of conspicuous works of art, innumerable small finds give an impression of a people whose way of life was much enriched by trade and familiarity with the countries of the Levant and even with Egypt. But undoubtedly the major discovery of the expedition was an abundance of tablets: over 5,000 texts in all, including in certain cases the entire archives of a single family over periods of as much as five generations.[221]

The main mound was called Yorghan Tepe, and beneath it lay the actual walled city with its palace and temple;[222] but there were also outlying mounds covering the remains of other palatial residences. To the temple some reference has already been made, since it was originally founded in the Early Dynastic period, at a time when the place was known as Gasur. It was finally rebuilt in Mitannian times, in a form which comprised two sanctuaries, and its remains were conveniently dated by a letter from the Mitannian king Shaushattar (c. 1460 BC). One shrine had internal walls faced with wooden panelling in the form of 'clapper-boards', pegged to the brickwork. Elsewhere the wall-faces were decorated with nail-shaped bosses of glazed terracotta and, suspended from these, some sort of woven fabric enriched with beads. Brightly coloured glazing, of the sort common in Egypt at this time, was also applied to other objects, such as small guardian figures of lions and, in one case, to a wall-ornament in the form of a boar's head. As for sculpture, the excavators had to be content with the eye-inlay of a life-size statue.

The palace was built around the usual broad open courtyards. In the largest of these, at the approach to the main reception suite, the walls seemed to have had some sort of painted wooden entablature beneath the eaves and, before the main entrance to the throne-room, a pair of free-standing brick piers may have supported a portico or ornamental baldachin. Everywhere there were elaborate provisions for drainage and sanitation, including at least one example of a toilet, flushed by piped water from above. A luxurious bathroom and lavatory were annexed to the royal apartments, and the vestibule through which these were approached was decorated with impressive mural paintings, incorporating foreign motifs such as guilloche ornament, acroteria, bucrania and 'Hathor heads'.[223] Main doorways had pivot-stones, in one of which the bronze 'shoe' of the door-pivot itself remained in place. The

125 Fragile pottery of the style known as 'Nuzi ware', with designs painted in white on a dark ground. Such vessels date from the time of the Mitannian kingdom (*c.* 1475–1350 BC), based in northeast Syria. (From Starr, 1938)

great thickness of the walls in the principal reception units could have implied an increase in their height to allow for clerestory lighting; but the excavators preferred to see in this a mere provision for security.

Several mansions in the northern suburb, including that of the 'Crown Prince' ('Governor of the City of Arrapha'), were the subject of special study. Those of two brothers called Tehip and Shurki Tilla between them produced 1,000 tablets. That of an individual called Zigi contained a formidable collection of copper objects, comprising arrowheads, spearheads, knives and much laminated armour plating, fused into heavy masses. But there were tools as well as weapons: scythes, punches, chisels and adzes – all discarded apparently at a time when the buildings were destroyed by fire.

Among the minor finds made in these palace buildings at Nuzi, one distinctive feature was an unusual type of pottery.[224] These finely made vessels were elegantly decorated with designs in white paint on a dark-coloured background. The commonest form was a tall cup with 'button base', and the patterns, usually in horizontal registers, included motifs till now unfamiliar in Mesopotamia, such as running spirals, guilloches and rosettes, as well as formalized birds and plants. Though this ware has been found as far south as the Kassite capital Dur-Kurigalzu and to the north at Tell Billa beyond Mosul, its affinities are with northern Syria, where it has appeared at such sites as Tell Atchana (Alalakh), and was supposed by Woolley (perhaps wrongly) to have originated in Crete. Mitannian cylinder-seals too, have more in common with those of northern Syria, and even Cappadocia. The designs are often overcrowded and confused; but certain motifs such as the stylized 'sacred tree' and the winged griffin survived in the imagery of later Assyrian ornament.[225]

125

Finally, there is the famous collection of texts from Nuzi. The excavations brought to light no less than 4,000 cuneiform tablets, of which almost 1,000 were found in the house of Tehip-Tilla. Their contents create an extraordinarily detailed picture of daily life in this part-Hurrian community of citizens. Legal and commercial transactions which they often record are of interest in themselves; but it is their incidental references to people, places and things that promote one's understanding of the social or environmental background against which they were written, and amplify the evidence provided by archaeological finds.

In an appendix to R. F. S. Starr's publication of the Nuzi excavation (1939), E. R. Lacheman summarizes most interestingly the 'evidences of material culture' to be derived from the texts: a most welcome addition to an archaeological report of this sort. It appears under headings whose variety alone prepares one for the wealth of information which they contain.

First then, Nuzi emerges as a walled city, with towers, bastions and gates whose names are mentioned. The palace is a great complex of buildings with annexes serving many purposes and a long architectural history. The temple known to the excavators was one of several shrines, piously served by the leading families, by suitable offerings and the gift of slaves. Accounts of the building or repair of private houses provide a glossary of architectural terms and structural details. Streets are frequently mentioned by name, and the topographical picture is supplemented by much detailed reference to the distribution of water: a small river serving a network of canals, reservoirs and bridges, each of them carefully named. Other landmarks were individual wells. Dealings in real estate and the transfer of land ownership reveal details of agricultural practices in a well-irrigated province, surrounded by uncultivated steppe-land, and there is a precise vocabulary of words commonly used for such purposes. One learns the relative popularity of various crops, of which barley is once more the most common, followed by wheat, emmer, sesame, poppy and flax. In a separate category are orchards and gardens, from which fruit, vegetables and flowers are listed by name, in careful inventories, and the wood of fruit-trees is recommended for specified purposes. Much information of a more technical character is provided under further headings, such as 'Chariots and Wagons', 'Furniture' or 'Clothing', and there is a section on tools, weapons and armour.

In the catalogue of subjects dealt with by the Nuzi texts, one regrets above all the paucity of references to political subjects and contemporary history. Indeed, the only piece of inscriptional evidence by which the Nuzi culture can be positively dated is, as we have said, a document from a room in the great house of Shilwi-Teshup: a well-known letter from Shaushattar, King of Mitanni, who ruled in the latter part of the 15th century BC.

The Middle Assyrian Period

For our knowledge of Assyrian archaeology during this period we are indebted almost exclusively to the work of the German excavators at Ashur (Qal'at Sharqat) on the Tigris. The decision to embark on this major enterprise was made in 1903, when, in the south, Robert Koldewey's expedition had already spent four years wrestling with the problems presented by the great ruinfields of Babylon. They had by then largely elucidated the site-plan, identified most of the principal buildings and were assured of success in their efforts to resurrect the remains of Nebuchadnezzar's capital city. Only in that year, it became evident that the unexpectedly high level of the sub-soil water-table was likely to preclude the investigation of any occupation level earlier than the 7th century BC. A supplementary operation was therefore suggested, at a site where such remains might be more accessible and, when Ashur was chosen, it was Walter Andrae who was entrusted with the new undertaking. From then onwards, until 1913, the two excavations continued simultaneously at sites 350 miles apart. Their combined accomplishment, both in the recovery of historical information and in the perfection of archaeological method, has since come to be generally recognized.[226]

CITY OF ASHUR

We have already mentioned the situation of Ashur, on an outcrop of limestone rising to a considerable height in the angle formed by two courses of the River Tigris. This gave the city natural *126–7* protection on two sides and, on the landward side, its defences were completed by a crescent-shaped array of powerful walls, enclosing an area three-quarters of a mile wide.[227] Andrae's principal excavations were carried out in the elevated part of the city to the north and northwest, where its temples and palaces were situated. He had assured himself that this was so by the now-standardized German method of cutting search-trenches (*suchgraben*) clean across the site from east to west at intervals of 100 m, corresponding to the grid-lines of his initial survey. At the same time the full circuit of the fortifications was traced, exposing the principal gates, river-side quays and other features. His deepest penetration was the sounding which revealed the Pre-Sargonid foundation of the Ishtar Temple. The latest architectural remains he encountered could be dated to the final phase of the Parthian period, about AD 256.

Andrae and Koldewey were both architects, and at Babylon their tendency to over-correct the evident faults of earlier excavators resulted in their concentration on the study of buildings rather than written texts.[228] At Ashur, the function of Andrae's epigraphical advisers gained in importance for reasons which soon became obvious. Over a period of some 2,000 years, successive kings had contributed to the restoration and multiplication of public buildings or fortifications; and the chronological sequence of their building-levels could only be determined with the help of associated inscriptions. These showed that many of them had continued to be rebuilt by Late Assyrian kings, long after the city had ceased to be their administrative capital. In the paragraphs that follow, this will explain the mention of royal names belonging more correctly to a later chapter.

FORTIFICATIONS

The landward rampart of the inner city was built and rebuilt by a number of kings, including Shamsi-Adad I in Hammurabi's time. Tukulti-Ninurta I (1244–1208 BC) provided it with an external moat, 20 m wide. A foundation inscription also records that Shalmaneser III (858–824 BC) completely reconstructed it, adding an outer wall which ran parallel to it but was diverted at its southern end to enclose an extension of the city. Meanwhile, in about 1300 BC, Adad-Nirari I had constructed a great quay of baked brick along the eastern river front, and this had been strengthened by several later kings as a secondary protection against flooding. A description of the town in the time of Sennacherib (704–681 BC)

126 The city of Ashur on the Tigris, in the Middle Assyrian period, as seen from the northwest. A drawing by Walter Andrae himself, towards the end of his ten-year excavation

127 Town plan of the city of Ashur, on its eminence at the junction between two branches of the Tigris. The *Bit Akitu* is outside the town to the northwest. (From Hawkes, 1974)

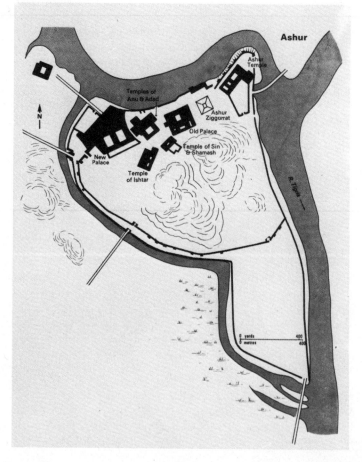

mentions thirteen gates in these fortifications, though the excavators were able to locate only eight (distinguished by numbers in the site-plan). The most important of these, used by travellers to the north, was known to the Assyrians as 'Gurgurri' (1 & 2). Between this and the western river-bed there was a kind of citadel (referred to by the Germans as the *Aussenhaken*), with gates at either end (3 & 4) through which a great procession passed out of the city at the time of the New Year's Festival (see below). Next there were gates in the north wall, a western gate known as 'Illat', and finally minor gates at the southern extremity of the city and its later extension (7 & 12).

TEMPLES AND PALACES

Approaching the city by river from the north, its massed buildings must have created an impressive silhouette – as one realizes from a well-known reconstruction drawn by Andrae himself.[229] The temples rose to a maximum height on the northernmost shoulder of rock, and there were three ziggurats. The greatest of these, which had been given its final form by Shamsi-Adad I, measured 60 m square and was originally dedicated to the Sumerian god Enlil, who, as a patron of Assyria was later replaced by the city-god Ashur himself. In its exposed position the tower was much denuded by weather and nothing remained of its stairways or auxiliary buildings. Out of 38 temples mentioned in the inscriptions, only 4 were fully excavated, the largest of which was again dedicated by Shamsi-Adad to Ashur and occupied the most prominent position on the northern height, with an enclosed precinct extending southward. Here, as in the later rebuildings of the old Ishtar Temple, something is to be learnt about the changing conventions that dictated the planning of sacred buildings. The Ashur Temple, as built by Shamsi-Adad, seemed to have two main sanctuaries, one at least conforming to the *breitraum* arrangement currently adopted in Babylonia. Many centuries later, Sennacherib added to it an eastern annex, with its cella set lengthwise on the main axis in the Assyrian manner. As for the Ishtar Temple, after the destruction of the 'Archaic' shrine, the Germans found traces of no less than six rebuildings, in the course of which even its dedication was changed. Yet, always annexed to it, was a small secondary shrine, where Ishtar continued to be worshipped, and which still retained the old *langraum* cella, with its 'bent-axis' approach following the Sumerian tradition.

Of the two other principal temples, both had dual dedications and unusual plans. One was the Anu-Adad shrine, with its twin ziggurats, identical *tieftempel* units in the Assyrian manner, and an enclosed forecourt: all contrived as a single architectural composition. The second double temple, dedicated to the moon- and sun-gods, Sin and Shamash, was first built by Ashur-nirari I (*c.* 1500 BC), but rebuilt to a different plan by Sennacherib. Both have twin Assyrian sanctuaries, approached through *breitraum* antecellas. A fifth cult-building, hardly to be regarded as a temple, was that known in Assyrian as the *Bit Akitu*, to which the cult-statues were brought in procession during the New Year's Festival. It was located 400 m outside the city to the north-west, and consisted of a

126

128

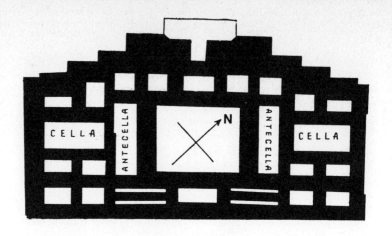

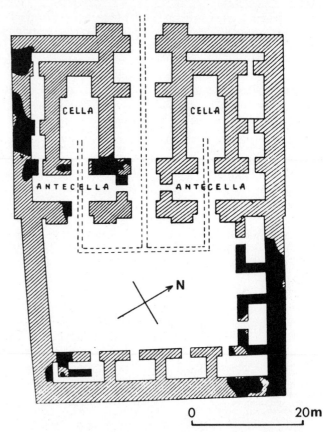

128 The Temple of Sin and Shamash at Ashur: *above*, foundation plan at the time of Ashur-nirari I (1500 BC); *below*, plan at the time of Sennacherib (704–681 BC). The long, axial sanctuaries are common to most Assyrian temples. (After Parrot, 1946)

0   20m

great square courtyard with lateral colonnades and a sanctuary on the main axis, more closely resembling a throne-room.

A further word should here be said about the *Akitu* or 'New Year's Festival', which acquired its complete ceremonial form during the early centuries of the 1st millennium BC. By that time it had replaced or assimilated the earlier Sumerian 'Spring Festival', associated with the 'Sacred Marriage' of god and goddess, symbolizing the recurrent cycle of creation and fertility. The feast now took place at the time of the spring equinox and lasted eleven days, each day marking a stage in a prolonged and complicated ritual performance. It was for the culminating phases of this ceremony that the *Bit Akitu* or Festival House provided a setting. Thither the statues of the gods were escorted, mounted on wagons or boats, having been temporarily removed from their temples, to be present at the celebration of a rite known as the 'Fixing of Destinies', in which the king himself played a leading role. Many details of the ritual used on these occasions are known from surviving texts; and at Ashur the paved way along which the procession passed out of the city has been revealed by excavation.

In contrast to the temples, there is little to be said about the secular buildings at Ashur. The so-called 'Old Palace', sited next to the main ziggurat, embodies a labyrinth of rectangular chambers and ranges of store-rooms, entered and lit from a succession of open courtyards. In this way it resembles the palaces of the Larsa period at Eshnunna, with which indeed its original foundation was contemporary. Here and there also, as in the palaces of Mari and Ur, private religious shrines are incorporated. The Ashur palace was still in use at the time of Tiglath-pileser I (1115–1077 BC); but during the Late Assyrian period, what remained of it seems to have been converted into a mausoleum. Ashur-nasirpal (883–859 BC) embellished one of its gateways with winged-bull sculptures and beneath it he constructed elegant tomb-chambers. These were found by the Germans to contain huge, monolithic sarcophagi, looted in antiquity but still bearing the names, among others, of Ashur-nasirpal himself and of Shamsi-Adad V (823–811 BC).

Meanwhile, on an artificial terrace in the northwest angle of the city wall, Tukulti-Ninurta I, after his conquest of Babylon, had built a 'New Palace' of which only the stone foundations remained. Not content with this, he also provided himself with a new residential suburb, 1.8 miles to the north of the city on the left bank of the Tigris, and named it 'Kar-Tukulti-Ninurta'. Here too he built a miniature ziggurat and, beside it, a temple with a Babylonian sanctuary and a cult-niche actually penetrating the façade of the tower itself. Andrae thought that in this case access to the upper terraces of the ziggurat was obtained by building a bridge over the street behind. For the rest, some of the most interesting discoveries at Kar-Tukulti-Ninurta were examples of figured ornament in coloured glaze on terracotta, sometimes in the form of upright wall-slabs ('orthostats'), and a panel built up out of polychrome glazed bricks.[230]

Some Finds at Ashur

We should now consider some of the finds at Ashur and the symptoms among them of ideas or innovations which can be accepted as characteristically Assyrian. In a study of this subject, Henri Frankfort claims that

... in the fourteenth century an art emerged which, for all its derivations, possessed an individual character, not only in style but also in subject matter. It depicted secular subjects with an interest in actuality for which no incident seemed too trivial. In religious matters on the other hand, it displayed a cold formalism, which did not allow man to meet the gods face to face, but only to perform the established rites before their statues and emblems.[231]

129 An altar of Tukulti-Ninurta I (1244–1208 BC) from Ashur, with a relief in which homage is paid only to the symbol of a god, in this case Nusku, set upon an image of the altar itself. Ht 53 cm

An example, frequently quoted, of this last tendency is the carved relief on an altar set up by Tukulti-Ninurta I. If one remembers the direct confrontation between man and god in the scene carved on Hammurabi's famous stela, here is a direct contrast. The Assyrian king is seen to approach and then kneel before an altar similar to that on which the picture is carved, and it is surmounted, not by a statue but by the traditional symbol of a particular god, in this case Nushku, one of three fire-gods manifest in the sacrificial flame. Perhaps this attitude to divinity is equally reflected in the planning of Assyrian temples described earlier, where the cult-statue is withdrawn to the furthest extremity of an elongated sanctuary. As for the god Ashur himself, he too more often appears as a symbol rather than in human form. His figure acquires wings, like the sun-disc of Egyptian Horus, and the disc has a bird's tail.

Another contemporary development can be seen in the carving of cylinder-seals, which now show a new upsurge of interest in design.[232] In the Larsa and Old Babylonian periods 'presentation scenes' had reached such a degree of monotonous uniformity that an inscription had often to be added giving the owner's name. This convention was now discarded and replaced by distinctive compositions in tabloid form. Some traditional 'combat scenes' can be seen to survive, but new subjects are abundant. A king hunts ostriches; a winged horse protects its foal from a lion, or stags graze

130

131

130 Middle Assyrian cylinder-seal. A late example of the 'presentation scene'. According to the inscription, the seal's owner, Hashhamer, Governor of Ishkun-Sin, is brought by a minor goddess into the presence of Ur-nammu, deified King of Ur (early 20th century BC)

131 Seal design showing a king or genius hunting ostriches (12th–11th century BC)

132 Another Middle Assyrian scene, described as 'the noble Pegasus defending his wingless foal from a lion . . .'

133 Seal design marking the transition from Middle to Late Assyrian styles (*c.* 900 BC). Kings and supporting genii face a sacred 'tree of life', with the bird-like symbol of the god Ashur above (cf. ill. 148)

among stylized trees and mountains. Added to these are the
hitherto alien motifs which we have seen at Nuzi, imported by way
133 of Mitanni from Syria: the 'sacred tree' and the 'winged griffin'.
Other Mediterranean forms of ornament are to be seen in the
glazed panels from Kar-Tukulti-Ninurta.

BUILDING PRACTICES
Our earlier account of buildings at Ashur was, for obvious reasons,
largely confined to variations in their ground-plans. Where façade
ornament and external appearance are concerned, occasional clues
are to be found among contemporary seal designs. This applies in
particular to the parapet treatment of buildings, whether religious
134 or secular. We suspect that the use of crenellations was introduced
at about this time from Egypt; and one 13th-century seal from
Ashur shows a double fortress wall, its parapet crenellated with
round-headed merlons.[233] Two other seals from the same site,
dated perhaps a hundred years later, show for the first time merlons
in the 'stepped' form familiar today.[234] One of these is of special
interest, first because the symbol of the dog-deity, Gula, proves the
building to be a temple rather than a fortress; which would mean
that the crenellations are probably ornamental. Secondly, it shows
architectural details, such as towers rising above the tops of the
walls, doorways and rectangular panels which might be windows.
Finally, in seals of this period, genii of the sort known as *apkallu*
133 sometimes appear: hybrid creatures with two pairs of wings,
winged and hawk-headed monsters, or bearded men sheathed in
the skins of fish. But these are to be seen more frequently in the
form of terracotta plaques or figurines, such as are sometimes found
buried beneath the floors of houses for apotropaic purposes. They
too take their place in the imagery of later Assyrian times.

134 Fortifications of an Assyrian
city, from a relief of Tiglath-
Pileser III, showing crenellated
parapets and towers as finally
standardized in Late Assyrian
times. (Drawing by R. Leacroft)

Chapter Nine

The Late Assyrian Period

Imperial History

Early in the 10th century at Ashur, a new dynasty was founded by a king called Ashur-rabi II and in a sense this marked the beginning of an important epoch in Mesopotamian history. The reign of his grandson, Adad-Nirari II (911–891 BC) saw the earliest stage in the revival of economic stability and military initiative which eventually led to the creation of an Assyrian empire. Adad-Nirari's first concern was to establish once and for all the essential frontiers of his kingdom, and this he accomplished by a series of successful campaigns and political manoeuvres. Cities like Arrapha (Kirkuk) in the east and Guzan (Tell Halaf) on the headwaters of the Khabur in the north, became strongpoints in a new defensive system, while small Aramaean principalities on the middle course of the Euphrates were annexed to protect his trade connections with Syria.

At an early stage in these operations, Assyria's southern frontier with Babylon was fixed by a treaty, the text of which has been preserved in a rather famous inscription known as the 'Synchronous History'. This document conveniently incorporates a chronological account of all previous border disputes between the two states. It may also be considered to correspond in time with the beginning of accurately dated history, since from now onwards we have the supplementary evidence of the so-called 'limmu-lists'. These lists record in chronological order the names of particular officials appointed annually to preside over the New Year's Festival. Since they had come to be used in dating legal agreements and other important documents, their historical significance is obvious.

Adad-Nirari's successor, Tukulti-Ninurta II made the first move in extending his father's frontiers to the north and, in doing so, found himself for the first time in contact with the Muski (or Phrygians?) who had replaced the Hittites on the Anatolian plateau, and also with the 'Nairi peoples', later consolidated into the state of Urartu. After this he contented himself with an operation of the sort which was later repeated at intervals by most of his successors: a general sweep around the eastern and southern provinces, checking on subject states from whom tribute had not been forthcoming, and making an admonitory gesture towards Babylon. On this occasion, he paused to inspect the remnants of the old Kassite capital at Dur-Kurigalzu.

But, from an archaeological viewpoint, the most important of these first 'Iron Age' kings of Assyria was Ashur-nasirpal (883–859 BC); for it was he who transferred the centre of government from Ashur itself to a hitherto less-important city at the junction of the Tigris and the Upper Zab. This was Kalhu, the Calah of Genesis, now known as Nimrud, which he enlarged and embellished to create a new Assyrian capital. Once this was done, and an improved military headquarters established, he set out on a campaign directed towards the Euphrates crossings in the northwest. Until now, the main barrier to progress in this direction had been a powerful state centred on Til Barsip (Tell Ahmar), near Carchemish, and its capture opened the way to Aleppo. From there his armies marched almost unopposed as far as the Mediterranean, and tribute was exacted from the coastal cities. Inaugurated in this way was the long saga of foreign conquest which, under Ashur-nasirpal's successors, brought Assyrian armies westward as far as Egypt.

For the time being, his hold on the Levantine cities at least must have been oppressive, for, in the reign of his son, Shalmaneser III, we hear of an anti-Assyrian coalition, headed by a prince called Adad-iri of Damascus (who is suspected to have been Benhadad of the Old Testament). This revolt was suppressed and the inland cities of Syria brought into subjection, along with Tabal, north of Aleppo and Que in Cilicia. Economically these conquests must have been greatly to the advantage of Assyria, since they ensured the freedom of trade-routes to the west and access to metal-sources in the Taurus Mountains. Similarly, in the south, Shalmaneser's suppression of a revolt by Chaldean chieftains against the friendly government in Babylon (celebrated on his throne base at Nimrud), enabled him to maintain contact with traders in the Arabian Gulf, who brought goods from India and Arabia by way of Dilmun (Bahrein).

It would be out of place here to pursue further the threads of Late Assyrian history in any great detail. Of its framework it may be necessary to recall only those elements which lend coherence to the archaeological record. The five reigns which followed that of Shalmaneser III represent a period of comparative inertia, during which imperial aspirations seem to have been temporarily in abeyance and little effort was made to counteract the erosion of newly acquired territories. To the north in particular, the now-powerful kingdom of Urartu, with its system of fortresses in the region of Lake Van, was pursuing a policy of expansion which threatened to deny the Assyrians access to Anatolia. Its territories now extended eastward to the shores of Lake Urmia and, by 745 BC when Tiglath-pileser III succeeded to the throne in Kalhu, the Urartian armies were engaged in a westward thrust towards Syria. Firm action was needed and Tiglath-pileser proved himself a ruler equal to the occasion. During his reign one sees Assyria recovering its lost territories and re-establishing itself as the leading economic and military power in the Near East. Contributary to this revival were the successful administrative reforms whereby he reorganized the whole system of government, both in the homeland and in the provinces. These were made effective by the establishment of posting-stages along the main caravan routes which enabled the

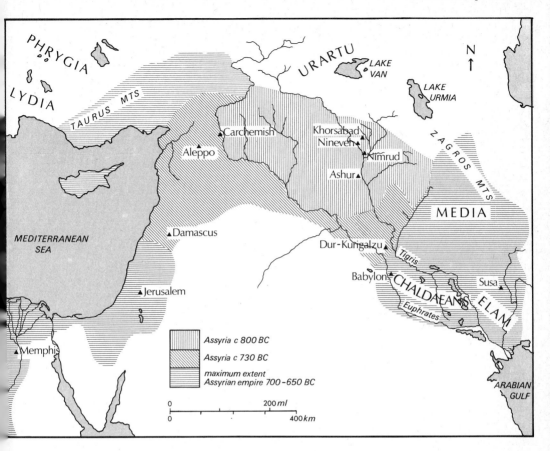

135 Map of the Assyrian empire.
(S. Ebrahim after Postgate, 1977)

king to be in continual contact with his provincial governors. The vassal states which they controlled were further protected by an outer tier of 'client kingdoms', with a greater measure of independence. By the time of his death in 727 BC Tiglath-pileser ruled an empire extending from the borders of Egypt as far as southern Babylonia, the only region still afflicted with political unrest. It was in this quarter that dissident tribesmen, now under the leadership of the formidable Marduk-apil-idinna (called in the Bible Merodach-baladan), were for many years to persist in defying the authority of Assyria.

We are now confronted with the names of four great rulers, in whose reigns one sees, as it has been said, 'not only the culmination of Assyrian power but the seeds of its disintegration'. Where Sargon is concerned, the circumstances of his accession and his subsequent military triumphs must, for our present purpose, be subordinated to his enterprise in providing himself with a new capital. At the site known today as Khorsabad, 12 miles northeast of Nineveh, he built himself a heavily walled city, more than 1 mile square, and named it Dur-Sharrukin. Its public buildings and fortifications were completed in a remarkably short time; but there is some doubt whether the accumulation of residents which would have created a populous city, could have been accomplished in the sixteen years of his reign. For he was seldom there and after his

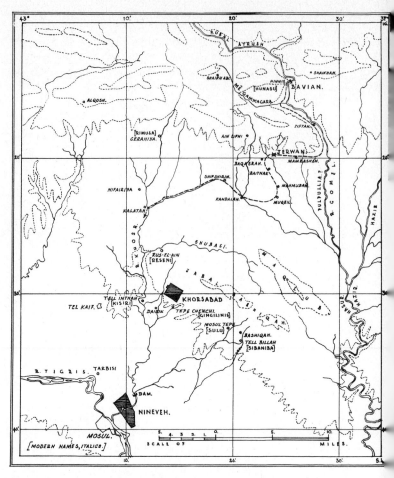

136 Map showing the line of Sennacherib's Canal, from the barrage and sluices at Bavian, passing over the Jerwan aqueduct and finally joining the course of the River Khosr to Nineveh. (S. Lloyd)

death in 705 BC the place was abandoned. His successor Sennacherib preferred to adopt the older city of Nineveh as his centre of government, thereby profiting from the obvious advantages of its central position on the east bank of the Tigris, and it was there that, for the third time in succession, a new and more splendid setting was contrived for the Assyrian court.

In a well-known text, Sennacherib reproaches his forbears for having neglected the upkeep of Nineveh. He adds a lengthy and rather detailed account of his own efforts to remedy this situation, and the magnitude of his undertaking is made apparent by the immensely extended area of the city whose ruins can be seen today from the west-bank eminences of modern Mosul. Its walls form an irregular rectangle almost $2\frac{1}{2}$ miles long, and on the side facing the river one sees the older mound whose shape and size he adapted to form an emplacement for his palaces and temples. Outside the walls, as we know from the same text, he laid out orchards and plantations with rare trees brought from distant provinces, and he added to these a zoological garden. Not content with the quality of 136 water in the Tigris he also constructed a canal, more than 50 miles long with stone aqueducts, to bring a cleaner supply from springs in the mountains to the northeast. At its remotest source, on a cliff-face near Bavian, its completion was commemorated by rock-carvings of the Assyrian gods and inscriptions, to which he added an account of his other political and military accomplishments.[235] In these texts and others from his palace at Nineveh, Sennacherib is convincingly presented as perhaps the greatest soldier-statesman since Hammurabi.

Only two notable figures remain in Late Assyrian history. One is Esarhaddon, who succeeded Sennacherib after his eventual murder by members of his own family. He it was who reached the ultimate goal of his country's imperial ambitions by invading Egypt. During the temporary absence of its Ethiopian ruler, Tarku or Tirhakah, he besieged and captured Memphis, thereafter adopting the title of the Pharaohs, 'King of Upper and Lower Egypt'. At Nineveh he had time to build himself a new administrative palace, in which he installed some of the loot from Egypt, before receiving the news that Memphis had been retaken by Tarku. He was on his way to deal with this situation when he died. In a document which has survived, Esarhaddon had long ago assured the accession to the Assyrian throne of his son Ashur-banipal, and it was he who was now compelled to reconquer Egypt. This time Memphis was destroyed. Ashur-banipal next turned his attention to the southeast frontier, where Elam was in revolt, having formed an alliance with Chaldea. Here too he scored a notable victory and it was his capture on this occasion of Susa, the Elamite capital, which was commemorated by a well-known relief carving in his palace at Nineveh.

Twenty-five years later, the Chaldeans played some part in the events which led to the final destruction of Nineveh. In 614 BC, a Median army under Cyaxares invaded the Assyrian homeland, capturing Nimrud and totally destroying the more ancient capital at Ashur. This brought them into contact with the Babylonians and a treaty was signed between Cyaxares and the Chaldean king Nabopolassar. During the following year, the Medes were also able to enlist the help of Scythian tribes to the north of their realm and the three peoples made common cause against Nineveh. The city fell after a surprisingly short siege in 612 BC and was largely destroyed. The remnants of the Assyrian court took refuge at Harran on the northwest frontier.

Early Excavations in Assyrian Cities

It has seemed necessary to present this rather threadbare account of the latest phase in Assyrian dynastic history in order to clarify the chronology and location of the discoveries which we are about to discuss. Their abundance and variety are today made apparent by the heavy volumes in which they are recorded, and by the accumulation around them of commentary literature. Here again it becomes clear that a selective analysis of the knowledge which they have helped us to acquire is the most that can usefully be attempted.

For our present purpose, then, a distinction must first be made between two classes of excavation, to which the ruins of Assyrian cities have on occasions been submitted – widely separated as they were in time, and variously dependent on the contemporary

137 Austin Henry Layard
(1817–1894) in Bakhtiyari dress.
A drawing by Ulrica Lloyd from
portraits in Layard's *Early
Adventures* and *Autobiography and
Letters*

understanding of archaeological intention. The first category of
course comprises the work of the great pioneer explorers in the
19th century, whose objective was the discovery and acquisition of
removable antiquities, with little attention to the setting in which
they were found. It started in 1842 with Botta's discovery of
Khorsabad, followed two years later by Layard's first excavations
at Nimrud. It lasted, with a brief interval during and after the
Crimean War, until the death in 1877 of George Smith, who had
found and identified the cuneiform version of the 'Deluge' story.

Excavations in the second category – of the sort with which we
are familiar today, paying proper attention to stratigraphy and
environmental evidence – were resumed in 1927, when American
archaeologists returned to Khorsabad, and later by British
excavators at Nimrud. To the lives and adventures of the earliest
excavators little attention will be paid here, except to admire in
retrospect their dedication and persistence in the face of sceptical
discouragement or deliberate obstruction. They were rewarded in
the end by popular reaction to the romantic appeal of their

138 Paul Emile Botta, discoverer and excavator of Khorsabad. Botta's pioneer work in Assyria received little recognition from the government of the Second Republic in France. He was relegated to a consular post at Tripoli in Syria and died in 1872

discoveries and could forget the ill-humoured contention and international rivalry which had marred their relations with each other, and which later deteriorated into an undignified scramble for archaeological loot. Their story has been told elsewhere, in narrative form by the present writer and, more objectively by French and German scholars.[236] Our present aim will be to examine the sites at which they dug, and to identify the monuments or buildings that they encountered, in the light of subsequent and more systematic investigations.

Nimrud (Kalhu)

At Kalhu, the greatly enlarged city designed by Ashur-nasirpal II (883–859 BC) during the early years of his reign, was approximately square in shape with a maximum dimension of almost 1.25 miles.[237] Its site was bounded on the west side by the Tigris and to the south by a canal, into which water was diverted from the Upper Zab river. In the southwest corner, a mound created by the remains

139

Plan of City Walls

139 Diagram showing the fortifications of Nimrud and its principal groups of buildings. The city was protected to the west by the Tigris and to the south by a wide canal. (After Hawkes, 1974). A, Fort Shalmaneser

140

140 Plan of the citadel mound at Nimrud after the conclusion of Mallowan's work there in 1963. Previous excavations by Layard, Rassam, Loftus and others took place intermittently between 1845 and 1854. Principal finds were made in the northwestern and southeastern groups of buildings. (From Mallowan, 1966)

of earlier settlements had been reshaped and revetted to form a raised citadel, within which the main palaces and temple buildings could be concentrated. But there was also, in the southeast corner, a walled enclosure containing the imperial arsenal.

It was the citadel mound which first attracted the attention of Layard when he started his excavations in November 1845.[238] As it exists today, partly eroded by the drainage of rainwater from the summit, one sees the rhomboid of its retaining-walls, dominated by the remnants of a small ziggurat in its north-west corner. Dramatically revealed by Layard's first trenches were the walls and sculptures of Ashur-nasirpal's own official residence (later known as the 'Northwest Palace'), overlooking the river directly south of the ziggurat. It was here that, in addition to wall-reliefs, he exposed for the first time doorways flanked by guardian figures of winged bulls or lions with tall 'genii' behind them. His work was for the time being confined to chambers around the ceremonial court of the building, and they contained figures of bronze, alabaster vessels and fallen fragments of mural paintings which he had no means of conserving.

Layard's first period of work at Nimrud lasted until 1847, by which time he had located and examined a number of other buildings. Again on the river-front was a so-called 'Western Palace' of Adad-nirari III and a 'Southwest Palace', built or restored by Esarhaddon, using sculptures intended for a building of Tiglath-pileser III. The name of this last king was also associated with that of Shalmaneser III on many inscriptions from a 'Central Palace': and it was in the environs of this building that Layard came upon the famous 'Black Obelisk' (now in the British Museum), with its scenes of tribute-bearers among whom 'Jehu, King of Israel' is named. Finally, beneath an eminence in the southeast corner of the mound, he cleared some rooms of a building attributed to a very late Assyrian king called Ashur-etililani, in which Mallowan, over a century later, made important finds. In 1847, with Rawlinson in Baghdad acquiring improved knowledge of cuneiform, Layard

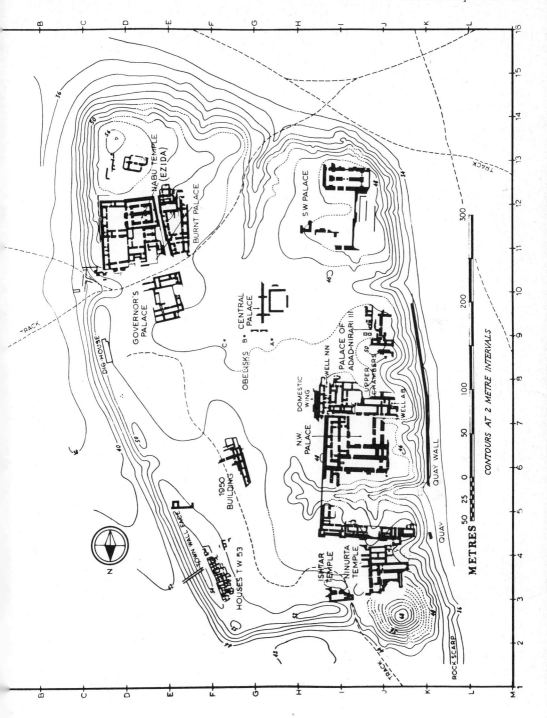

was able to satisfy himself that the site he was excavating was Kalhu, rather than Nineveh.

Layard returned to Nimrud in 1849, after publishing his book, *Nineveh and its Remains*, and he brought with him an artist (Cooper, later replaced by Bell), to take over the task of drawing the reliefs which had been occupying too much of his time. During the following two years he made further finds in the Northwest Palace, including some hundreds of bronze objects, with ornaments of ivory and even of glass. At the foot of the ziggurat he also discovered a temple dedicated to Ninurta, with inscribed paving slabs presenting the annals of Ashur-nasirpal's reign and, in its sanctuary, an almost undamaged statue of the same king, which has tken its place in the British Museum as a rare example of Assyrian sculpture in-the-round. But, during 1850 as we shall presently see, he had begun a secondary excavation in the palace mound at Nineveh, where his discovery of Sennacherib's palace brought his archaeological field-work to an end.

From 1852 to 1854 Layard's work in Assyria was taken over by his assistant Hormuzd Rassam, brother of the locally born British Consular representative in Mosul, who from then onwards became known for the ruthless pragmatism of his archaeological methods and disregard for the finer points of international ethics.[239] At Nimrud, in the southeast part of the citadel he located the Nabu Temple complex, more recently and more methodically excavated by Mallowan's expedition. There he found statues, two of which were respectively dedicated 'for the life of' Adad-nirari III and of his mother Sammuramat (Semiramis): also a stela of Shamsi-Adad V. But he was by now too preoccupied with excavations at Nineveh to absent himself for long from Mosul. In 1854 Rawlinson entrusted the work at Nimrud to W. K. Loftus, who is better known for his earlier soundings at sites of Sumerian cities in the south.[240] Loftus made one more important find in a building to the west of the Nabu Temple, now known as the 'Burnt Palace'. This was a fine group of carvings in ivory, which, after a belated study by the British Museum in the 1950s, made possible the first stylistic analysis of craftsmanship in this medium.

Khorsabad

Three years before Layard's discovery of Nimrud, Paul Emile Botta was appointed French Consul in Mosul. Already in 1842, he had started without much success to make soundings in the Küyünjik mound at Nineveh, when his workmen told him of ancient sculptures recently found at Khorsabad: a large mound on the River Khosr, 12 miles to the northeast. In March 1843 he transferred his activities to this site and was soon busily excavating in the building which we now know to have been the palace of King Sargon II. His success was immediate and his finds very similar to those which were to astonish Layard two years later at Nimrud. In the following year he had the good fortune to be joined by E. Flandin, a remarkable draughtsman, who systematically recorded the reliefs and other sculptures now brought to light in almost overwhelming numbers.[241]

138

At Khorsabad Sargon had selected a site where, as at Nimrud, there already existed a small ancient mound of the sort which could conveniently be reshaped to form a raised emplacement for his palace buildings. The city which he laid out took the form of a *143* square, with sides measuring rather more than a mile each, and was surrounded by towered walls with seven gateways. The palace platform was set astride the northwest wall and its inner part was surrounded (as American excavators discovered in the 1930s), by an inner citadel at ground level, containing other public buildings. Also as at Nimrud there was an 'imperial arsenal' in the southern corner of the town. In conformity with Assyrian tradition, Sargon's palace itself was planned around two main courtyards, the innermost of which was used for ceremonial purposes. Where Botta's excavations are concerned, it is made clear in the five-volume record of his work, which he and Flandin published in 1849–50, that they were limited to the projecting suite of state-rooms on the northwest side. They lasted until 1846; but after the political events of 1848 in Paris, Botta was for some reason disgraced and sent to an obscure consular post in the Levant. By then, like Layard, he had come to understand that the city which he had been excavating was not, as he had thought, Nineveh.

At Khorsabad in 1852, Botta was replaced by Victor Place. The artist Felix Thomas accompanied him as principal assistant, and it is to him that we owe the only surviving records of major finds made by the French expedition during that and the following year.[242] The entire plan of the palace was now traced and the better- *143–4* preserved sculptures extracted for transport to Paris, together with many smaller finds. According to Place's own calculation, at the end of 1853, he had cleared 209 chambers, grouped around 31 courts, in addition to 3 temples and a small ziggurat. He had traced the circuit of the city walls – 24 m thick on stone foundations – and he had examined 7 gateways, 3 with sculptured portal figures and 1 (no. 3 on his plan), with its vaulted archways and archivolts ornamented in coloured glaze, almost intact. By 1855, with his records completed, he was ready to return to France, and it was in that year that the great disaster took place. The story is today generally well known. The Khorsabad sculptures travelled safely as far as Baghdad, where the 235 cases were loaded, together with antiquities from other sources, on to a large country boat and two *kelek* rafts, bound for Basrah. Near Kurnah, where the Tigris is joined by an effluent from the Euphrates, the convoy was attacked by hostile tribesmen and all five vessels were capsized. Fortunately, an earlier consignment, shipped to France by Botta in 1847, had arrived safely, but today this modest collection, together with two winged-bull figures in the British Museum, represent all that remains of the French finds at Khorsabad.[243]

Nineveh

The ruins of Nineveh, as we have mentioned, received attention from both English and French excavators during the period of activity which we have been discussing. Its city walls, now some *141* distance from the Tigris, form an irregular rectangle, almost $7\frac{1}{2}$

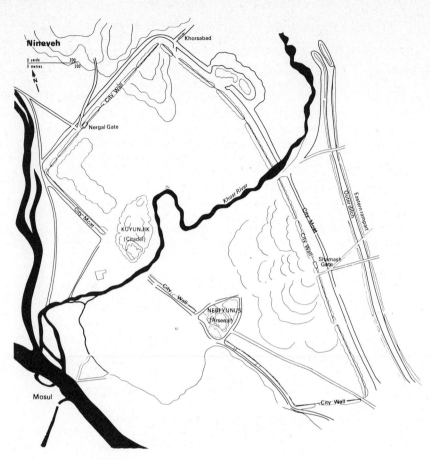

141 The city plan and fortifications of Nineveh in Late Assyrian times. Excavations in the second half of the 19th century took place principally on the main citadel mound, *Küyünjik*. The smaller mound, *Nebi Yunus*, is still inhabited, being the site of an important Moslem shrine. An earlier course of the Tigris skirted the city wall to the southwest, which now marks the limit of modern Mosul. (From Hawkes, 1974)

miles in circumference, with an outer rampart and ditch on the eastern side.[244] The palace mound, known by the Turkish name, *Küyünjik*, marks the line of the western wall, facing the river. One mile to the south, a second, smaller mound covers the ruins of the Assyrian arsenal, and at its summit today the houses of an Arab village cluster around a Moslem shrine, associated with the name of the Prophet Jonah (*Nebi Yunus*). Entrances to the city firmly identified are, in the north wall the Nergal Gate, with its guardian figures still preserved, and to the east the Shamash Gate.[245] These and others, together with the adjoining fortifications, have recently been exposed and partially restored.

During his first campaign at Nimrud, Layard had found time to continue Botta's soundings in the Küyünjik mound at Nineveh; but it was not until June 1847 that his expectations in that quarter were realized. In the southern corner of the citadel, he came upon the walls of an enormous building which proved to be *142* Sennacherib's principal palace; but he was compelled to postpone its further exploration while he returned temporarily to London. When he resumed work there in 1849, he was at first disappointed to find evidence that the palace had been destroyed by fire – perhaps during the sack of Nineveh in 612 BC. The damage, however, proved to be less than he had expected, and much of the sculpture

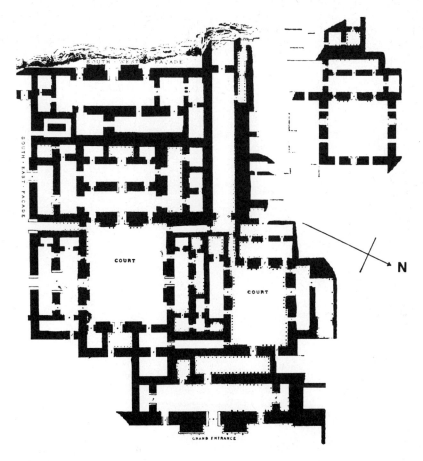

142 Plan of Sennacherib's palace at Nineveh. Unhappily no complete record has been kept of all the excavations in the Küyünjik mound and even the relative positions of some major buildings are today uncertain. (After Paterson, 1912)

had survived. In the 71 chambers which he investigated, over 2,000 sculptured slabs were exposed, while two small rooms (numbered 40 and 41 in his plan), were found to contain great quantities of tablets, comprising a part of Sennacherib's library – a prodigious store-house of contemporary knowledge, with detailed records of contemporary events.[246] At this time, Layard also made a less-successful attempt to excavate in the unoccupied part of the Nebi Yunus mound. Here he found inscriptions of Adad-nirari, Sennacherib and Esarhaddon, but was forced by the hostility of the inhabitants to discontinue his work. In 1851, he finally returned home, leaving the excavations in charge of Hormuzd Rassam.

Layard had reached an understanding with Victor Place that British excavations should be restricted to the southern half of the Küyünjik mound and Place now asserted his right to explore the northern part. Rassam, who returned to Mosul in 1852, contested this agreement, and, having eventually resorted to the expedient of working under the cover of darkness, had the good fortune to discover the great northwest palace of Ashur-banipal, which he claimed for the British Museum. In addition to the famous 'Lion Hunt' sequence of sculptures, the building also proved to contain the remaining half of Sennacherib's library. This was the triumphant culmination of the British excavations at Nineveh.

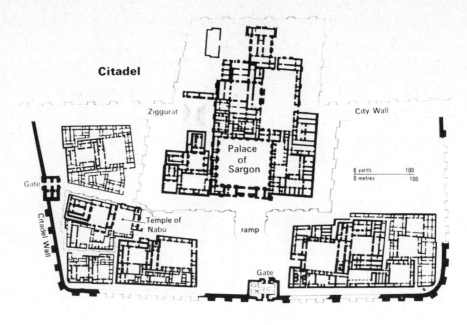

Citadel

Ziggurat

City Wall

Palace
of
Sargon

| 0 yards | 100 |
| 0 metres | 100 |

Gate

Citadel Wall

Temple of
Nabu

ramp

Gate

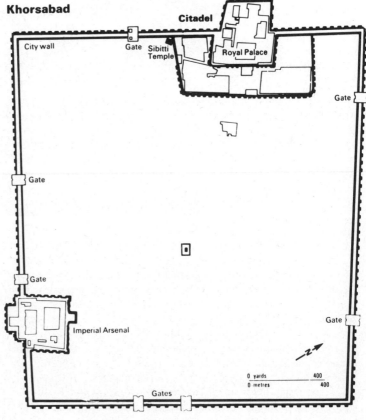

143 Ground plan of Sargon II's
capital city, Dur Sharrukin, at
Khorsabad, with fortifications
enclosing an area over one mile
square. The detailed plan (*above*)
includes the royal palace on its
platform, level with the city
walls, excavated by Botta and
Place and later re-examined by
Gordon Loud. Beneath this at
ground level is the fortified
citadel excavated by Loud in the
1930s, comprising a number of
minor palace and other public
buildings. (From Hawkes, 1974)

Khorsabad

Citadel

City wall

Gate

Sibitti
Temple

Royal Palace

Gate

Gate

Gate

Gate

Gate

Imperial Arsenal

Gate

| 0 yards | 400 |
| 0 metres | 400 |

Gates

They were completed in 1874 by George Smith, whose methodical search through the spoil from Rassam's excavations resulted in the recovery of a missing fragment from the 'Deluge' text.

It should be added, however, that a highlight in Rassam's own subsequent explorations was his discovery in 1878 of Imgur-Enlil, a 'country seat' of the Assyrian kings at Balawat, 25 miles east of Mosul. From a low mound at this site he extracted two pairs of huge bronze gates, set up respectively by Ashur-nasirpal and Shalmaneser III at the entrances to a palace and temple.[247] These, together with a third pair found by Mallowan, will presently be referred to in greater detail.

American Excavations at Khorsabad

From the above account of excavations in the ruins of Late Assyrian cities, it will already have become evident that secular buildings now take precedence over temples. The king-emperors of this age were more concerned with the construction of fortifications and the planning of pretentious royal palaces than with the religious shrines which were occasionally annexed to them. As one ruler succeeded another, the palaces themselves multiplied in numbers and were enlarged or reconstructed, usually without respect to the overall planning of the great platforms on which they stood, and their ultimate destruction added to the confusion of their surviving ruins. This was the case at Nimrud, and to an even greater extent at Nineveh, where the architectural record has to this day remained regrettably incomplete. If, by contrast, we turn to Khorsabad, we find a city built, occupied and abandoned in the space of a single

144 A reconstruction of the Royal Palace and citadel buildings at Dur Sharrukin by William Suddaby after Loud and Altmann. On the left, the raised temple of Nabu can be seen, connected to the palace platform by a bridge

generation. Its remains, uncomplicated by problems of stratig-raphy, have been excavated and recorded with great thoroughness over a long period of time. For our present purpose, therefore, it may be accepted as a model most effectively illustrating the principles of planning and construction favoured by contemporary builders.

143–4   The American excavators who returned to Khorsabad in 1928 did much to amplify the finds of their French predecessors. After a preliminary clearance of an 'undecorated' city-gate (no. 7), they set about re-excavating parts of the palace, at the same time removing certain sculptures rejected by Botta for lack of transport facilities.[248] In 1930, a second gate ('A') was found, ornamented with winged bulls and genii, which led in its turn to the discovery of an inner citadel, surrounding the palace at ground level. Under the direction of Gordon Loud, the following years were spent in exposing the many buildings enclosed by the citadel wall, while at the same time examining the great 'arsenal' establishment in the southern corner of the city (known to Place as 'Palace F').[249]

In the course of Loud's work in the citadel, a new survey was undertaken, which involved checking and correcting Place's palace plan.[250] From this a striking inference could be made regarding the inadequacy of Assyrian building methods in their initial stages. Even the platform itself proved to be asymmetrically planned, while the layout of buildings in the citadel appeared haphazard to the point of inconvenience. At the approach from Gate 'A', a large temple, dedicated to the god Nabu, was sited at an awkward angle beside a paved street. This building was raised on a platform of its own to the level of the palace, from which it could be reached directly by a bridge over the road. Beyond it there was an open space from which a broad ramp led up to the main portal of the palace, and facing this – again off-centre – a secondary citadel gateway. Elsewhere within these inner walls, Loud excavated five minor palaces, whose plans had been adapted with obvious difficulty to the sites available. This curious absence of preliminary planning would appear to have been characteristic of monumental building at all periods in Mesopotamian history.

In the main palace, as we have said, the ceremonial apartments and state-rooms were planned around an inner courtyard, dominated on one side by sculptural composition of winged bulls and other figures, guarding the three entrances to the throne-room. This huge rectangular chamber had walls about 12 m high, decorated with mural paintings from pavement to ceiling, and at one end a throne emplacement with relief carvings. At the other, a vestibule led to a stairway, giving access to the flat roof, and a doorway near the throne brought one through a long robing-room to the private courtyard around which the residential apartments were grouped. This arrangement of a throne-room with subsidiary chambers and stairway seems to have been an architectural convention universally adopted in all Assyrian palaces, and here at Khorsabad it can again be recognized in the 'reception suites' of minor buildings in the lower citadel. A second convention of the same sort dictates the composition of an isolated group of state-rooms on the northwest side of Sargon's palace, where doorways lead out on to an open terrace. Loud found an identical arrangement of chambers in the residential part of the southern arsenal.[251]

Where religious buildings are concerned, the Nabu temple with its two outer courtyards and conventionally planned sanctuary is the most conspicuous. But Loud also re-excavated the assemblage of three smaller temples annexed to the palace on the southwest side; and one of these – the Sin Temple – revealed a well-preserved façade. Reeded panels on either side of the arched doorway sprang from small projecting platforms, faced with glazed-brick ornament in bright colours. Beside each of these was a tall artificial palm-tree and a female statue of the 'flowing-vase' type – all extremely reminiscent of the mural painting from Mari on which we have earlier commented. The small ziggurat adjoining these temples was too denuded to examine further. But if Place's reconstruction can be relied upon, it had a spiral ascending stairway dividing it into successive stages, each painted a different colour.[252]

Regarding the arsenal-palace (*ekal masharti*) at Khorsabad, which Loud took to be the residence of Sennacherib at the time when he was crown-prince, one point of interest could now be established. Stone column-bases found by Place in its ruins had brought to mind an inscription in which Sargon claimed to have built a palace of the Syrian kind, known as *bit hilani*, with a columned loggia in front of the throne-room. But Loud was able to show that the position of the columns in the building did not conform to this theory, and Sargon's *hilani* must therefore be sought elsewhere.[253] Little more need be added about the plan, since, as we shall presently see, an arsenal building of the same sort was later completely excavated by Mallowan at Nimrud.

Building Construction

At Khorsabad, walls of every description were built of mud brick. Contrary to the usual practice, mortar was here very seldom used, the bricks being only partially dried after casting, and laid in a soft, pliable condition. Kiln-baked bricks were used in great quantities for facings and pavements. The city walls, which were over 20 m thick, were revetted at their base with dressed stonework up to a height of 1.10 m. Behind this facing, undressed stone was roughly laid to form a base for the brick upper structure, which terminated in a crenellated parapet with stone merlons. Here, as elsewhere in Assyria, stone which may be described as gypseous alabaster (now known as 'Mosul marble'), was easily obtained from local quarries, if necessary in very large blocks. The palace platform had a facing of stone in blocks up to 2.7 m long, weighing as much as 23 tons apiece. For the rest, stone was mainly used for portal sculptures and for the 'orthostat' slabs on which the reliefs were carved. These latter were exclusively placed inside the building, to form an ornamental 'dado' along the bases of the walls. The Americans discovered that the rows of slabs were set in place and their reliefs carved *in situ*, *before* the brick upper structure was built.[254] Where slabs occurred on both faces of a wall, the space in between was filled with rubble, composed partly of masons' chippings. Another

145 One of a pair of winged and
human-headed bulls with
attendant genii from the
southwest gate into the citadel at
Khorsabad (now at the entrance
to the Iraq Museum in Baghdad)

use of stone was for the thresholds of important doorways, where huge slabs were laid, carved with designs representing carpets.[255]

With regard to roofing, traces were found in the city gates of barrel-vaulting in brick, and 'pitched-brick' vaulting was used in the drainage system of the palace platform. But in the palace itself Loud satisfied himself that flat ceilings were the rule, sometimes with painted beams. For wood was comparatively plentiful. Cedar, cypress, juniper and maple were among the species recognized, and from fallen beams he calculated that it was available in scantlings capable of spanning the widest chambers.

Late Assyrian Sculpture

Sculptures in-the-round of this period are for some reason remarkably rare. A few isolated portraits of royalty have survived, the best-preserved examples being rather more than half life-size. That of Ashur-nasirpal II, found in the Ninurta Temple at Nimrud, which may be taken as typical, has been described as 'dull and impersonal'; yet the figure of this king, bare-headed and draped in the simple fringed shawl which was the court-dress of Assyria, has an indisputable dignity.[256]

By contrast, the most conspicuous and characteristic class of sculptures in this category are the *lamassu* guardian figures with which the gateways and palaces of Assyrian cities were adorned. These hybrid colossi – winged and human-headed bulls or lions – were usually 'double-aspect' figures, set facing outwards against the reveals of doorways, with a fifth leg, intended to rationalize their appearance from in front as well as from the side. Each of these monolithic monsters was carved, partly in relief and part in-the-round, from a single slab of stone measuring up to 5.5 m square. Roughly shaped in the quarry, it was transported to its destination, often by river, and set in place for the final carving to be done.[257]

The most spectacular achievement of Late Assyrian sculptors was in the realm of relief-carving. Their contrivance of pictorial designs in this medium for the decoration of interior wall surfaces was in itself a great technical accomplishment; but their capacity for abstract expression elevated the products of their craftsmanship into the realm of creative art.

As for the subject of the reliefs, from the time of Ashur-nasirpal onwards, they were primarily concerned with the king's victorious campaigns against the armies and cities of dissident dependencies. This theme tends to become almost monotonously repetitive. As Frankfort has put it: 'We see the march of armies, subjugating, burning and punishing in country after country.' The war-chariot is a recurrent motif, and one sees them advancing against a retreating enemy, while infantry dispatch the wounded, left upon the field. 'Opposition is centred on a city; it is taken, its leaders are impaled or killed in other ways, then the inexorable chariotry presses on again.' Variety is obtained by suggesting the geographical background against which these events take place, and the national characteristics of Assyria's various enemies. Details of these are carefully and vividly presented, with a reality which is the more

145

146

146 Relief from Sennacherib's southwest palace at Nineveh, depicting the transport by raft of a winged bull (*lamassu*) figure from a quarry in wooded country. The sculpture has already been roughly shaped and will be completed *in situ*. Ht 135 cm

148

150-1

147 Relief from the 'Central Palace' of Tiglath-Pileser III (744–727 BC) at Nimrud, showing an attack on a walled city. Scaling ladders and a battering-ram are used, with covering fire from archers. In a mountainous setting (below) enemies are slain and (above) naked captives impaled on stakes

148 Relief from the 'Northwest Palace' of Ashur-nasirpal II (883–859 BC) at Nimrud. Figures are shown of the King, worshipping before a 'sacred tree', supported by winged gods, each holding a cone and *situla* (metal bucket); above, the god Ashur in a winged sun-disc (compare the slightly earlier seal design in ill. 133)

149 Reliefs from the 'North Palace' of Ashur-banipal (668–627 BC) at Nineveh. Above, a lion-hunt in progress; below, a ceremony in which the king pours libations over his victims

remarkable if one remembers the limitations of the medium in which these artists worked, and their ignorance where the principles of perspective were concerned. Under these circumstances, the ingenious devices by which spatial recession could be suggested, particularly in depicting landscapes, are unparalleled in pre-Greek art.

On the whole, the king's military campaigns took place during fixed seasons of the year. During the intervals between these, he would seek distraction in hunting, and this was another subject much favoured in the reliefs. It is perhaps best illustrated in the carvings of a later historical phase, but there is one good sequence of hunting pictures from the time of Ashur-nasirpal.[258] These do not in fact represent an event taking place in open country, but in an enclosure formed by the shields of soldiers, within which lions were released to be shot at by the king from his chariot. After the hunt he is seen pouring libations over the bodies of his prey, attended by courtiers and musicians. Usually at this time, the slabs were about 2 m high and the pictures arranged in two horizontal registers. But the culminating scene in this sequence, where the king rests and takes refreshment after the hunt, occupies the full height of the stone. It is a sort of epilogue, in which we are reminded of the divine protection which he enjoys, by the figures of benevolent genii on either side. Similar figures, facing a 'tree-of-life', appear again in a great self-contained panel behind the actual throne in the throne-room of the Northwest Palace at Nimrud.[259] It has the character of a rather splendid wall-tapestry, and its composition is repeated elsewhere in the embroidered design on Ashur-nasirpal's mantle.[260] Strangely enough religious symbolism of any sort appears only rarely in these sculptures.

In the reign of Shalmaneser III, a variant form of relief ornament is seen for the first time, in the great bronze gates of Balawat. These

150 Reconstruction of the Balawat Gates (lower half shown only) in the British Museum

are double doors of wood, with each 'leaf' measuring 1.8 m wide by 6.1 m high, and each is supported at the side by a circular pivot-shaft of the same material. They are ornamented with separate, horizontal bands of bronze plating, 28 cm wide and hardly more than 2 mm thick, running from side to side and continuing around the pivot-shaft. These bands are modelled by a *repoussé* process with scenes in relief similar to those elsewhere carved in stone, and, as there are two registers to each strip, the height of the actual design cannot exceed 13 cm. The scenes here chosen are once more of a narrative or episodic character, but lively and revealing.[261] A victory is won over the Chaldeans among the palm-groves of lower Mesopotamia; on the Mediterranean coast, the island fortress 151 of Tyre is captured and the tribute of its ruler brought ashore in boats to the Assyrian camp; in southern Urartu, the army's advance is hampered by hills and forests. But here in the north, a more strange episode is also depicted. The king has discovered what he takes to be the source of the Tigris, in a mountain cave. With the soldiers up to their waists in water he makes appropriate sacrifices, while a sculptor carves a rock-relief to commemorate the occasion.[262] The third pair of gates from Balawat, now restored and returned to the Iraq Museum, add new instalments to the same pictorial history.[263]

After the Assyrian revival in the mid-8th century BC, Tiglath-pileser III built himself a provincial palace at Til Barsip (Tell 152 Ahmar) on the Euphrates in Syria, in which mural paintings were substituted for relief sculptures in stone.[264] The designs were in red,

151 A detail from the Balawat Gates. An episode in Shalmaneser III's campaign of 858 BC on the Levant coast. The city of Tyre, on its rocky island (top left), sends tribute by boat to placate the king. Below, he is seen in his chariot, passing on to further conquests, and his camp (bottom left) is left empty. Ht 27 cm

152 Detail from a mural painting in the 'Governor's Palace' at Til Barsip on the Middle Euphrates (reign of Tiglath-Pileser III, 744–727 BC). The murals (substitutes for stone reliefs) are painted in black, red, and blue on a white plaster background

blue and black on a background of white plaster, and their subjects very similar to those of the stone reliefs. Episodes in the king's military campaigns alternated with hunting scenes, and paintings of winged genii took the place of portal sculptures. Reconstructed in the Louvre, these murals were not reproduced in colour for publication until comparatively recently.[265]

Stone reliefs from palaces of Tiglath-pileser's successors in the 8th and 7th centuries show changing characteristics. In the state-rooms at Khorsabad, narrative is replaced by static compositions, representing court ceremonial. The huge figures of the king and his courtiers, some 2.75 m high, follow or confront each other in hierarchical formality, and one notices the coloured paint which is sparingly applied to their hair, beards and the exposed parts of their bodies. The possibilities offered by these larger slabs were later to be exploited by the artists of Sennacherib's time for pictorial compositions of another sort. Historical episodes could now be elaborated on a much less restricted scale and concurrent incidents added to a central theme. For this purpose, the division of a picture into horizontal registers was often abandoned. A single design might now extend to the full height of the slabs, while new formulae could be devised to imply relative distance or dramatic priority. New details of landscape added to the panoramic effect of these compositions.

It would be impossible here to enumerate the many and various subjects chosen by the artists of this period.[266] Almost all are concerned with violence and the destructive effects of punitive warfare. Some are lent special interest by their accompanying inscriptions, which identify historical events and even individual personalities. After the capitulation of Lakish in Palestine, Sennacherib may be seen receiving his officers and their suppliant

153 Relief carvings of a winged god and gift-bearers from the Palace of Sargon II at Khorsabad. In this case the orthostat slabs are over 3 m high

153

154 (*Right*) Part of a sculptured scene from Sennacherib's palace at Nineveh, identified from inscriptions as the capitulation of Lakish in Palestine. In a hilly landscape with vines and olives, the King, seated on an elaborate throne before his tent, receives his commanders while Jewish prisoners bow before him. His chariot awaits him below (*Left*) The captive people of Lakish are tortured or deported, together with their families and belongings. Early in the 7th century BC attempts of this sort were made to evoke pictorially the setting in which events took place

155 Relief from the 'North Palace' of Ashur-banipal at Nineveh. In a vine-arbour, to the sound of music, the king and queen celebrate a victory over the Elamites. Hanging in a tree (left) is the severed head of their enemy Te-umman, King of Elam

156 Sandstone stela of Ashur-nasirpal II, whose portrait appears inset beneath the symbols of his gods, Sin, Ashur, Shamash etc. Around this figure are 153 lines of inscription celebrating the completion of his capital, Nimrud, in 879 BC and recording the attendant festivities

captives; or he is shown, during one of his campaigns in the marshes of southern Mesopotamia, watching from an island while his soldiers pursue the enemy in boats through the reed-beds and fishy waters of the lagoon. Ashur-banipal celebrates the capture of Susa to the sound of music, with a quaint bird's-eye view of the city behind him, contemplating the gruesome aftermath of heavy fighting; or accompanied by his wife, he relaxes on a couch in an arbour of vines.[267]

In this last phase of Assyrian relief carving, the drawing of animals receives particular care and attention. It reaches a peak of accomplishment in the time of Ashur-banipal, when hunting scenes, depicting lions, wild asses or gazelles, became popular subjects. For here – perhaps deliberately – a note of pathos is introduced, and one's sympathy is aroused for the 'dying lioness' or for the 'onager mare' who is compelled to abandon her foal.

The more practical value of the reliefs, from an archaeological viewpoint, is the wealth of detailed evidence which they provide about the appearance and characteristics, not only of the Assyrians but of neighbouring peoples with whom warfare brought them into contact. Painstaking study of these pictorial records has by now acquainted us with every smallest detail of military equipment, and of common practices in its use which the written texts alone could never have made clear.[268] Regarding those aspects of Assyrian life which the reliefs illustrate, little remains to be learnt.

British Return to Nimrud

Some account must now be given of the finds made by a British expedition under the leadership of M. E. L. Mallowan, which *139–40* returned to Nimrud in 1949 and worked there for a further fourteen years.[269] Mallowan at first concentrated on the Northwest Palace, where the 'central ceremonial' block of buildings, excavated by Layard, had included a great throne-room.[270] His first important find was indeed made in a side-chamber adjoining the throne itself. This was a commemorative *156* stela of Ashur-nasirpal II, bearing an effigy of the king in relief and

an inscription of 153 lines covering both sides of the stone. It is a monument of special interest, because it records the ceremonies and festivities arranged to celebrate the formal opening of the palace in the year 879 BC, and it includes details of the food prepared for the entertainment of 69,574 persons over a period of ten days. Other information of this sort enabled Mallowan to calculate the approximate population of Calah itself, after Ashur-nasirpal had made it his new capital. The figure at which he arrived (a minimum of 86,000 including children), makes an interesting comparison with the 'six score thousand' inhabitants which are attributed to Nineveh in the Old Testament (*Jonah*, IV, 11).

Meanwhile, in the eastern 'domestic wing' of the palace, two deep wells were investigated. In one of these ('AB'), which had been partly excavated by Layard, a find was made whose significance became clear after it had been examined in the British Museum laboratory. This was a 'book', composed of fifteen or more 'leaves', joined by golden hinges to open inwards and outwards, rather like a Japanese screen. The 'leaves', of wood and ivory, had raised edges to protect a surface of wax, on which inscriptions were engraved in cuneiform. Together they composed a written document of several thousand lines. The 'cover' bore the name of Sargon II, together with the title of the text and a note to say that the 'book' should be kept in the 'King's new palace at Dur Sharrukin [Khorsabad]'. Until that time, contemporary evidence of writing on a wax surface had been found only in Phrygia. But Mallowan was reminded of a later Babylonian inscription, in which the officer who read the omens to the king was instructed, when the reading was over, to 'close the book'; a phrase which was difficult to understand, supposing that it was a *tablet* from which he was reading.

It was from a second well in this part of the palace ('NN') that Mallowan recovered several objects, now considered to be the greatest masterpieces in the category of 'Nimrud Ivories', presently to be discussed. First came the strikingly beautiful female head, perhaps an ornament from some piece of furniture, which came to be known by the excavators as 'Mona Lisa'.[271] Measuring 16 × 13.3 cm, the ivory of which it was made had matured to a warm brown colour and the features, lightly stained with

157

157 Reconstructed part of a 'book', found in a well at Nimrud, consisting of wax-covered 'boards' of ivory, hinged to unfold. The wax was darkened in colour with a yellow 'orpiment' (sulphide of arsenic) to make the inscription more easily readable. The size of each board was 33.8 × 15.6 cm. (From Mallowan, 1966)

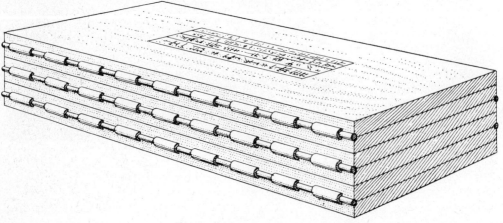

158 Ivory head of a woman, perhaps from a piece of ornamental furniture, found in a well beneath the 'Northwest Palace' at Nimrud. The hair, eyebrows and pupils are stained a darker colour. Known to the excavators as the 'Mona Lisa', this carving probably dates from the late 8th century BC. Ht 16 cm

appropriate colouring, have been compared by Mallowan stylistically to those of archaic Greek sculptures. There was a second head of the same sort, much more crudely carved, and both are dated to about 700 BC. Even more aesthetically effective than either of these objects were the two ivory (or rather chryselephantine) plaques, representing a lioness killing a negro, against a formal background of lotuses.[212] They are about 10 cm high, elaborately enriched with gold leaf and coloured incrustations. The *cloisonné* process by which they are decorated has been closely studied in the British Museum.[273]

Other buildings of the citadel which Mallowan excavated included the northern wing or Chancery of the Northwest Palace, and the Ninurta Temple at the foot of the ziggurat; the southwest complex, consisting of Loftus' Burnt Palace and the Nabu Temple (*Ezida*) with the neighbouring Governor's Palace; a large group of private dwellings and the great Quay Wall, supporting the western or river-side of the citadel platform. All these building remains were methodically recorded and successive phases in their architectural history distinguished. During these years, Mallowan

159 Ivory plaque from the same well at Nimrud as ill. 158, depicting a lioness killing a young negro in a thicket of lotus and papyrus plants. The flowers are inlaid with lapis and carnelian, mounted in gold by a *cloisonné* process; prominent features such as the boy's curls and his trousers are gilded. Ht 10.5 cm

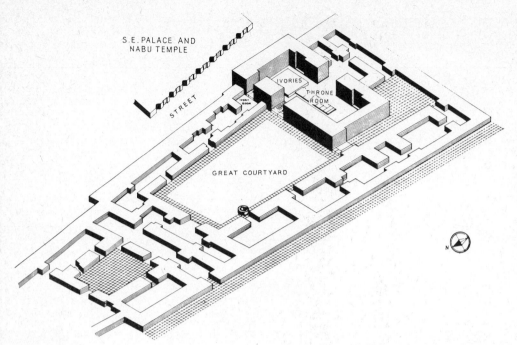

S.E. PALACE AND
NABU TEMPLE

IVORIES

THRONE
ROOM

IVORY
ROOM

STREET

GREAT COURTYARD

N

160 Projected plan of the 'Burnt Palace' at Nimrud (*c.* 612 BC), where ivories were first discovered by Loftus in 1854. (From Mallowan, 1966)

161 Plan of Fort Shalmaneser at Nimrud. To the north and west are three courtyards, surrounded by workshops, stores and offices. One of these (southwest) is divided into long magazines, one of which was the main source of ivory. Separated from these by a parade ground is the king's residence, composed of a throne-room and standard suites of royal apartments.

was not primarily searching for large statues or reliefs, but his work was amply rewarded by finds on a smaller scale: bronze vessels or weapons, fine ivory carvings and deposits of unbaked tablets, objects of a sort which earlier excavators had been incapable of preserving. But his most notable discoveries were made after the expedition had transferred its activities to the huge, and hitherto unexcavated, group of buildings in the remote southeast corner of the outer town. This was the 'Imperial Arsenal' (*ekal masharti*) of Shalmaneser III.[274]

Buildings answering to this description have been found to exist in all three of the Late Assyrian capitals. The arsenal at Nineveh remains buried beneath the modern buildings of Nebi Yunus; but an inscribed prism from that quarter gives a description of its reconstruction in the reign of Esarhaddon.[275] Another passage defines the purpose served by such a building, stating that it was 'for the ordinance of the camp, for the maintenance of the stallions, mules, chariots, weapons, equipment of war and spoils of the foe of every kind'. It also records how, annually at the time of the New Year's Festival, the establishment was subject to inspection by the king himself, for whom residential quarters were provided.

The Arsenal at Nimrud, known to the excavators as Fort Shalmaneser, occupied a rectangular site measuring 300 × 200 m, enclosed on the east and south sides by the city wall and elsewhere by its own massive fortifications. David Oates, who took charge of its excavation in 1958, thought that it had also been provided with an 'outer bailey', and there is evidence of a similar arrangement at Khorsabad. The fortress itself was divided into five main sections. In the centre there was a broad parade-ground, with a throne-dais on one side for the king. Two large courtyards to the north of this were surrounded by the functional accommodation of an official

161

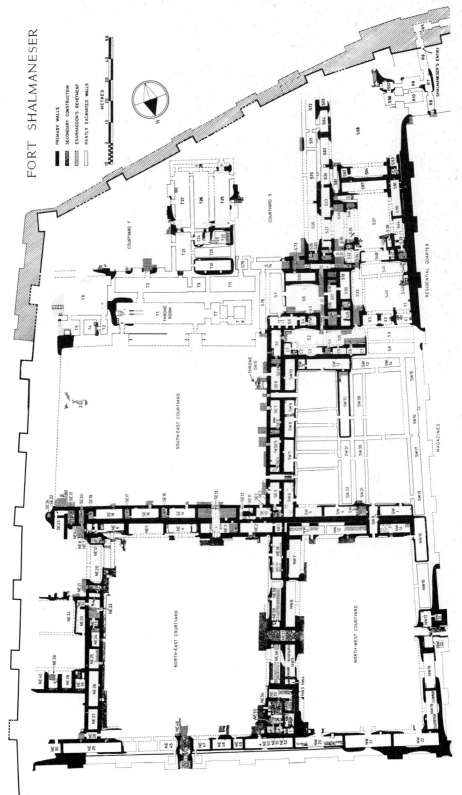

FORT SHALMANESER

■ PRIMARY WALLS
■ SECONDARY CONSTRUCTION
▨ ESARHADDON'S REVETMENT
☐ PARTLY EXCAVATED WALLS

METRES
10   20   30   40   50

N

COURTYARD T

COURTYARD S

THRONE
ROOM

THRONE
DAIS

SHALMANESER'S ENTRY

RESIDENTIAL QUARTER

SOUTH-EAST COURTYARD

MAGAZINES

NORTH-EAST COURTYARD

NORTH-WEST COURTYARD

162 Part of the huge stone base for the king's throne at Fort Shalmaneser, sculptured in relief all round with processions of tribute bearers and court officials. Here in the centre Shalmaneser himself is seen greeting with a handshake Marduk-Zakir-Shumi, King of Babylon

entrepôt: workshops for carpenters, smiths, leather-workers or armourers, often with their tools and appliances preserved among the litter of scale-armour and, in one case, a royal statue under repair. Elsewhere, stores for food and wine adjoined the administrative offices and adjutant's quarters. A third court to the west of the parade was divided into spacious magazines, arranged around smaller light-wells. The entire south side of the building was occupied by the royal residence, of which the ceremonial section, with its entrance from the parade-ground, was composed of two elements, their plans conforming precisely to architectural conventions which we have already observed at Khorsabad and elsewhere: namely, a 'reception suite' with its huge rectangular throne-room and a projecting wing containing state apartments.

In the throne-room the stone dais itself had survived, and proved to be decorated with spirited relief carvings representing the receipt of tribute from Syria and Chaldaea. The principal subject was an encounter between Shalmaneser and the contemporary ruler of 162 Babylon, in which the two kings actually *clasp hands*.[276] Almost equally impressive was the pictorial panel in glazed brick, fallen from above the doorway in an adjoining chamber, in which the figure of the Assyrian king appears in duplicate beneath a winged disc.[277]

At Fort Shalmaneser, however, the most rewarding discovery of all was the contents of storage chambers in and around the 'southwest courtyard', on the western side of the parade-ground.[278] They contained a vast collection of ivory carvings, mostly of the sort which were used to decorate furniture, chariots or parade harness. Piled or scattered at all levels in the debris which filled the rooms, they consisted of plaques in high or low relief, *ajouré* figures of animals or men and some subjects carved in-the-round – the work of Phoenician or Syrian craftsmen, looted from the cities of the west. From the thousands of fragments recovered, some hundreds of items have now been restored and most of them published.[279]

We have already had reason to mention a study of Late Assyrian ivories made by R. D. Barnett during the years preceding Mallowan's excavation at Nimrud.[280] This was based on a collection which had been retained for almost a century in the British Museum, and it proved to be derived from two sources: Layard's finds in the Northwest Palace and Loftus' discoveries in the Burnt Palace. Unlike these early excavators, Barnett was now able to compare these ivories with more recent finds of the same sort from sites in Palestine, Syria, Anatolia and even from Cyprus. At an early stage in his study of their stylistic characteristics, it became abundantly clear that in both groups the majority of designs were the work of Phoenician craftsmen in the coastal cities of the Levant. This was notably so in the group from the Northwest Palace, which consisted mainly of furniture enrichment, like the parts of a 'royal throne' said by Layard to have been found in 'Well AB'. Some examples of 'standard designs', such as the 'woman-at-the-window' (the Phoenician goddess Astarte) or the 'cow turning its head to lick a suckling calf', were marked by their makers with a sign corresponding to a letter in the Phoenician alphabet. In others, 'Egyptianizing' designs pointed to the same origin. By contrast, in the Loftus group Barnett professed also to recognize a 'Syrian' style, forming an independent unit associated with some more inland centre, in which non-Phoenician motifs were used and the designs applied to different forms of object. These included caryatid figures, model shrines and *pyxis* vessels for ointment. He also suspected the presence in this group of objects manufactured in Assyria itself, perhaps by imported craftsmen.

163
165

163 Ivory ornament with tenons for attachment to furniture. The Phoenician motif known as 'courtesan at a window' was popular in the Levant and elsewhere. This fragment, dated *c.* 700 BC, is from the 'Northwest Palace' at Nimrud

164 Ivory figure, carved in the round, of a Nubian leading an oryx while carrying a live monkey and a leopard-skin. A 'luxury object' from Fort Shalmaneser

165 Another motif, popular among Phoenician ivory-carvers over a period of several centuries and with Egyptian overtones, is the 'cow suckling its calf'. This *ajouré* (open-work) example is from Fort Shalmaneser (*c.* 700 BC)

166

164

Barnett's *Nimrud Ivories* was eventually published in 1957 and during the years that followed, as we have seen, a great volume of new material became available. Mallowan, in the study of his own finds which appeared nine years later, was able to confirm many earlier conclusions; but he was cautious in accepting Barnett's firm distinction between Phoenician and 'Syrian' work, on the grounds that a free interchange of craftsmen may have taken place at that time in all markets west of the Euphrates. On the other hand, he also was able to detect a whole school of imported artists and indigenous carvers, owing little except their technique to foreign influence. Regarding the purpose and setting of the ivories, Mallowan gained the impression that this highly prized, luxury material was applied as a veneer to every conceivable form of furniture. One room at Fort Shalmaneser (no. SW7) contained a great number of panels, juxtaposed in their original setting, and these at least could be identified as the elaborate ornamental backs – and sometimes sides – of beds, couches and chairs. In this connection, he could point to the furniture so carefully depicted in a relief, already mentioned, in which Ashur-banipal and his wife are resting after the capture of Susa. He lists some of the other purposes and classes of objects for which ivory carving was used, and makes an interesting comparison with a surviving inventory of spoil, brought back by Sargon II from the cities of Urartu, where ivory was as popular as in Assyria itself.

In considering the Levantine style of carving and its background, one is reminded that the Phoenician craftsmen by whom it was perfected were renowned, even in the Old Testament, for their skill and ingenuity. Nevertheless, where design was concerned, one also notices that they lacked any authentically native tradition. Just as in Europe the artists of the Renaissance turned to ancient Greece for their inspiration, so for the Phoenicians, Egyptian art provided the source of a ready-made idiom. Egyptian art, however, was based on religious imagery and on a huge repertory of symbolic and mythical forms. For the Phoenicians neither the religion nor the symbolism was their own, and little attempt was made to understand them. Their adaptation of Egyptian imagery was accordingly often incorrect and occasionally clumsy. Surprisingly, its visual effect remained unimpaired. [281]

Chronologically, the Nimrud ivories could logically be dated to any period between Ashur-nasirpal's reign and the eventual destruction of his capital. Adad-nirari III is known to have acquired an ivory bed and a couch from the king of Damascus in about 800 BC. But Mallowan considers the bulk of his finds to be later than this and dates much of it to the reign of Sargon II. The extinction of the Syrian elephant towards the end of the 8th century may have increased the shortage of ivory.

166 A magnificent ivory bed-head from Fort Shalmaneser, composed of 12 panels, each with the figure of a bearded warrior and magical tree, those in the centre surmounted by sun-discs. Dated by Mallowan to 730 BC

Chapter Ten

Babylon: The Last Mesopotamian Monarchy

A Dynastic Revival

After the fall of Nineveh, the Medes withdrew to consolidate their conquests in eastern Anatolia, leaving the Babylonian ruler in full control of Assyria. For the moment, however, Nabopolassar was compelled to devote his energies primarily to the revival of the southern Mesopotamian economy and the restoration of cities whose civic amenities had been neglected during the period of Assyrian domination. Meanwhile, the most formidable threat to the newly acquired Assyrian provinces was from the Egyptians, who had already established a military outpost on the Euphrates crossings at Carchemish. It was the crown-prince, Nebuchadrezzar ('Nebuchadnezzar' of the Old Testament), who was entrusted with the task of confronting their armies and recovering the cities of northern Syria. In this he was initially successful but, long after he had himself become king, he continued to be involved in a perpetual struggle to protect the trade-routes on which the prosperity of Babylon depended. It was during one of his successful campaigns in the Levant that the city of Jerusalem was taken and some thousands of Jews deported to Babylonia. At home, during the intervals of peace, he devoted much of his time to completing the work of his father Nabopolassar, in rebuilding the old Sumerian cities; and at Babylon itself, the magnificent layout of pretentious public buildings and fortifications which have been revealed in our own time can be attributed for the most part to Nebuchadnezzar's ambitious planning and precocious ingenuity.

As for Nabonidus, the last independent ruler of Babylon, he appears by contrast to have been both eccentric and ineffectual: a 'deviationist', whose enigmatic behaviour and frequent absence from his kingdom remain to this day something of a puzzle to historians. Apart from his rejection of Marduk, the time-honoured patron of Babylon, in favour of the god Sin, whom he worshipped at Harran, recently found inscriptions have provided an account of his prolonged and totally inexplicable sojourn in central Arabia. [282] A group of historical relics, found at Ur, were identified by Woolley as Nabonidus' private collection of antiquities.

At home in Babylon during Nabonidus' reign, political events were overshadowed by the ominous expansion of the Persian empire under its first great Achaemenid ruler. In 539 BC, the armies of Cyrus II, supported by dissident peoples of Assyria, marched upon Babylonia. Frontier defences were hastily manned by the crown-prince (Belshazzar of the Old Testament), who had deputized for Nabonidus during his long absences; but these were soon overrun, and within days the city of Babylon itself was peacefully occupied, almost without opposition, by the Persian army.[283] On instructions from Cyrus, violence was avoided and where possible the inhabitants persuaded to accept their new ruler as some sort of 'liberator'. Three thousand years of self-rule in Mesopotamia thus ended in a curious anti-climax.

We have three different sources of information regarding the city of Babylon as it existed during these final years of independence. One is to be found in the writings of the Neo-Babylonian rulers themselves, which include (in a document known as the *Steinplatten* inscription), Nebuchadnezzar's own account of how he built the city. But at this time in the 6th century BC there is another form of evidence which would not previously have been available: namely the eye-witness accounts, written by contemporary travellers of other nationalities who had actually visited Babylon. From the Hebrew writers of the Old Testament little can be learnt in this respect, since their short and unwelcome association with the city apparently left no time for detached observation. In the case of the Greek travel-writers, however, the situation is quite the reverse. Herodotus, and to a lesser extent Ctesias, have bequeathed to us long and detailed descriptions, not only of the city and its buildings but of the 'manners and customs of the Babylonians'.[284]

Textual information of this sort was of course available to the earliest explorers of the actual ruins in the 19th century, from Claudius James Rich onwards.[285] But their actual excavation had to await the turn of that century, when Robert Koldewey and his German colleagues submitted the site to a systematic investigation, which lasted thirteen years. The results of their excavations are the third and by far the most important source of our present knowledge about Babylon.[286]

The German Excavation

The patience and ingenuity which the German excavators devoted to their prolonged task at Babylon have been remembered with admiration by later generations of archaeologists and are manifest in the results of their work. Koldewey was well provided with architectural assistants, and there was some good-humoured rivalry between them and the epigraphic specialists upon whom he relied to interpret the evidence of the written texts. Yet it is to the collaboration of both that we owe the remarkably detailed information available today, regarding every aspect of a city of which, hardly a century ago, few traces remained visible above ground. Koldewey and Andrae between them were the first excavators in the Near Eastern field properly to understand the problems of stratification, and they were the first to train a gang of expert wall-tracers. From most points of view, their methods attained a higher standard of efficiency than anyone could have expected at that early period in the history of archaeological technique. Yet, with all this industrious activity and the expense which it involved, Koldewey, at least, could never afterwards regard his excavations at Babylon as having been in any sense completed. When he started he had estimated that five years would be necessary for the work, yet, fourteen years later in 1913, one finds him writing in one of his reports that 'approximately one half of the work considered necessary or desirable has now been completed'. The German excavations at Babylon were in fact never afterwards resumed on any considerable scale.

It should be remembered that Koldewey's interest in the site was not originally confined to the ruins of the Neo-Babylonian town. He had hoped to find, buried beneath them, remains of the 2nd-millennium city which had been the capital of Hammurabi's empire. By the end of his first campaign, however, he already realized that in this respect a disappointment was in store, owing to the high level of the sub-surface water-table. Instead, therefore, he resolved to extend his excavations laterally over the whole area of the later city, in the hope of recovering as much of its plan as possible. This of course proved to be an immense task, which involved continuous residence at the site in all seasons, interrupted only by rare visits to his home.

Some idea of the enormous scale on which the 6th-century fortifications of Babylon were built can be inferred from Herodotus' own first-hand account. He gives an overall description of the area enclosed by the walls, adding a characteristically careful explanation of their disposal and construction, with detailed dimensions which have proved to be approximately correct. One needs only to glance at the site-plans in the German publication to see the Greek traveller's impressions transformed into an accurate topographical record.[287]

The City

The old 'Inner City' can be seen on the right bank of the Euphrates, making an irregular square, with sides rather more than a mile

167 Babylon at the time of Nebuchadnezzar II (605–562 B C) with fortifications extended to enclose the Summer Palace (*a*) in the north. (After R. Leacroft)

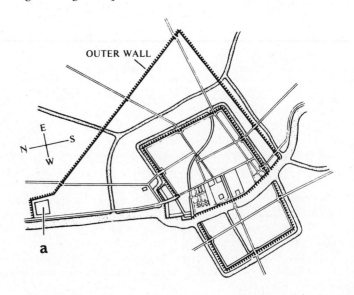

OUTER WALL

a

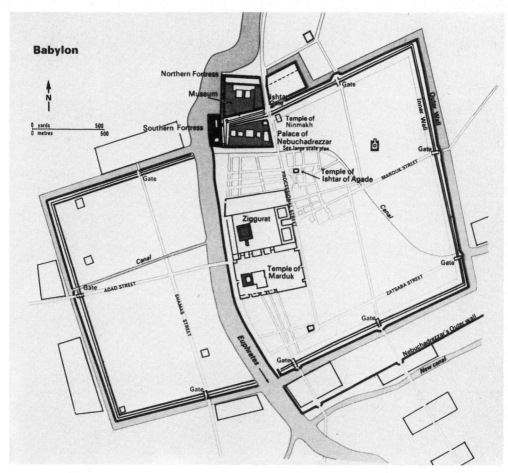

long. In Nebuchadnezzar's time these walls were extended to enclose a further large area on the western side of the river, and the square thus became a rectangle with a longest dimension of $1\frac{1}{2}$ miles. In the western sector the excavations were restricted to soundings, whereby it was possible to establish the extent of the walls and to obtain some idea of the street planning. For the rest, the work was concentrated on the older part of the town to the east; and here a very careful study was made of the fortifications. They consisted of a double line of walls, the innermost of which had a thickness of 6.5 m and was probably higher than the outer one, which measured no more than 3.7 m. Both were built of sun-dried bricks and strengthened at intervals by projecting towers, doubtless with turrets projecting above the crenellated battlements. The space between them, as Herodotus had recorded, gave room for a protected military roadway at parapet level. At the foot of the outer wall there was a moat, which varied from 20 m to 80 m wide, leaving and returning to the river at either end. The 'scarp' or inner face of the moat was strengthened by a wall of kiln-baked bricks, set in bitumen. Koldewey also confirmed the testimony of Herodotus, that 'there was free passage for boats and craft of all kinds around the moat', and one is left to assume that it must

168 Plan of the old Inner City of Babylon, with the western suburb, showing the Procession Street and principal buildings. (From Hawkes, 1974)

168

therefore have been bridged where the main gateways occurred. There were in all nine of these, named after the patron gods of other cities to which the roads led, and they were provided with outer guard-rooms and roomy inner gate-chambers. Four of them were excavated.

The whole of this inner fortification was built by Nabopolassar and Nebuchadnezzar between the years 625 and 562 BC. Along the east bank of the river, where streets came down to the waterside, a new wall was later built by Nabonidus with a broad quay for shipping at its foot.

172   The main palace of the Babylonian kings was situated in the northwest corner of the old city, at a point where the walls themselves were further protected by a colossal bastion overlooking the river and an external citadel. It was here also that the great
171   highway from the north passed through the famous 'Ishtar Gate' into the inner city, of which it became the main artery. This 'Procession Street', along which the statues of the gods were carried at the time of the New Year's Festival, continued southward along the eastern wall of the palace, crossed a canal called *Libilhegalla* and skirted the walls of the ziggurat enclosure, *Etemenanki*. At the city centre it turned westward, passing on its left the great temple of Marduk, *Esagila*, and came down to the Euphrates, which it crossed upon a bridge supported by five stone piers, to enter the western sector of the city.[288]

Finally, we must refer to the outer enceinte, which created a huge extension of the city on the eastern bank. This great moated rampart was built to enclose, in the far north, Nebuchadnezzar's
167   'Summer Palace', and it returned to the river south of the inner city. It has sometimes been thought that it had been intended to repeat this outer triangle on the west side of the river, making the enlarged city into a gigantic square; but there is no evidence that this was ever done. The two short sides of the existing triangle measure $2\frac{1}{2}$ miles each; so the complete square would have enclosed $6\frac{1}{4}$ square miles of country.

Buildings

The northern highway rises steeply before reaching the Ishtar Gate; so that the gate itself and the Procession Street are paved at a level several metres higher than the surrounding buildings. The pavement itself was of limestone slabs, over one metre square, and bordered with flags of red breccia. Beneath this, the Germans were able to expose the foundations of the gate and street-walls; and they found that Nebuchadnezzar (as mentioned in his *Steinplatten* inscription), had carried them down to a depth of 15 m: almost as far as the clean soil beneath the mound. Since the quarrying activities of local builders before Koldewey's arrival had left practically nothing standing above pavement level, these foundations are today all that remains to be seen by modern visitors to the site. They did, however, enable the excavators to recover the plan of the gate itself, with its imposing towers and high vaulted inner chambers, as can be judged by the remarkable reconstruction afterwards made in the Berlin Museum.

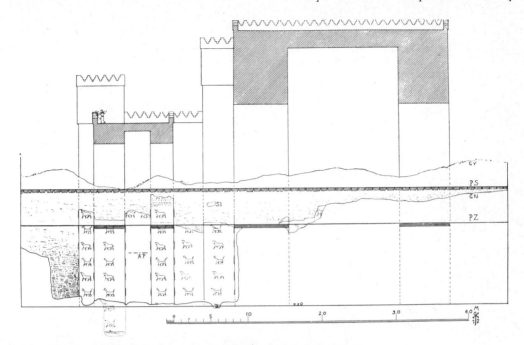

169 Drawing of the restored Ishtar Gate, as seen from the north. The raised Procession Street is shown in section, with decorated foundations beneath it. (From Koldewey, 1926)

170 Relief figure of a *sirrush* dragon in moulded brickwork, from the façade of the Ishtar Gate at Babylon. The reliefs were covered with brightly coloured glaze: brown and yellow on a background of peacock blue. Ht 92 cm

    Now, regarding the façade ornament for which these buildings are so justly famous: the whole of the gate itself and the adjoining walls of the Procession Street had outer faces ornamented with designs in brightly coloured glazed brickwork. Repeated at regular intervals were the figures of lions, bulls and *sirrush* dragons, sometimes represented in flat glaze – at others in glazed relief. The reconstruction of these designs was made possible by the survival of a small section which remained standing at the base of one tower. As to the process by which this brick ornament was glazed and

169

170

171 Reconstructions in the Berlin Museum of (left) the ornamental façades of the Ishtar Gate, and (right) a glazed brick panel from the outer face of the great throne-room, facing the third and largest courtyard in Nebuchadnezzar's palace

assembled, Koldewey in his report speculates at great length, but with a certain lack of clarity. One is left to suppose that it resembled in most respects that used by the Assyrians at Khorsabad and in Fort Shalmaneser at Nimrud.

The same form of façade ornament seems to have been used in certain parts of the royal palace ('Southern Citadel', as the Germans refer to it). A tall panel recovered from a wall outside the throne-room is of special interest, in that classical motifs are adapted to the design, suggesting that some contact now existed between Babylon and Greece. Otherwise, the planning and architecture of this building show no departure from Mesopotamian tradition except for its colossal size. There were five successive courtyards, arranged on a single axis, and the largest of these (63 × 58 m) in the centre of the building, was entered through a sort of 'Sublime Porte'. On its south side, and occupying rather more than its complete width, was the principal throne-room, which, like all the other important reception rooms, was thus given a northward exposure for the sake of coolness in summer. The remaining space was filled with domestic and administrative offices. One other feature, in the northeast corner of the building, aroused special interest. Here was a self-contained group of subterranean store-chambers, heavily vaulted and containing much fallen stonework. It was thought by the excavators that this curious structure might represent an emplacement on which the famous 'Hanging Gardens' could have been built, as described by Herodotus. Their theory was given increased credibility by the discovery at one point of a deep well, surmounted by a triple chamber, which might have accommodated apparatus for drawing water for the gardens above. In more recent years, however, scholars have found reasons to doubt this interpretation.

As we have already mentioned, the Procession Street, in its passage westward towards the bridge, passes between the ziggurat enclosure, *Etemenanki* and the Marduk Temple, *Esagila*, which respectively represent the *hochtempel* and *tieftempel* of Mesopotamian religious convention. If one remembers that these two buildings must have demonstrated the culmination of a great architectural tradition, it is distressing to realize that for all practical purposes their physical remains are today non-existent. The ziggurat enclosure, more than 500 m square, has an inner and an outer temenos wall. Around these a complex of administrative buildings were successfully excavated; but in the case of the great staged tower itself its structure had been totally quarried away by brick-robbers, so that all that could be learnt about it archaeologically had to be inferred from the negative impression left in the ground – today a deep, marshy pit. Based on Herodotus and other ancient writers, a variety of reconstructions have been proposed, of which the most convincing are those which most closely resemble the Third Dynasty tower at Ur.[289] *Esagila*, on the other hand, presented a different problem. Its ruins were buried beneath 21 m of later debris, topped by the Islamic shrine of Hajji Amran, and its excavation, which involved the removal of 30,000 cubic metres of earth, could be achieved only by tunnelling along the base of the walls. At least it was possible to determine the size of the

172 Plan of Nebuchadnezzar's palace, adjoining the Ishtar Gate. The throne-room, with its three portals and dependent suite of apartments, faces the great courtyard, which is approached from the east through a 'sublime porte'. The group of vaulted store-houses, once thought to have supported the 'Hanging Gardens', is located in the northeast corner of the building. (After Koldewey, 1925). *a*, Ishtar Gate; *b*, Ninmakh Temple

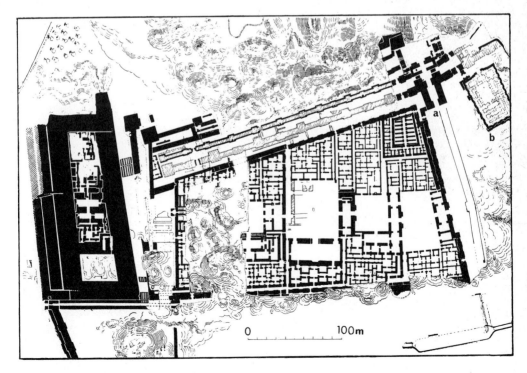

0   100m

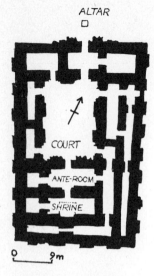

ALTAR
☐

COURT

ANTE-ROOM

SHRINE

0   9m

173 Plan of the Ninmakh
Temple, also near the Ishtar
Gate: a building characteristic of
the Late Babylonian period,
which has recently been
reconstructed *in situ*. (After
Macqueen, 1964)

174 Façades of Neo-Babylonian
temples at the summit of the
Harsagkalama mound at Kish,
still standing up to 5.6 m high.
Shown by foundation deposits to
be the work of Nebuchadnezzar

building, which measured 86 × 78 m. But conflicting conclusions
about its planning become apparent when one observes that the
reconstruction in the final report and the great scale-model in the
Berlin Museum disagree, even in regard to the position of the main
sanctuary. As to its traditionally rich furnishings, one must once
more be content with the stories, among other marvels, of a seated
statue of gold, 6 m high, and a throne of gold, weighing $18\frac{1}{2}$ tons.

In addition to the Ninmakh Temple adjoining the Ishtar Gate,
which has already been mentioned, a number of other minor
shrines were excavated. They can all be seen to conform to the now
generally accepted arrangement of entry, courtyard and sanctuary,
all on the same axis, but with variously developed subsidiary
chambers. In some respects more interesting were the private
dwelling-houses, some with pretentious appointments of a sort
which one would expect in a capital city. Like town-houses in all
periods of Mesopotamian history their ground-floor rooms had no
outward exposure and obtained light from a central court. A
strange form of external façade ornament – if so it may be called – is
frequently to be seen in buildings of this sort, and would appear to
have been an innovation in Neo-Babylonian times. Successive tiers
of bricks are set at a slight angle to the true line of the wall-face,
creating a 'dog-tooth' pattern of vertical ridges. It is a practice
which may originally have been adopted when an irregular shaped
site resulted in a disparity between the oblique angle of the outer
wall and the rectangular rooms which it contained. For the rest,
Herodotus had spoken of houses with 'two or three storeys' and,
though the excavators found this difficult to confirm, it could at
least be seen that, like the much earlier houses excavated by
Woolley at Ur, these too must have been provided with rooms on
an upper floor, entered and lighted from a wooden gallery around
the court.[290] Private chapels, sometimes with burials beneath
them, suggested another aspect of Babylonian domestic life.

Evidence of large-scale building activities in the time of the Neo-
babylonian kings is by no means limited to the capital itself.
Something has already been said about Nebuchadnezzar's
ambitious reconstruction of the city walls at Ur, with their
imposing gateways and protected harbours for ships trading on the
Euphrates. On a new site in the city, a huge building known as the
Palace of Bel-shalti-nannar also appeared at this time;[291] while at
Kish, on the Harsagkalama mound colossal temples were built,
whose walls still remain standing many metres high. At almost
every other Sumerian city derelict stacks of kiln-baked bricks,

stamped with Nebuchadnezzar's name, testify to his repair of some ancient shrine and the belated renewal of its splendour.

In summarizing the results of the prolonged excavation at Babylon, it is indeed surprising to find so little to record in the realm of sculpture or among the various products of contemporary craftsmanship. The German excavators would have been the first to admit their considerable disappointment in this respect; and it is reflected in the commentary of a more recent writer. He says: 'There is a scarcity of works of this period, which makes it impossible to estimate its artistic achievement', and he adds:

There was an intense literary activity, and it was from Neo-Babylonian sources that the Hellenistic world acquired its knowledge of astrology and other Mesopotamian sciences; but Neo-Babylonian art did not affect the West. It was from Assyria that Greece and Etruria obtained their models during their 'orientalizing period', through the intermediacy of the Phoenicians.[292]

Postscript

These pages have been written at a time when the excavation of historical sites in Mesopotamia seems to have lost impetus. Some new discoveries continue to be reported, of a sort which may serve further to illuminate the early history of Near Eastern civilization, but the locations in which they are made – often beyond the immediate territories of the old Mesopotamian kingdoms – may point to a new widening of historical perspective. One instance may here be cited of an excavation at present in progress, whose relevance in this respect may be thought to have particular significance. At a site called Tell Mardikh, 31 miles to the southwest [1] of Aleppo in Syria, the ruins have been found of a city called Ebla, some of whose rulers in the late 3rd millennium were already known by name. Of a slightly later period, contemporary with the Larsa and Amorite dynasties of Babylonia, architecture and sculpture have been found, which rivals in interest and accomplishment that currently known in Mesopotamia. But an even greater discovery is now added to these: an archive of tablets numbering many thousands, some of them with over a thousand lines of writing. Here then, is a completely new field of philological study. Written in a hitherto unfamiliar language of the West Semitic type, their transcription will be facilitated by the inclusion among them of plentiful vocabularies with Sumerian equivalents. But, quite apart from their linguistic significance, the archaeological setting in which they were found may in itself suggest a genuine 'breakthrough' into a new realm of discovery. The point which they serve to make clear is, in the excavator's words, that 'south Mesopotamia was not the sole progenitor of literacy and civilization for the whole Near East; similar processes were operating over a much wider area, from the Levant to Elam'.[293]

Over the past century, as we have attempted to show in these pages, the Mesopotamian contribution has been studied with devoted thoroughness. As a specialized subject, the possibilities which it offers are still unlimited; but clearly it has everything to gain from collateral research among the remoter byways of Near Eastern antiquity.

Notes on the Text

1 The best commentary on the geography of Iraq is in Brice (1966, chs. 11 and 21).

2 But see Roux (1960, pp. 20–31).

3 Lees and Falcon (1952, pp. 24–39).

4 Jacobsen (1960, pp. 174–83).

5 See Adams (1958, pp. 101–4).

6 See Jacobsen (1958a, p. 1251).

7 See Oates, D. (1968, fig. 2, p. 14).

8 See chronological table in Solecki (1971, fig. 8, p. 182).

9 See Coon (1963, map 8, on p. 320). But see a summary of recent conclusions regarding climatic changes during the Upper Palaeolithic in Singh (1974, pp. 5–6).

10 Garrod (1930, p. 8).

11 Solecki (1971); note in particular map 2, on p. 17.

12 Their work is fully reported in Braidwood and Howe (1960).

13 Childe (1950), quoted in Singh (1974, p. 4).

14 Braidwood (1974a).

15 Mellaart (1967).

16 Singh (1974); for a fuller account see Mellaart (1975) or D. and J. Oates (1976).

17 Lamberg-Karlovski (1974).

18 Braidwood (1974b).

19 Mortensen (1964, p. 32 ff.).

20 Braidwood (1960, p. 173).

21 An analysis and discussion of all these soundings is presented in Perkins (1949), and by A. Porada in Ehrich (1965).

22 The German reports have been published at great length, mostly in the series *Uruk Vorläufige Berichte* (titles vary), and *Abhandlungen der Deutsche Orient Gesellschaft*, in progress since 1929. An almost up-to-date summary in English is to be found in Mallowan (1970, ch. 8/1, p. 360 ff.), and in Frankfort and Davies (1971, ch. 12). But note also the more recent find of a level IVa–b palace, in Lenzen (1974, p. 111).

23 Mackay (1931) and elsewhere.

24 See Lloyd and Safar (1947, p. 84 ff. and 1948, p. 115 ff.); also Lloyd (1947 and 1948).

25 Delougaz and Lloyd (1942).

26 These and other proposed changes in stratigraphical terminology are well shown diagrammatically by E. Porada in Ehrich (1965, p. 176).

27 Heinrich (1957).

28 Safar (1950, p. 27 ff).

29 Van Buren (1972).

30 Ziegler (1953).

31 Oates, Joan (1960, pp. 32–50).

32 See 'Excavations in Iraq, 1971–72', *Iraq*, 34, pt 2 (1972), p. 149.

33 Lloyd and Safar (1943, p. 131 ff.).

34 Heinrich (1957).

35 Van Buren (1952, p. 76 ff.).

36 *Riemchen* in German, meaning 'prismatic', is the name used by the excavators for the small, rectangular mud bricks characteristic of the Uruk period.

37 Delougaz and Lloyd (1942).

38 Mostly accounts and inventories.

39 A full discussion of this script will be found in Falkenstein (1936).

40 Roux (1964, p. 82).

41 General reference books for cylinder-seals are Frankfort (1939) and Amiet (1961).

42 Some fine examples are illustrated in Frankfort (1955, pl. 1 ff.).

43 Well illustrated in Delougaz (1952).

44 E.g. in Frankfort (1951).

45 See Falkenstein (1955, p. 269 ff.).

46 See Lamberg-Karlovski (1974).

47 Cf. Kramer (1963, p. 111 ff.).

48 Cf. D. and J. Oates (1976, p. 136).

49 See Lloyd (1960).

50 Oates, Joan (1976, pp. 20–31), with map, fig. 1, p. 23, and Burkholder (1972, pp. 264–9). The writer is indebted to Dr Oates for the further information which follows.

51 For a comparative analysis in detail of the evidence from these excavations, in northern Iraq, see Perkins (1972). Also to be recommended is the site-by-site commentary in

Mallowan (1970, ch. 8/2, p. 376 ff.).

52 Mallowan and Rose (1935).

53 See Speiser (1935) and Tobler (1950).

54 Herzfeld (1950).

55 Thompson and Mallowan (1932, p. 71 ff.).

56 Lloyd and Safar (1945, p. 255 ff.).

57 Summary reports in English: Munchajef and Merpert (1969 onwards).

58 Preliminary reports: Kirkbride (1972 onwards).

59 Of the animal bones 68·5% were onager and 15·9% gazelle.

60 See Braidwood *et al.* (1952, p. 1 ff.).

61 Preliminary reports by B. Abu-al-Soof and others in *Sumer*, 21 (1965) to 24 (1968).

62 See Oates, Joan (1966).

63 See Oates, Joan (1969) and Braidwood (1944, pp. 47–72).

64 E.g. at Yanik Tepe in Azarbaijan: Burney (1964).

65 Cf. Mallowan (1970, ch. 8/2, footnote no. 2 on p. 383).

66 See Mallowan (1947, p. 1 ff.).

67 See Braidwood (1944, pp. 47–72).

68 Typical examples of Samarra and Tel Halaf painted pottery are well illustrated in colour in Strommenger (1964, pl. II).

69 Lloyd (1938, p. 123 ff.).

70 See Ucko (1968).

71 Munchajef and Merpert (1971, pl. V, fig. 2 and pl. VII, fig. 10).

72 Oates, Joan (1969a) and illustrations reproduced in Singh (1974, figs. 59a–d, 60 and 61).

73 Typical figurines from these two sites are illustrated side-by-side in Strommenger (1964, pl. 6).

74 See Speiser (1935, pl. CXLII, p. 36) and Barnett (1966).

75 Syria and Iran are covered rather more fully in Mallowan (1967).

76 Two of these are illustrated in colour in Strommenger (1964, pls. III and IV).

77 See Le Breton (1957, p. 79 ff.), with diagrams of comparative chronology.

78 Lamberg-Karlovski (1970).

79 Jacobsen (1939). Simply presented in Woolley (1965, pp. 21–6).

80 A useful English translation is Sandars (1960).

81 There is a summary of the evidence in Gadd (1971, ch. 13, p. 93).

82 Sollberger (1960, p. 69 ff.).

83 Hall and Woolley (1927).

84 See Kramer (1965).

85 Delougaz and Lloyd (1942, fig. 115, p. 134), and alternative dating in Ehrich (1954, table on p. 176).

86 This subject has been exhaustively studied in Mallowan (1964, p. 62 ff.). At Kish he noted several alternative 'Flood-levels'.

87 See Kramer (1956, p. 290).

88 See Sollberger (1954–6, p. 10 ff.).

89 See Edzard (1959, p. 9 ff.).

90 See Kramer (1952).

91 The relevant final publications of the Khafaje excavations are, Delougaz (1940) and Delougaz and Lloyd (1942).

92 For burials, see Delougaz *et al.* (1967).

93 Delougaz and Lloyd (1942).

94 Delougaz and Lloyd (1942).

95 Woolley's preliminary reports were published under the heading 'Excavations at Ur', in the *Antiquaries Journal*, 3 (1923), to 14 (1934), and republished in a single volume by Benn, London (Woolley 1954). Of the final publications, Woolley (1934), Woolley (1939) and Woolley (1974) are relevant to this chapter.

96 Site-plans are reproduced in colour in Hawkes (1974, p. 173).

97 For the identity of these animals, see Dyson (1960, p. 102 ff.).

98 Cf. Gadd (1960, p. 51).

99 See Hall and Woolley (1927).

100 See Delougaz (1938, p. 1ff.).

101 Mackay (1929): also Waterlin and Langdon (1930–4).

102 See Moorey (1966, p. 83) and Lloyd (1969, p. 40).

103 De Sarzec and Heuzey (1884–1912).

104 Jacobsen (1958, pp. 127–9).

105 See Crawford (1974, p. 29 ff.).

106 Parrot (1948).

107 For easy reference, see siteplan in Hawkes (1974, p. 174).

108 For preliminary reports, see Haines (1956, 1958, 1961), and Hansen and Dales (1962).

109 See Hansen (1965, pp. 201–13).

110 See Hansen (1963).

111 For plan in colour, see Hawkes (1974, p. 181).

112 See Andrae (1922). The results of this excavation are summarized in English in Mallowan (1971, ch. 16, p. 298), and in French (with plan) in Parrot (1946, p. 224 ff. and fig. 52).

113 Cf. Edzard (1959, p. 9 ff.).

114 Preliminary reports on A. Parrot's excavations at Mari

appeared annually in *Syria* and other journals, from 1935 onwards. Their final publication is in the series *Mission Archéologique de Mari*, of which vol. 1 (1956), vol. 2, pts 1–3 (1958), vol. 3 and vol. 4 (both 1967) are relevant. Vol. 2, pt 2 and vol. 4 are reviewed in English in Mallowan (1969). The Ishtar Temple is described (with plan) in Mallowan (1971, p. 291 ff.).

115 See Moortgat (1959–67). The results are discussed in Mallowan (1966a) and Mallowan (1971, ch. 16).

116 Mallowan (1971, ch. 16).

117 E.g. Moortgat (1959–67) and elsewhere.

118 Cf. Ehrich (1965, p. 162).

119 Cf. Frankfort (1954, p. 23 ff.). All Early Dynastic sculpture from the Diyala sites is published by the same writer in Frankfort (1939 and 1943).

120 Andrae (1922).

121 See Frankfort (1939 and 1943).

122 Illustrated in Frankfort (1954, pl. 9b).

123 Illustrated in Frankfort (1954, pl. 13).

124 See Frankfort (1939, footnotes on pp. 51 and 54).

125 Well illustrated in Strommenger (1964, pls. 88–100 and in colour, pl. XX).

126 Strommenger (1964, p. 401) refers to this individual as 'he'. But see also Barnett (1969, p. 96). A statue from the same provenance, showing a headless couple holding hands, represents a convention occasionally seen elsewhere.

127 Frankfort (1954, pl. 26b).

128 See Hansen (1963, p. 146).

129 Frankfort (1954, pl. 33b).

130 Frankfort (1954, pl. 33a).

131 Hansen (1963). He detected two main phases in their stylistic development, equating the first with the earlier half of the 'ED II' period, and the second with a transitional phase extending to cover 'ED IIIa'. This suggests a sub-division of the 'ED II' period, which would conform to the German system of chronology outlined above on p. 110.

132 Hansen (1963, pl. VI). See also below, p. 131.

133 Illustrated in detail in Strommenger (1964, pls. 66–9).

134 Lamberg-Karlovski (1974, p. 283).

135 Strommenger (1964, pls. 38–9). See also Delougaz (1960).

136 The making and use of these bricks is explained in Delougaz (1933).

137 E.g. in Sin Temple VIII at Khafaje, in level VIII of the Inanna Temple at Nippur and, most notably, in Palace 'A' at Kish.

138 Delougaz and Lloyd (1942, pl. 23).

139 Delougaz and Lloyd (1942, pl. 12).

140 Delougaz and Lloyd (1942, fig. 203, p. 263).

141 Haines (1961).

142 Delougaz, Hill and Lloyd (1967, pl. 36).

143 Strommenger (1964, fig. 17, p. 391).

144 Safar (1950, fig. 3).

145 Parrot (1972, fig. 2, p. 285).

146 The seals of all three phases are described and illustrated in Frankfort (1939).

147 These two figures were associated by an earlier generation of archaeologists with Gilgamesh and his companion Enkidu of the famous epic; but the equation is today trea-

ted with some reserve. Compare Frankfort (1939, p. 62).

148 The most important commentary on objects under this heading is to be found in Woolley (1934).

149 The most satisfying reconstruction of such a headdress is perhaps to be seen in the Iraq Museum exhibit, mounted by an Iraqi sculptor on an imaginary head and shoulders. It is shown here, ill. 85. See also Maxwell-Hyslop (1960).

150 Frankfort (1954, pl. 20a).

151 Best illustrated in Strommenger (1964, pl. 72, and colour pls. X and XI).

152 Parrot (1962, pls. 11 and 12 and fig. 11, p. 164).

153 Compare the top left-hand figure in the 'Peace Scene' of the 'royal standard', ill. 87.

154 Barnett (1969). The anatomy of these instruments, in relation to the known principles of Sumerian music, was first discussed in Galpin (1929). A more up-to-date commentary on them is to be found in Rimmer (1960).

155 Strommenger (1964, pl. XIV in colour).

156 A long and very detailed study of Early Dynastic pottery, with colour illustrations of painted wares, at this and earlier periods, may be found in Delougaz (1952). See also Strommenger (1964, pls. VIII and IX).

157 See Mallowan (1964, p. 142 ff.).

158 Strommenger (1964, pl. 41).

159 George Roux (1964) competently summarizes the information at present available on this subject.

160 Saggs (1962, p. 272 ff.).

161 These two rock reliefs are discussed stylistically in Bar-

relet (1959, p. 20). See also Strommenger (1936, p. 83 ff.).

162 Hilprecht (1903).

163 Scheil (1902).

164 Banks (1912).

165 Waterlin and Langdon (1930–4). See also Moorey (1966, pp. 18–51) and Lloyd (1969, pp. 40–8).

166 Woolley (1934).

167 Delougaz, Hill and Lloyd (1967, p. 186 ff. and pl. 37).

168 Delougaz, Hill and Lloyd (1967, p. 196 ff.). The present writer, who was responsible for the excavation of the Northern Palace at Tell Asmar, finds the argument for this theory unconvincing. Delougaz dates the building to a so-called 'Proto-Imperial' period, defined by Th. Jacobsen, in *Assyriological Studies*, no. 11, table II, as lasting from the reign of the Lagashite king, Entemena, to the first years of Sargon-of-Akkad.

169 Delougaz, Hill and Lloyd (1967, pl. 64).

170 Delougaz, Hill and Lloyd (1967, p. 54 ff. and pl. 20).

171 Mallowan (1947, p. 26 ff. and 63 ff.). Plan also reproduced in Strommenger (1964, fig. 18, p. 403).

172 Mallowan (1932, pl. L), also (1936), p. 104 ff. and pls. V–VII. Illustrated in colour in Strommenger (1964, pls. XXII–XXIII).

173 Originally published in *Mémoires du Délégation en Perse*, vol. I, 1900, pl. X.

174 E.g. two fragments published in Strommenger (1964, pls. 114–15).

175 Strommenger (1964, pls. 118–19), also discussed in Barrelet (1959).

176 Compare Akkadian seals illustrated in Frankfort (1939),

Moortgat (1940) and Wiseman (n.d.).

177 See Frankfort (1934).

178 Frankfort (1933, pp. 47–53, figs. 30–3), also Gadd (1933), and Corbieau (1937, p. 1 ff.).

179 Starr (1939).

180 Lambert and Tournay (1951).

181 De Sarzec and Heuzey (1884–1912), also Parrot (1948).

182 What follows is partly taken from an abbreviated account in Parrot (1946, pp. 127 ff.).

183 These statues were first published in de Sarzec and Heuzey (1884–1912). They are well illustrated in Strommenger (1964, pls. XXVI and 133–7).

184 Crawford (1974) and the accompanying footnotes.

185 Woolley's preliminary reports, as has been said, were published immediately after the end of each season's digging. Mallowan, in his introduction to the Memorial Volume, *Iraq*, vol. 22, published soon after Woolley's death in 1960, recalls how these articles were often 'written on board ship as he travelled home'. For the titles of volumes in the final publication (*Ur Excavations*), see Bibliography.

186 See Woolley (1974, pls. 53 and 61).

187 See Woolley (1939). Woolley's several perspective restorations have been widely published and are well known.

188 The only parallels in architectural history for this practice are to be seen in the mausolea of Augustus and Hadrian at Rome. See Bannister-Fletcher (1961, p. 237, figs. b and c).

189 See Woolley and Mallowan (1974, pl. 54).

190 See Frankfort, Lloyd and Jacobsen (1940, pl. 1 *passim*).

191 A good account of Mesopotamian history in the 2nd millennium BC is to be found in Roux (1964).

192 Published as the *Archives Royales de Mari*, Paris 1950 onwards (transliterations and translations).

193 See D. Oates (1968, p. 31 ff.).

194 See Parrot (1938, pp. 308–10).

195 See McEwan (1958).

196 Frankfort *et al.* (1940).

197 Turner (1968).

198 Frankfort *et al.* (1940, pl. 7).

199 Frankfort (1936, p. 74 ff.).

200 See Smith and Baqir (1946); Baqir (1948 and 1959); Gurney (1950).

201 See Woolley (1954, fig. 12, p. 176).

202 E.g. in Woolley (1935, pl. 12).

203 Preliminary reports in *Syria* (1935–67) and *Annales Archéologiques de Syrie* (1951–67). Final publication: see Bibliography under Parrot.

204 Illustrated in colour, e.g. in Strommenger (1964, pls. XXVIII and XXIX) and in Parrot (1961).

205 See Barrelet (1950).

206 See Parrot (1967a).

207 Annual reports by Oates, D. in *Iraq*, 27–34 (1965–72).

208 See Oates, D. (1967, p. 70 ff.). He refers to similar façade ornament at Ur, 'flanking the entrance to the bastion of Warad-Sin, which was built *c.* 1830 BC'. Cf. Woolley (1939, p. 42–3).

209 See Oates, D. (1973, p. 183).

210 All these sculptures are well illustrated in Strommenger (1954, figs. 148–54). But see J. R. Kupper in *Revue*

d'Assyriologie, 15 (1971), p. 113 ff.

211 The 'Burney Plaque', illustrated here, ill. 118, and in Frankfort (1954, fig. 56).

212 Strommenger (1964, pl. xxvii).

213 Strommenger (1964, fig. 170).

214 Baqir (1944, 1945 and 1946a).

215 Baqir (1946a).

216 Baqir (1946a, pls. XI–XIV).

217 E.g. Frankfort (1954, pl. 71).

218 Baqir (1945, pls. 17 and 21).

219 Frankfort (1954, pls. 70b and 70c).

220 Starr (1938).

221 For once, a very revealing analysis of their contents is appended to the main publication (Starr 1938, vol. 1, p. 528 ff.).

222 Starr (1938, general plan in folder).

223 Strommenger (1964, fig. 40, p. 430).

224 Frankfort (1954, fig. 64, p. 142); also Mallowan (1939, pp. 887–94), and Ceccini (1965).

225 Strommenger (1964, fig. 179, bottom row).

226 Published by W. Andrae in *Wissenschaftliche Veröffentlichungen der deutschen Orient Gesellschaft*, no. 10 (1909), no. 23 (1913), no. 24 (1913), no. 39 (1922), no. 58 (1935), and summarized by him in Andrae (1938).

227 Andrae's site plan is reproduced in Strommenger (1964, fig. 46, p. 434).

228 Earlier excavators at Ashur had included Rich, Layard, Place, Rassam and finally George Smith of the British Museum. See Lloyd (1955).

229 Reproduced in Strommenger (1964, fig. 47, p. 435), from Andrae (1938).

230 Andrae (1925). Examples illustrated in Frankfort (1954, pls. 74 A–B).

231 Frankfort (1954, p. 65).

232 See Frankfort (1939) and Porada (1948).

233 Weber (1920, p. 105, no. 531).

234 Moortgat (1944, p. 43, figs. 45b and 46).

235 See Jacobsen and Lloyd (1935). For other rock-reliefs of Sennacherib, see Bachmann (1927).

236 Lloyd (1947 with illustrations, and 1955).

237 For the site of Nimrud and its surroundings, see Mallowan (1966b, vol. 1, ch. 1) and Oates, D. (1968, ch. 3).

238 Layard's two principal books are Layard (1950 and 1953).

239 Rassam's excavations are recorded, as a rule rather briefly, in Rassam (1897).

240 Loftus (1857).

241 Botta and Flandin (1849–50).

242 Place (1867–70).

243 See Gadd (1936, p. 57). These two figures were purchased from the French Consular Agent in 1849 and sawn into four pieces each. They were transported safely by sea from Basrah to London, though the ship was reported to be 'well down in the water'.

244 An early survey was published in Jones (1857).

245 See Finch (1948, p. 9 ff.) and Madhloum (1967 or 1968).

246 See plan in Layard (1853, vol. 1, facing p. 67).

247 See plan of Ashurbanipal's palace in Rassam (1897, facing p. 8); for Balawat, King (1915), also Barnett (1973).

248 See Loud (1936).

249 See Loud and Altmann (1938).

250 Since Loud and Altmann (1938) is a heavy volume, Loud's plans may more conveniently be consulted in e.g. Strommenger (1964, pp. 445–7).

251 See Turner (1970, p. 177 ff.).

252 Reproduced in Frankfort (1954, fig. 32, p. 79).

253 For the *bit hilani*, see Frankfort (1952).

254 See Loud and Altmann (1938, p. 19).

255 Reproduced in Frankfort (1954, fig. 40, p. 103).

256 Reproduced in Frankfort (1954, pl. 82).

257 The pair of bulls from Gate 'A', now at the entrance to the Iraq Museum, measured 4.4 m square and weighed over 20 tons. The single bull, with head facing sideways, from the throne-room entrance, now in the Oriental Institute Museum, Chicago, was 4.7 m square, and the largest fragment weighed 14 tons. Other fragments remain *in situ* of an even larger bull, measuring 5.5 m square.

258 Frankfort (1954, pl. 87).

259 Frankfort (1954, pl. 90).

260 Frankfort (1954, fig. 41, p. 104).

261 Strommenger (1964, pl. 209–14).

262 King (1915).

263 See Barnett (1971, p. 442 and notes).

264 Thureau-Dangin and Dunand (1936).

265 See Parrot (1961, pls. I–IV and figs. 109–20, 266 and 336–48).

266 Some of the best photographs are those taken by Max Hirmer to illustrate Strommenger (1964).

267 Strommenger (1964, pl. 241).

268 E.g. Madhloum (1964).

269 See Mallowan (1966).

270 See plan of the citadel in Mallowan (1966, fig. 1, p. 32).

271 See Mallowan (1966, vol. 1, facing p. 128).

272 See Mallowan (1966, vol. 1, Frontispiece).

273 See Plenderleith's report, quoted by Mallowan: Mallowan (1966, p. 139).

274 Preliminary reports by D. Oates in *Iraq* and *Illustrated London News* from 1957 to 1963. Finally published in Mallowan (1966, vol. 2).

275 See Turner (1960, p. 68 ff.).

276 Well illustrated in *Illustrated London News*, 1 December 1962.

277 See Mallowan (1966, vol. 2, fig. 373, p. 453).

278 In the second volume of Mallowan's major work on the excavations at Nimrud, he deals with two groups of ivories, one from rooms NW.15, SW.2 and SW.7, the other from rooms SW.12, SW.37. This last is one of the eight magazines – each almost 30 m long – of which the storage space in the Southwest courtyard is composed. The remainder are marked on the plan 'partly excavated'.

See Mallowan (1966, folding plan no. 8).

279 The final publication of the ivories (Commentary, catalogue and Plates), has appeared in a succession of fascicles under the title *Ivories from Nimrud (1966, 1970 1974)*.

280 Barnett (1957).

281 It has been compared to the 'Chinoiserie' phase of English ornament in the 18th century.

282 See Gadd (1958, p. 35 ff.).

283 Herodotus (*History*, Bk 1, ch. 191 ff.), and Xenophon (*Cyropaedia*, Book VII, ch. V, 10), maintain that Cyrus diverted the course of the Euphrates, so that his troops could enter the city along its dry bed. Koldewey (in F. Wetsel, *Die Stadtmauern von Babylon*, Leipzig 1930, p. 53), was inclined to believe that something of this sort did in fact happen. Others have doubted it.

284 Herodotus' account (Bk 1, ch. 178 ff.), is very fully discussed and compared with the excavators' findings in Ravn (1942), a book in English which is unfortunately difficult to obtain. Koldewey's semi-popular account of his work appeared in 1914, poorly translated into English. A better summary is to be found in MacQueen (1964).

285 See Lloyd (1947).

286 Koldewey's own reports appeared in the *Mitteilunger der deutschen Orient Gesellschaft* (MDOG), in the years between 1899 and 1932.

287 For the site plan before excavation, see Koldewey (1925, fig. 1), and for the inner city after excavation, *ibid.*, fig. 256.

288 Herodotus (*History*, Bk 1, ch. 186), describes how this bridge was built by 'Nitochris'.

289 Various reconstructions are illustrated side-by-side in Ravn (1942, pls. 14 and 15).

290 Discussed fully in Ravn (1942, p. 67 ff.).

291 Woolley's plan of the Neo-Babylonian temenos at Ur appears in Woolley and Mallowan (1962, pl. 60), and that of the Bel-Shalti-Nannar palace in *ibid.*, pl. 70. For the plan of the outer city wall, see Hawkes (1974, p. 173).

292 Frankfort (1954, p. 108).

293 See reports on this excavation by Paolo Matthiae *et al.*, under the heading *Missione Archaeologica Italiana in Siria*, Istituto di Studi del Vicino Oriente, Universita, Rome 1966, onwards. For the discovery of archives: P. Clough in *The Times*, 15 January 1977.

Bibliography

General Recommendations

BEEK, M. A. *Atlas of Mesopotamia*, London 1962.

EHRICH, R. W. (ed.) *Chronologies in Old World Archaeology*, Chicago 1965.

ELLIS, R. S. *A Bibliography of Mesopotamian Archaeological Sites*, Harrassowitz, Wiesbaden 1972.

HAWKES, JACQUETTA *The First Great Civilizations*, London and New York 1973.

KRAMER, S. N. *The Sumerians*, Chicago 1963.

LLOYD, SETON *Foundations in the Dust*, Oxford 1947.

MALLOWAN, M. E. L. *Twenty-Five Years of Mesopotamian Discovery*, British School of Archaeology in Iraq, London 1956.

OPENNHEIM, A. L. *Ancient Mesopotamia*, Chicago 1964.

PARROT, A. *Archéologie Mésopotamienne*, vol. 1, *Les Etapes*, Paris 1946; vol. 2, *Technique et Probèmes*, Paris 1953.

PERKINS, A. L. *The Comparative Archaeology of Early Mesopotamia*, Studies in Ancient Oriental Civilization, no. 25, Chicago 1949.

ROUX, GEORGE *Ancient Iraq*, London 1964.

SAGGS, H. W. F. *The Greatness that was Babylon*, London 1962.

STROMMENGER, E. *The Art of Mesopotamia*, London 1964.

Other References

ADAMS, R. M. 'Survey of Ancient Water Courses and Settlements in Central Iraq', *Sumer*, 14 (1958).

ADAMS, R. M. and NISSEN, H. J. *The Uruk Countryside*, Chicago 1972.

AMIET, P. *La Glyptique Mésopotamienne*, Paris 1961.

ANDRAE, W. *Die archäischen Ischtar Tempel*, Mitteilungen der deutschen Orient-Gesellschaft, Berlin 1922.

——*Farbige Keramik aus Assur* (Coloured Ceramics from Assur), Berlin 1925.

——*Das Wiedererstandene Assur*, Leipzig 1938.

BACHMANN, W. *Felsreliefs in Assyrien*, Leipzig 1927.

BANKS, E. J. *Bismaya or the Lost City of Adab*, New York 1912.

BANNISTER-FLETCHER *A History of Architecture*, London 1961.

BAQIR, T. 'Iraq Government Excavations at 'Aqar Quf, 1942–43', *Iraq*, Supplement (1944).

——'Iraq Government Excavations at 'Aqar Quf; Second Preliminary Report', *Iraq*, Supplement (1945).

——'Iraq Government Excavations at 'Aqar Quf; Third Interim Report', *Iraq*, 8 (1946a).

——'Tell Harmal: A Preliminary Report', *Sumer*, 2, pt 2 (1946b), 226.

——*Tell Harmal*, Baghdad 1959.

——'A New Law Code from Tell Harmal', *Sumer*, 4, no. i (1948).

BARNETT, R. D. *A Catalogue of the Nimrud Ivories in the British Museum*, London 1957.

——'Homme Masque ou Dieux-Ibex', *Syria*, 43 (1966).

——'New Facts about Musical Instruments from Ur', *Iraq*, 31, pt 2 (1969).

——'Le Palais et le Royauté', *Proceedings of the XIXe Rencontre Assyriologique Internationale*, Paris 1971.

——'More Balawat Gates', *Studies Dedicated to F. M. T. de L. Bohl,* Brill, Leiden 1973.

BARRELET, M.-TH. 'Une Peinture de la Cour 106 du Palais de Mari', *Studia Mariana*, Brill, Leiden 1950, pp. 9–35.

——'Quelque Sculptures Mésopotamienne de l'Epoque d'Akkad', *Syria*, 36 (1959), 20 ff.

BOTTA, P. E. and FLANDIN, E. *Monuments de Ninive* (5 vols.), Paris 1849–50.

BRAIDWOOD, R. J. 'The Iraq-Jarmo Project', in G. R. Willey (ed.), *Archaeological Researches in Retrospect*, Cambridge (Mass.) 1974(b).

BRAIDWOOD, R. J. *et al.* 'Baghouz; New Chalcolithic Material of the Samarra Type and its Antecedents', *Journal of Near Eastern Studies*, 3 (1944).

——'Matarra: A Southern Variant of the Hassuna Assemblage, Excavated in 1948', *Journal of Near Eastern Studies*, 11 (1952).

——*Prehistoric Investigations in Iraqi Kurdistan*, Chicago 1960.

——'The Beginnings of Village Farming Communities in South-eastern Turkey', *Proceedings of the National Academy of Sciences, U.S.A.*, 1974(a).

BRICE, W. C. *South-west Asia.* A Systematic Regional Geography, no. 8, London 1966.

BURKHOLDER, G. ''Ubaid Sites and Pottery in Saudi Arabia', *Archaeology*, 25 (1970).

BURNEY, C. A. 'Yanik Tepe', *Iraq*, 23, pt 2 (1961) and 26, pt 1 (1964).

CECCINI, J. M. *La Ceramica di Nuzi*, Rome 1965.

CHILDE, GORDON. 'The Urban Revolution', in *Town Planning Review*, 21 (1950), 3–17.

COON, CARLETON. *The Origin of Races*, London 1963.

CORBIEAU, S. *'Indus Parallels'*, *Iraq*, 4, (1937), 1 ff.

CRAWFORD, V. E. 'Lagash', *Iraq*, 36 (1974).

DELOUGAZ, P. 'Plano-convex Bricks', *Studies in Ancient Oriental Civilization*, no. 7, Chicago 1933.

——'A Short Investigation of the Temple at Al 'Ubaid', *Iraq*, 5 (1938).

——*The Temple Oval at Khafaje*, Oriental Institute Publications, no. 53, Chicago 1940.

——*Pottery from the Diyala Region*, Oriental Institute Publications, no. 63, Chicago 1952.

——'Architectural Representation on Steatite Vases', *Iraq*, 22 (1960).

DELOUGAZ, P. and LLOYD, S. *Pre-Sargonid Temples in the Diyala Region,* Oriental Institute Publications, no. 58, Chicago 1942.

DELOUGAZ, P., HILL, H. and LLOYD, S. *Private Houses and Graves in the Diyala Region*, Oriental Institute Publications, no. 88, Chicago 1967.

DYSON, R. H. 'Shub-ad's Onagers', *Iraq*, 22 (1960).

EDZARD, D. O. 'Enmer-baragisi von Kis', *Zeitschrift für Assyriologie* von Vorderasiatische Archäeologie, no. 53, Berlin 1959.

FALKENSTEIN, A. *Archäische Texte aus Uruk*, Berlin 1936.

——'Zu den Tafeln aus Tartaria', *Germania*, 43 (1965).

FINCH, J. P. G. 'The Nergal Gate', *Iraq*, 10, pt 1 (1948).

FRANKFORT, HENRI. *Archaeology and the Sumerian Problem*, Studies in Ancient Oriental Civilization, no. 4, Chicago 1932.

——*Tell Asmar, Khafaje and Khorsabad.* Oriental Institute Communications, no. 16, Chicago 1933.

——'Gods and Myths on Sargonid Seals', *Iraq*, 1, pt 1 (1933).

——*Progress of the Work of the Oriental Institute in Iraq, 1934–35*, Oriental Institute Communications, no. 20, Chicago 1936.

——*Sculpture of the Third Millennium B.C. from Tell Asmar and Khafaje*, Oriental Institute Publications, no. 24, Chicago 1939(a).

——*Cylinder Seals*, London 1939(b).

——*More Sculpture from the Diyala Region*, Oriental Institute Publications, no. 60, Chicago 1943.

——*Birth of Civilization in the Near East*, London 1951.

——'The Origin of the Bit Hilani', *Iraq*, 14 (1952), 120–31.

——*Art and Architecture of the Ancient Orient*, Harmondsworth 1954, 4th rev. impression 1970.

——*Stratified Cylinder Seals from the Diyala Region*, Oriental Institute Publications, no. 72, Chicago 1955.

FRANKFORT, HENRI, LLOYD, S. and JACOBSEN, TH. *The Gimilsin Temple and Palace of the Governors at Tell Asmar*, Oriental Institute Publications, no. 43, Chicago 1940.

FRANKFORT, HENRI and DAVIES, L. 'The Last Predynastic Period in Mesopotamia', in *Cambridge Ancient History*, vol. 1, pt 2, ch. 12, Cambridge 1971.

GADD, C. J. 'Seals of Ancient Indian Style Found at Ur', Proceedings of the British Academy, vol. 18, 1933.

——*The Stones of Assyria*, London 1936.

——'The Harran Inscriptions of Nabonidus', *Anatolian Studies*, 8 (1958).

——'The Spirit of Living Sacrifices in Tombs', *Iraq*, 22 (1960), 51 ff.

——'The Cities of Babylonia', in *Cambridge Ancient History*, vol. 1, pt 2, ch. 13, Cambridge 1971.

GALPIN, F. W. 'The Sumerian Harp of Ur', *Music and Letters*, 10 (1929).

GARROD, D. A. W. *The Caves of Zarzi and Hazar Merd*, in Bulletin of the American Schools of Prehistoric Research, no. 6, 1930.

GURNEY, O. R. 'Laws of Eshnunna', *Symbolae Hrozny* (1950).

HAINES, R. C. 'Nippur', *Illustrated London News*, 18 August 1956, 6 September 1958 and 9 September 1961.

HALL, H. R. and WOOLLEY, C. L. *Ur Excavations*, vol. 1: *Al ʿUbaid*, London and Philadelphia 1927.

HANSEN, D. P. 'Votive Plaques from Nippur', *Journal of Near Eastern Studies*, 22 (1963).

HAWKES, JACQUETTA (ed.) *Atlas of Ancient Archaeology*, London 1974.

HEINRICH, E. *Bauwerke in der altsumerischen Bildkunst,* Berlin 1957.

HERZFELD, E. E. *Die Ausgrabungen von Samarra*, vol. 5: *Die Vorge-schichtlichen Töpfereien von Samarra*, Berlin 1930.

HILPRECHT, H. V. *Exploration in Bible Lands during the Nineteenth Century*, Philadelphia 1903.

JACOBSEN, TH. *The Sumerian King-list*, Assyriological Studies, no. 11, Chicago 1939.

——'Salt and Silt in Mesopotamian Agriculture', *Science*, no. 128, (1958a).

——'Girsu', *Revue d'Assyriologie*, 52 (1958b).

——'The Waters of Ur', *Iraq*, 22 (1960).

JACOBSEN, TH. and LLOYD, S. *Sennacherib's Aqueduct at Jerwan*, Oriental Institute Publications, no. 24, Chicago 1935.

JONES, FELIX. *The Topography of Nineveh*, Bombay 1957.

KING, L. W. *Bronze Reliefs from the Gates of Shalmaneser*, London 1915.

KIRKBRIDE, D. 'Umm Dabaghiyah', *Iraq*, 34 (1972) onward.

KOLDEWEY, R. *The Excavations at Babylon* (Engl transl.), London 1914.

——*Das Wiedererstehende Babylon*, Leipzig 1925.

KRAMER, S. N. *Enmerkar and the land of Aratta*, Philadelphia 1952.

——'Dilmun: Quest for Paradise', *Antiquity*, 27, no. 146 (1963).

——*From the Tablets of Ur*, Indianapolis, Colorado 1965.

LAMBERG-KARLOVSKI, C. C. *Excavations at Tepe Yahya, Iran,* Cambridge (Mass.) 1970.

——'Excavations at Tepe Yahya', G. R. Willey (ed.), *Archaeological Researches in Retrospect*, Cambridge (Mass.) 1974.

LAMBERT, M. and TOURNAY, J. R. 'La Statue B de Gudea', *Revue d'Assyriologie*, 45 (1951).

LAYARD, A. H. *Nineveh and its Remains* (2 vols.), London 1850.
——*Discoveries in the ruins of Nineveh and Babylon*, London 1853.
LEACROFT, H. and R. *The Buildings of Ancient Mesopotamia*, Leicester 1974.
LE BRETON, L. 'The Early Periods of Susa: Mesopotamian Relations', *Iraq*, 19 (1957).
LEES, G. N. and FALCON, N. L. 'The Geographical History of the Mesopotamian Plains', *The Geographical Journal*, 118 (1952).
LENZEN, H. J. 'Die Architecktur in Eanna in der Uruk IV Period', *Iraq*, 36, pt 1/2 (1974), p. 111 ff.
LOFTUS, W. K. *Travels and researches in Chaldaea and Susiana*, London 1857 (republished 1971).
LOUD, GORDON. *Khorsabad*, vol. 1, Oriental Institute Publications, no. 38, Chicago 1936.
LOUD, GORDON and ALTMANN, C. B. *Khorsabad*, vol. 2, Oriental Institute Publications, no. 40, Chicago 1938.
LLOYD, S. 'Some ancient sites in the Jebel Sinjar District', *Iraq*, 5 (1938).
——'The Oldest City: A Pre-Sumerian Temple at Eridu', *Illustrated London News*, 31 May 1947.
——'The Oldest City of Sumeria: The Origin of Eridu', *Illustrated London News*, 11 September 1948.
——'Ur-Al 'Ubaid, 'Uqair and Eridu', *Iraq*, 22 (1960).
——'Back to Ingharra', *Iraq*, 31, pt 1 (1969).
LLOYD, S. and SAFAR, F. 'Eridu', *Sumer*, 3 (1947) and 4 (1948).
——'Tell 'Uqair: Excavations by the Iraq Government Directorate of Antiquities in 1940–41', *Journal of Near Eastern Studies*, 2, no. 2 (1943), p. 131.
——'Tell Hassuna: Excavations by the Iraq Government Directorate of Antiquities in 1943–44', *Journal of Near Eastern Studies*, 4 (1945).
MACKAY, E. *A Sumerian Palace and the 'A' Cemetery at Kish, Mesopotamia*, Chicago 1929.
——'Excavations at Jemdet Nasr', in *Field Museum: Anthropological Memoirs*, nos. 1–3 Chicago 1931.
MACQUEEN, J. *Babylon*, London 1964.
MADHLOUM, T. 'Excavation of Nineveh', *Sumer*, 23 (1967).
——'Nineveh', *Sumer*, 24 (1968).
——*The Chronology of Neo-Assyrian Art*, London 1970.
MALLOWAN, M. E. L. 'Excavations at Brak and Chagar Bazar', *Iraq*, 9 (1927).
——'White Painted Subartu Pottery', in *Mélanges Offerts à M. René Dussaud*, vol. 2, 1939.
——'Noah's Flood Reconsidered', *Iraq*, 26, pt 2 (1964a).
——'Ninevite 5', in *Vorderasiatische Archäologie Studien und Aufsatze*, Festschrift Moortgat, Berlin 1964(b).
——'Tell Chuera: Fourth Campaign', *Iraq*, 28, pt 1 (1966a).
——*Nimrud and its Remains* (2 vols. and plans), London 1966(b).
——Review of *Mission Archéologique de Mari*, vol. 4, in *Bibliotheca Orientalis*, 26, no. 1/2 (1969).
——*Cambridge Ancient History*, vol. 1, pt 1, Cambridge 1970, ch. 8, 'The Development of Cities from Al 'Ubaid to the end of Uruk V': section 1, 'Babylonia and Mesopotamia', section 2, 'Assyria', section 3, 'Syria', section 4, 'Iran'; vol. 1, pt 2, 1971, ch. 16, 'The Early Dynastic Period in Mesopotamia'.
MALLOWAN, M. E. L. and ROSE, J. C. 'The Excavations of Tell Arpachiyah', *Iraq*, 2, (1935).
MCEWAN, C. *et al.* *Soundings at Tell Fachariya*, Oriental Institute Publications, no. 79, Chicago 1958.
MELLAART, J. *Çatal Hüyük*, London 1967.
——*The Neolithic of the Near East*, London 1975.

✕ MOOREY, P. R. S. 'A Reconstruction of East Kish', *Iraq*, 26, pt 1 (1966).

MOORTGAT, A. *Vorderasiatische Rollsiegel*, Berlin 1940.

——'Assyrische Glyptik des 12 Jahrhunderts', *Zeitschrift für Assyriologie*, 48 (n.f. 14) (1944).

——'Tell Chuera in Nord-Ost Syrien', Preliminary Reports in *Wissenschaftliche Abhandlungen für Arbeitgemeinschaft*, Köln 1959–67.

MORTENSEN, P. 'Additional Remarks on the Chronology of Early Farming Communities in the Zagros Area', *Sumer*, 20 (1964).

MUNCHAJEF, R. and MERPERT, N. IN *Sumer*, 25 (1969) onwards.

——'Early Agricultural Settlements in the Sinjar Plain, Northern Iraq', *Iraq*, 35, pt 2 (1973), p. 93 ff.

OATES, DAVID. 'Tell Rimah, 1966', *Iraq*, 29, pt 2 (1967).

——*Studies in the Ancient History of Northern Iraq*, British Academy, London 1968.

——'Early Vaulting in Mesopotamia', in *Archaeological Theory and Practice: Essays Presented to W. F. Grimes*, London 1973.

OATES, JOAN. 'Ur and Eridu: the Prehistory', *Iraq*, 22 (1960).

——'Tell-es-Sawwan Figurines', *Iraq*, 28, pt 2 (1966).

——'Goddess of Choga Mami', *Illustrated London News*, 28 September 1969(a).

——'Choga Mami, 1967–8': A Preliminary Report, *Iraq*, 31, pt 2 (1969b).

——'Prehistory in North-eastern Arabia', *Antiquity*, 50, no. 179 (1976).

OATES, D. and J. *The Rise of Civilization*, Oxford 1976.

PARROT, ANDRÉ. 'Mari et Chagar Bazar', *Iraq*, 19 (1938).

——*Tello: Vingt Campagnes de Fouilles, 1871–1933*, Paris 1948.

——*Mission Archéologique de Mari*: vol. 1, *Le Temple d'Ishtar*, Paris 1956; vol. 2, pt. 1, *Le Palais: Architectur*, Paris 1958(a); vol. 2, pt 2, *Le Palais: Peintures Murales*, Paris 1958(b); vol. 2, pt 3, *Le Palais: Documents et Monuments*, Paris 1958(c); vol. 3, *Les Temples de Ishtarat et de Nini-Zaza*, Paris 1967(a); vol. 4, *Le Trésor d'Ur*, Paris 1967(b).

——*Nineveh and Babylon*, London 1961.

——'Les Fouilles de Mari: Vingtième Campagne', *Syria*, 39 (1962).

PLACE, V. *Ninive et l'Assyrie, avec des Essaies de Restauration par Félix Thomas*, (3 vols.), Paris 1867–70.

PORADA, E. *Corpus of Ancient Near Eastern Seals in North American Collections*, vol. 1, Washington 1948.

POSTGATE, N. *The First Empires*, Oxford 1977.

RASSAM, H. *Asshur and the Land of Nimrod*. New York 1897 (republished 1971).

RAVN, O. E. *Herodotus' Description of Babylon*, Arnold Busck, Copenhagen 1942.

RIMMER, J. *Ancient Musical Instruments of Western Asia*, London 1960.

ROUX, GEORGE. 'Recently Discovered Sites in the Hammar Lake District', *Sumer*, 16 (1960).

SAFAR, F. 'Eridu: A Preliminary Report on the Third Season's Excavations', *Sumer*, 6 (1950).

SANDARS, N. K. (transl.) *The Epic of Gilgamesh*, Harmondsworth 1960.

DE SARZEC, E. and HEUZEY, L. *Découvertes en Chaldée*, Paris 1884–1912.

SCHEIL, V., 'Une Saison de Fouilles à Sippar', in *Memoires Publiées par les Membres de l'Academie Française d'Archéologie Orientale du Caire*, vol. 1, 1902.

SINGH, P. *Neolithic Cultures of Western Asia*, London 1974.

SMITH, SIDNEY. 'Diniktim', *Sumer*, 2, no. 2 (1946), p. 19ff.

SOLECKI, RALPH S. *Shanidar: The Humanity of Neanderthal Man*, London 1971.

SOLLBERGER, E. 'Sur la Chronique des Rois d'Ur et Quelque Problèmes Annexés', in *Archives für Orientforschung*, no. 17, 1954.

——'Notes on the Early Inscriptions from Ur and Al 'Ubaid', *Iraq*, 22 (1960).

SPEISER, E. A. *Excavations at Tepe Gawra*, vol. 1, Philadelphia 1935.

STARR, R. F. S. *Nuzi* (2 vols.), London 1938.

STROMMENGER, E. 'Akkadian Sculpture', in *Baghdader Mitteilungen,* no. 2, pt 1, 1936.

THOMPSON, R. CAMPBELL, and MALLOWAN, M. E. L. 'The British Museum Excavations at Nineveh, 1931–32', in *Liverpool Annals of Archaeology and Anthropology*, vol. 20, 1932.

THUREAU-DANGIN, F. and DUNAND, N. *Til Barsip*, Paris 1936.

TOBLER, A. J. *Excavations at Tepe Gawra*, vol. 2, Philadelphia 1950.

TURNER, G. 'Tell Nebi Yunus: The Ekal Masharti of Nineveh', *Iraq*, vol. 32, pt 1 (1970).

——'The State Apartments of Late Assyrian Palaces', *Iraq*, 32, pt 2 (1970).

——'Late Assyrian Palaces and their Mesopotamian Antecedents', Ph.D. thesis, London Institute of Archaeology, 1967.

UCKO, P. J. 'Anthropomorphic Figurines', *Royal Anthropological Society, Occasional Papers*, no. 24, London 1968.

VAN BUREN, E. D. 'Places of Sacrifice (Opferstätten)', *Iraq*, 14 (1952).

——'Fish Offerings', *Iraq*, 10, pt 2 (1948), p. 101.

WATERLIN, L. C. and LANGDON, S. *Excavations at Kish*, London 1930–4.

WEBER, O. 'Altorientalische Siegebilder', in *Der Alte Orient*, vols. 17–19, Leipzig 1920.

WETSEL, F. *Die Stadtmauern von Babylon*, Leipzig 1930.

WISEMAN, D. J. *Cylinder Seals of Western Asia*, London (n.d.).

WOOLLEY, C. L. 'Excavations at Ur', *Antiquaries Journal*, 3 (1923), to 13 (1934a).

——*Ur Excavations*, vol. 2: *The Royal Cemetery*, London and Philadelphia 1934(b).

——*Ur of the Chaldees*, London 1935.

——*Ur Excavations*, vol. 4: *The Early Periods*, London and Philadelphia 1956.

——*Ur Excavations*, vol. 5: *The Ziggurat and its Surroundings,* London and Philadelphia 1939.

——*Ur Excavations*, vol. 6: *The Buildings of the Third Dynasty*, London and Philadelphia 1974.

——*Ur Excavations*, vol. 6: *The Buildings of the Third Dynasty*, London and Philadelphia 1965.

——*Excavations at Ur* (preliminary reports collected in a single volume), London 1954.

WOOLLEY, C. L. and MALLOWAN, M. E. L. *Ur Excavations*, vol. 9, *The Neo-Babylonian and Persian Periods*, London and Philadelphia 1962.

ZIEGLER, C. *Die Keramik von Haggi Mohammed*, Berlin 1953.

Photographic Acknowledgments

Index

Numerals in *italics* refer to the illustrations

A'Annipadda, 91, 103
Abargi, *79*
Abbevillian, 21
Abu-al-Soof, B., 72
Abu-Shahrain, Tell, *see* Eridu
'aceramic periods', 32
Achaemenids, 222
Acheulian, 21
Adab, 90, 139
Adad-Nirari I, 179
Adad-Nirari II, 187
Adad-Nirari III, 194
Afghanistan, 82, 85
Agade, 137–9, 150, *see also*
    Akkad
Agga of Kish, 92, 93
Agrab, Tell, 36, 98; Shara Temple,
    98, *55*, 120, *74*, 142; sculpture,
    113, 117, *70*, 120, 128, *86*
Akalamdug, 102, 103
Akkad, 20, 137; Akkadian period,
    36, 66, *69*, 97, 106, 109, 135 ff.,
    137, 139; archaeology, 139;
    graves at Ur, 139; language,
    137; sculpture, *93*, 138, 142, *96*,
    144; seals, 144, *98*
Alalakh (Atchana), 158, 177
Aleppo, 29, 188, 231
Ali Kosh, 33
altars, 184
Altmann, C. B., *144*
Al 'Ubaid, *see* 'Ubaid
Amanus, 138
Andrae, W., 10, 90, 108, 112, *126*,
    181
Ani, 19
Anu Area, *see* Uruk
apkallu, 186
'Aqar Quf, 161, *121, 174*
Aral Sea, 23
Arabia, 188
Arabian Desert, 13
Arabian Gulf, 15, *31*, 64, 138, 149,
    160, 188
'Ark', the, 13

Arpachiyah, 65–7, 74, *36*
Arrapha, 177, 187, *see also* Kirkuk
'arsenal', 202, 216, *161*
Ashur, 10, 16, 107, 108, 135,
    137, 157, 179ff., *126, 127*; Ishtar
    Temple, 108, 112, 120, *127*,
    181; other temples and palaces,
    181ff., *127, 128*
Ashur-banipal, 191, 199
Ashur-etililani, 194
Ashur-nasirpal, 183, 188, 193;
    'Stela of', *156*, 212
Ashur-rabi II, 187
Asiab, Tepe, 27, 32
Asmar, Tell, 36, 39, 160; Abu
    Temple, 94, 97, 120; Archaic
    Temple, 97; Single Shrine
    Temple, 97; Square Temple,
    97, *54*, 112, 113, *64*; Gimil-Sin
    Temple and palaces, 155, *106*,
    161; houses, 141; Northern
    (Akkadian) Palace, 122, *140*,
    141, *94*; sculpture, 112, 113, *64*
'assembly, general', 88
Assyria, 19, 65, 107, *passim*;
    Assyrian empire, *135*
Aurignacian, 21, 22, 25
Azarbaijan, 32, 33, 158

Babylon, 10, 57, 157; city of, 224;
    Northern Palace, 228, 229, *171,
    172*; Summer Palace, 224, *167*;
    walls of, 223ff., *167, 168*; First
    Dynasty of, 157
Babylonia, 18, 172
Baghad, 18, *55*, 80; antique
    dealers of, 93, 149
Baghouz, 72, 79
Bahrein, 64, *31*, 138
Bahriyat, *see* Isin
Balawat, Gates of, 201, 206, *150,
    151*
Balik, 108
Baluchistan, 118
Bandar Abbas, 33
Banks, E. H., 139
'banqueting scene', 116, *79, 87*

Baradost, 24, 25
Barnett, R. D., 131, 219
basketwork, 31
Bau, 127
Bavian, *136*, 191
Bedouin, 138
Beidha, 27, 29, *5*
Beldibi, 24
Bel-shalti-nannar, Palace of, 230
Belshazzar, 222
Berlin Museum, 226, 230
Berossus, 88
Billa, Tell, 177
Bisitun, 24, *3*
Bismaya, 139
bit akitu, 181–3, 203
Black Sea, 23
Botta, E., 192, *138*, 196, 197
bow-drill, 61
Braidwood, R. J., 25, 26, 30, 33,
    35, 71
Brak, Tell, 66, 76, 147; Eye
    Temple, 76, *39*, 77, *46*, 85;
    Akkadian Palace, 95, 141, 142
bricks, 'cigar-shaped', 73;
    gypsum, 52; 'hog-backed', 28;
    kiln-baked, 119, 152; 'plano-
    convex', 119, *73*; *riemchen*, 21;
    stamped, 153, 230; sun-dried,
    41, 72
British Museum, 58, 59, 101, 131,
    149, 194, 196, 197, 199, 219
'brocade style', 124
'bucranium', 80
burials, 46, 47, 72, 74, 81, 82, 96,
    99ff., 139, 183, 230; infant, 92;
    pigmented, 47
'Burnt Palace', 196, *160*, 219
Burushanda, 138
Bus Mordeh, 33

canals, 17
Cappadocia, 158, 177
Carchemish, 16, 158, 188, 222
Carmel, Mount, 22, 23, 26
Caspian Sea, 23
Caucasus, 85
Cauvin, J., 29
cedar, 204
cemeteries, 45, 64, 86
Chagar Bazar, 158
Chalcolithic period, 32, 33, 35, 65,
    69, 72, 77
Chaldea, 188, 191, 218
chariot burials, 106
Chemchemal, 33, 35
Chicago, Oriental Institute of, 91,
    93, 96

Childe, Gordon, 26
Choga Mami, 66, 72, 73, 83, *45*
Choga Mish, 87
Cilicia, 188
cire perdue, 86, 128
city-states, 135
'Cliff, the', 12
climate, 17
coastline, 15
composite objects, 131
'cone-mosaic', 50–2, *21*, 54, 129
continuity (religious beliefs), 63
Coon, Carleton, 24
copper, 25, 30
Crawford, V. E., 150
Crete, 138, 177
Crimean War, 192
crop-yields, 18
Cros, G., 149
Ctesias, 223
Ctesiphon, Arch of, 115
cult statues, 108, 112, 114
Cyaxares, 191
cylinder-seals, 59; Protoliterate,
    59, 60, *28*, *29*; ED II and III,
    124, 125, *78–81*, 127; Akkadian,
    144, *98*; Mitannian, 177;
    Middle Assyrian, 184, *130–3*
Cyprus, 138, 218
Cyrus, 222
Çambel, H., 30
Çatal Hüyük, 27, 30, *6*
Çayönü, 27, 30

Dagan, 138; Temple of, 167
Dalma, 33
Damascus, 188, 221
Darband-i-Gawr, 138
date-palms, 19
Deh Luran, 33
Delougaz, P., 94, 103, 114
'Deluge' text, 201
democracy, Sumerian, 88, 89
de Morgan, J., 86, 142
Dilmun, 188
Diwaniyah, 107
Diyala, 18; Diyala sites, 36, 55,
    91–3, 99, 107, 108, 112, 141,
    160, 161
Diyarbakir, 30, 80, 138
domes, 67, 74, 99
domestication of animals, 26, 32,
    33
domestication of plants, 26, 31,
    33, 34
doors, 119, 208, *150*, *151*
Dumuzi, 57

Dur-Kurigalzu, 160, 172, 187 *see*
ʿAqar Quf
Dur-Sharrukin, *see* Khorsabad

Eanna Precinct, *see* Uruk
Eannatum, 106, 116, 149
Early Bronze Age, 65
Early Dynastic period, 36, 66, 88,
99, 107, 108, 110; pottery, 132,
133, *92*; sculpture, 112, 113,
passim, *64 passim*; seals, 124,
78–81; sites, 92ff.; terminology,
91, 110
Ebih-il, 114
Ebla, 231
E-dub-lal-makh, 153
Egypt, 62, 184, 188, 191, 221, 222
einkorn, 30
ekal masharti, 216, *161*
Elam, 85, 138, 142, 147, 151,
157–9, 191, *155*
elephant, Syrian, 221
Elâziğ, 16
En, 88, 89
Enki, 57
Enlil, 57, 103, 107, 117
Enmebaragisi, 93
Enmerkar, 93
ensi, 88, 89, 122
Enuma Elish, Epic of Creation, 167
E-nun-makh, 153
Erech, 45
Eridu, 15, 39ff., 57, 66, 81;
cemetery, 45–7; palaces, 122,
123, *77*; temples, 39, *8*, *10*, 43,
11, *32*, 75; pottery, 36, 39, *12*,
44, 45
Eshnunna (Tell Asmar), 96, 157–9
Etana, 144
E-temen-anki, 226, 229
Ethiopia, 191
Euphrates, 12, 16, 19, 72, 99,
105–7, 114, 138, 158, 222, 230;
crossings, 80
'extensive' cultivation, 18
'eye' or 'spectacle' idols, 77, *46*, 85
'Eye Temple', 77, *39*
Eynan (Ain Mallaha), 28

Faish Khabur, 19, *2*
Farah, 90–2; 'Farah period', 110
Fertile Crescent, 19
fireplaces, 72
fish, 19; offerings, 16, 55
Flandin, E., 196, 197

'Flood', the, 90–2, 106; floods,
river, 16
'Flowing-vase goddess', 166, *113*,
167, 169, *120*, 172, 203
'Fort Shalmaneser', *161*, 216;
throne-base, *162*, 218; glazed
brick, 218
foundation deposits, 124
foundations, sand, 94, *53*, 96;
Babylon, 169
Frazer, Sir James, 57
French excavations, 86, 105, 108,
124, 147, 157, 192, 193, *138*

Gadd, C. J., 88
gaming-boards, 129
Ganj Dareh Tepe, 32
Garrod, A. E., 21–3, 25, 26
Gasur, 147
Gawra, Tepe, 66, 67; 'acropolis',
67, 75, *32*; 'round house', 75, *37*
'Gawra period', 67, 75, *38*, 76, 81,
82, 85, *47*
gazelles, 29, 35
German excavators, 38, 108, 110,
178, 193, 223
Gilgamesh, 48, 49, 90, 91, 92, 93;
Epic, 103
Gimil-Sin, 155, *106*, 161
Gi-par-u, 153
Girsu, 107, *103*, 150
glazed ornament, 183, 218, 227,
170, *171*
glockentopf, 81
Godin Tepe, 87
Grai Resh, 66, 81
Gravettian, 21–3, 25
Greek art, 221, 228, 230; writers, 88
Gudea, 147, *101*, *102*, 149, 150
Gula, 186
Guran, Tepe, 27, 32, 34
Gutians, 139, 147
Guzan, *see* Halaf

Hacılar, 27
Haines, R. C., 107
Hajji Firuz, 33
Hajji Muhammad, 36, 45, 66, 81
Halaf, Tell, period, 27, 67, 74;
pottery, 66–8, *43*, *79*, *44*, 80, 81
Hall, H. R., 107
Hamad, 13
Hammurabi, 157, 171, *108*; 171,
159, 184
'Hanging Gardens', 228, *172*
Hansen, D. P., 116

Hariri, Tell, *see* Mari
Harmal, Tell, 160; laws of, 162;
　lions, 171, *119*
Harran, 13, 191, 222
Harsagkalama, 105
Hashhamer, *130*
Hassuna, 25, 34, 35, 66, 69–70;
　pottery, 'Standard', 69, 77, *40*,
　79; 'Archaic', 69, 77, 79
Hatra, 70
Hazar Gölü, 16
Hazar Merd, 22, 23, *3*
Hebrew scriptures, 92, 223
Herodotus, 18, 223, 229
Herzfeld, E., 68, 72
Hiba, Tell al-, 106, *103*, 150
Hill, Harold, 162, *109*
'hilly-flanks zone', 19
Hilprecht, H. V., 139
Hittites, 160, 187
Homs, 158
Howe, B., 25
Hurrians, 138, 149, 158, 159
'husking-trays', 70

Iakhdunlim, 158
Ibiqadad II, 161
Idi ilum, 169
Ilushuilia, 161
'Imdugud-Sikurru period', 110,
　117
Imgur-Enlil, 201
Inanna, 49, 57, *25*, 59, 107
India, 188
Indo-European, 160
inlaid ornament, 129, 130
Iran, 26, 32, 80, 85, 87
Iraq, Antiquities Directorate, 25,
　39, 69, 151, 174; modern, 12,
　18, 25; Museum, 52, 69, 102,
　142, 144, 203, 208; northern, 19
Iron Age, 188
irrigation, 16, 17, 31, 33, 72
Ischali, 160, 161, *109*
ishakku, 106
Ishtar, 49, 108, *100*
Ishtar Gate, 226, *169, 171*
Ishtar-Kititum Temple, 161, *109*
Israel, 194
Istanbul Museum, 138
ivory, 215, 219ff.

Jacobsen, Th., 18, 88, 89, 106, 150
'Jaffar phase', 33
Jarmo, 25 33, *7*, 35, 66, 71, 72;
　ancient environment, 35

Jazirah, *2*, 14, 19, 70, 77
Jehu, 194
Jemdet Nasr, 38; period, 36, 38,
　40, 49, 54, 55, 66, 71, 72; seals,
　29; pottery, 61, 62, *10*
Jericho, 27, 28, 33
Jerusalem, 222
Jews, 222
Jonah, 198
Jordan, 28
Jordan, J., 38, 60

Kalhu (Calah), *see* Nimrud
Kanesh, 158
Karaindash, Temple of, 172
Karim Shahir, 22, 23
Karkheh, 15, 86
Karun, 15, 86
kaunakes, 114, 130, 144, 171
Kayseri, 138
Keban dam, 6
Kenyon, K. M., 28
Kermanshah, 24, *3*, 32
Khabur, 10, 76
Khafaje, 36, 55, 58, 92, 94, 103,
　120; houses, 142; Oval Temple,
　36, 94, *51–3*; pottery, 132;
　sculpture, 112–14, *6*?, Sin
　Temple, 36, 40, 55, 93, *50*, 120
Khanikin, 19
Khosr, 196, *136*
Khuzistan, 15, 85, 87
'king' figure, 58–60
King-list, 88, *49*, 90, 92, 93, 105,
　106, 108, 139
kingship, 88, 135
King-of-Battle, epic of, 138
Kirkbride, D. (Mrs H. Helbaek),
　29, 70, 72
Kirkuk, 33, 71, 147, 187
Kish, 36, 38, 90, 92, 105, 120, 139,
　230, *174*
Koldewey, R., 10, 90, 188, 223ff.
kudurru, 122, 175
Kufah, 13
Kültepe, 158
Kurdistan (Iraq), 19, 21, 25, 26, 32
Kurigalzu, 153, 174
Kurnah, disaster, 197
Küyünjik, 25; Ishtar Temple, 69,
　142; sounding at, 69, 198, *141*

Lacheman, E. R., 178
Lakish, siege of, *154*, 211
lamassu, 141, 202
Lamberg-Karlovsky, C. C., 118

land, ownership of, 122
langraum, 162
Larsa, 57, 90, 157, 159; period, 160, 161
Law, Antiquities, 10
Layard, A. H., 192, *137*, 194, *140*, 195 *passim*
lead, 70
Le Breton, L., 87
Leiden, conference at, 38
Lenzen, H. J., 48
Levant, 26, 27, 32, 188, *151*, 219
Lilith, 171, *118*
limmu-lists, 187
'Lion Hunt', 199
Lloyd, S., 39, 52, 69
Loftus, W. K., 196, *140*, *160*
Loud, G., 89, *144*, 202ff.
Louvre, the, 116, 138, 144, 147, 159
lugal, 88, 89
Lugal-zaggesi, 137
Lullubi, 138
Luristan, 138

Mackay, E., 105
Magan, 138, 149
Magdalenian, 22, 24
Makran, 38
Mallowan, M. E. L., 10, 25 *passim*
Malyan, 87
Mandali, 72
Manishtusu, 138, 142
Mardikh, Tell, 231
Marduk, 57, 222, 226
Marduk-apal-idinna (Merodach-baladon), 189
Marduk-nasir, *122*
Mari, 10, 19, 90, 107, 108, 135, 136, 157; archives, *158*; Ishtar Temple, 108, 157; inlays, 130, *89*, 131; murals, 116, *113*; palace, 122, 124, 164ff., *111*, *112*; 'Palais Présargonique', 124
Matarrah, 71
marsh-dwellers, 25, 41, 58
mausoleum (Ur III), 151–3, *105*, 155
Medes, 191, 222
megaron, 38, 76, 109
Mellaart, J., 30, 31
Meluhha, 138
Memphis, 191
Mersin, 31
Mesannipadda, 91, 92, 106, 108, 110
'Mesilim' period, 110

Meskalamdug, 102, 103, 107, *69*, 117, 127, *90*, 142; style, 110
Mesolithic, 27
Mesopotamia, 12, *2*; northern, 65, 67, 107, 108
metal, 65, 81, 113, *82*, *83*, 127, 128, *86*
Metropolitan Museum, 106, 150
Mitanni, 160, 176ff., 186
M'lefaat, 22
Mohenjo-daro, 118, 147
'Mona Lisa', 214, *158*
Moorey, P. R. S., 105
Moortgat, A., 40, 109, 110
Mosul, 68, 70, 167, 189, 196, 197
Mousterian, 21, 22, 24
mudhif, 41
Muqayyar, *see* Ur
mural paintings, 31, *6*, 52, 71, *33*, 166, *113*
Mureybet, 27, 29
Mursilis I, 160
musical instruments, 100, 116, *87*, 131, *90*
Muski, 187
Mycenae, 67

Nabonidus, 222, 226
Nabopolassar, 191, 222, 226
Nabu Temple, Khorsabad, 202; Nimrud, 196, *140*
Nairi peoples, 187
Nannar, 57, 153, 156
Naram-Sin, 138, 139; Stela of, 138, 142, *96*
Nasiriyah, 15
Natufian, 26, 28, 29, *5*
'natural habitat zone', 26
Neanderthal, 21, *14*
Nebi Yunus, 198, *141*, 199, 216
Nebuchadnezzar (Nebuchadrezzar), 99, 151
Neo-Babylonian period, 106, 151, 222ff.
Neolithic man, 21; period, 27, 28, 31–3, 70, 77; 'Revolution', 26
New Year's Festival, 127, 182, 183, 187, 226
New York University, 106
Niffer, *see* Nippur
Nimrud, 16, 188, 192, 193ff., *139*, 140, 141; buildings, 212ff.; ivories, 214, 215, 219ff., *163–6*
Nineveh, 16, 25, 65, 189, 190, *136*, 197, *141*; 'Ninevite One', 69; 'Ninevite Five', 132, 134; fall of, 198; population, 214; sounding at, 66, 69

Nin-gal, 153, 156
Ningirsu, 117, 127, 147, 149, 150
Nin-khursag, 57, 103, 167
Ninmakh Temple, 230, *173*
Ninni-Zaza, 167
Nintu, 57, 114
Ninurta, 57, 196
Nippur, 36, 57, 91, 107, 137, 139
Nisibin, 160
Noah, Babylonian, 92
Nöldeke, N., 38
nomads, 26, 29
Nusku, 184

Oates, D., 167, 216
Oates, D. and J., 11, 30, 75
Obelisk, 'Black', 194
obsidian, 32, 70
Old Testament, 12, 171, 188, 189,
214, 221–3
Oman, 138
omens, 44
onager, 71, *33*, 128, *86*
opferstätten, 55
Oppenheim, Max von, 66
orthostats (slabs), 203

palaces, 106, 122, 140, 155, 161,
*76, 106, 141, 142, 144, 171,
172,* 200
Palaeolithic period, 21, 22, 24;
terminal, 27
Palegawra, 22, *3*, 25
Palestine, 22, 219
parapet design, 184, 186
Parrot, A., 10, 108, 150, 157, 164
Parthian period, 179
Pennsylvania, 176
Perigordian, 22
Persians, 222
phalanx, 116, 117
Pliny, 12
'polos' headdress, 114
pottery, Halaf, 66–8, *43,* 79, *44,*
80, 81; Eridu, 36, 39, *12,* 44,
45; S. 'Ubaid, 37–9, 44, *12, 13,*
45, 47; N. 'Ubaid, 65–7, 75, 80,
81; Protoliterate, 61, *10,* 132;
ED I and II, 132, *92;* ED III,
134
Predynastic, 65
'Pre-pottery Neolithic', 28, 30, 33
Pre-Sargonid period, 91, 108, 111
priests, 57, *28,* 112, *83; baru,* 44

private houses, 141, 162, *110,* 230
Procession Street, 226, *168,* 227,
172
Proto-Elamite script, 87
Protoliterate period, 40, 54, 55,
67, 82, 103, 118, 124
Proto-Neolithic, 28
Pu-abi, 125
Pusur-Ishtar, 169

Qal'at Sharqat, 107
Qatnah, 158
Que, 188

'ram' ornament, 132, *90*
Rapiqu, 141
Rassam, H., 49
Ras Shamra, 80
Rawa, 19
Rawlinson, G., 194
'reception suite', 124
reed architecture, 41, *9,* 59, *28, 29*
religion, 43, 55, 57, 122, 172
Reza'iyeh, *see* Urmia
Rich, C. J., 223
riemchen, 118
Rimah, Tell, 158, 167ff., *114, 115*
Rimush, 138
rivers, 12, *2,* 15
rock reliefs, 138
Romania, 62
roofs, 119, 204
Rowanduz, 24, *3*
Rowton, 110

'sacred herd', 59
'sacred marriage', 88, 127, 182
sacrifices, 44
Safar, Fuad, 39, 52, 69, 150
Saggs, H. W. F., 44, 88, 122
Sakçagözü, 31
salinization, 17
Samarra, period, 70, 71, 73;
pottery, 66, 68, 71, 72, 77, *41,
42,* 78, 80
Sammuramat, *see* Semiramis
Sarab, Tepe, 32; 'Venus', 32
Sargon-of-Akkad, 91, 135, 137,
139, 142
Sargon II, 189, 196
Sarzec, E. de, 106, 147, 149, 150
Sawwan, Tell-es-, 35, 66, 71, 73,
35, 74, *45*
'scarlet ware', 132, 134, *92*
scribes, 90, 122

sculpture, 31, 56; Protoliterate, 56, 58, *25*, *26*, 59, *27*, 112, *63*; Early Dynastic, 59, 97, 108, 109, *62*, 111, 112, *64*; Mari, 114, *65*, *66*; relief, 114, *67–9*, 115–17, *70*, *71*; Akkadian, *93*, 138, 142, *96*, *97*, 144; Gudea, 47, *101*, *102*, 149; Ur III, *107*, 155; second millennium, 108, 116–19, 122–4, 184, *129*; Late Assyrian, 204ff., *146ff.*; metal, *83*, 128, *86*, *93*

Scythians, 191

Sea-Land, 160

'Sea-of-the-West', 138

Semiramis, 196

Sennacherib, 179, 190, 191

Shaduppum, *see* Harmal

Shalmaneser I, 160

Shalmaneser III, 179, 188; Fort, 216, *161*

Shamash, 57, *81*, *108*

Shamash Gate, 198, *141*

Shamsi-Adad, 158, 167, 174, 196

Shanidar, Cave, 22, 23, *3*

Shar-gali-sharri, 139

Shatra, 106

Shatt-al-Arab, 86, 107

Sha'ur, 86

Shaushattar, 176, 178

Sheil, V., 139

Shilwi-Teshup, 178

ships, 38

Shuaira, 109, *62*

Shubad, *see* Pu-abi

Shubat-Enlil, 158

Shuruppak, *see* Farah

Shutruk-nakhkhunte, 142

Sialk, 87

silver-mines, 138

Sin, 57, 93; of Harran, 222

Sinjar, 70, 77, 81, 158, 167

Sinkara, *see* Larsa

Sin Temple (Khorsabad), 203

Sippar, 57, 90, 139, 142

sirrush, 227, *170*

Smith, G., 192, 201

Solecki, 23

Solutrian, 22, 24

Soviet archaeologists, 70

Speiser, E. A., 67

stamp-seals, 67, 70, 85, *47*

Standard (Ur), 103, 130, *87*, *88*

Starr, R. F., 176, 178

'steatite bowls', 117, *71*

'Steinplatten' inscription, 223

Stela of Hammurabi, *108*

Stela of Ur-nammu, 155

'Stela-of-the-Vultures', 106, 116, *69*, 142

Stone Age, Old, 21, 22, 25

stones, gem-, 82

stone, building-, 119, 203

Strabo, 12

suchgraben, 179

Sumer, 15, 18

Sumerians, 37, 39, 107; origins, 62, 63, 137

'Summer Palace', 226, *167*

Susa, 32, 86; pottery, 86, *48*, 137, 142, 144, 171

Susiana (periods), 27, 85, 87

Syria, 10, 16, 29, 85, 108, 138, 157, 177, 186, 219, 231

Syrian Desert, 20, 136

Tabal, 188

tablets, archaic, 55, 56, *24*; cuneiform, *49*, 122, 157; ivory, 214

Tammuz, 57, 59

Tarsus, 31

Taurus, 17, 26, 138, 188

Tell Afar, 70

Telloh, 106, 107, *69*, 147, 149, 150

temples, 119; Eridu, 41, *10*, 43, 49, 50; Early Dynastic, 93, *50*, 98, 108, 119; Ur III, 155, *106*; Larsa period, 161, *109*; second millennium, 167, *114*; Mid-Assyrian, *126*, *127*, 181ff.; Late Assyrian, 196, 202, 203, *160*; Neo-Babylonian, 230, *174*; 'platform', 52, 103, 105, 119; size, 121; function, 122

terminology (Uruk period), 40; pre-Sargonid, 110

'terrazzo pavements', 30

'Tête au Turban', 150

texts, written, 9

'tholoi', 67, 74, *36*, 75

Thomas, Felix, 197

tieftempel, 153, 181, 229

Tiglath-Pileser I, 183; III, 186, 188, 189

Tigris, 12, 16, 93, 106, 108, 179, 190, 193

Til Barsip (Tell Ahmar), 188, 208

Tilla, Tehip and Shurki, 177

timber, 138, 204

'tortoise jars', 81

'tree-of-life', *133*, 206

T-shaped buildings, 73, *35*

'Tummal' inscription, 92

Tutub, *see* Khafaje

Tyre, *151*, 208

ʿUbaid, Tell Al, 25, 36, 37, 47,
103; culture, 47; Nin-khursag
Temple, 36, 37, 90, 103, *60*,
105; 'northern', 65–7, 75, 80,
81; period, 27, 36, 38, 63;
pottery, 37–9, 44, *12*, *13*, 45,
47; settlement, 36, 37, 63, *31*,
103, *60*; small objects, 46
Uhaimir, 105
Umma, 107, 116
Umm Dabaghiyah, 35, 66, 70, 71,
33, 72, *34*, 73, 77
ʿUqair, Tell, 36; Painted Temple,
36, 52, *22*, *23*; Jemdet Nasr
chapel, 36, 54; ʿUbaid
settlement, 36, 52, 63; small
objects, *14*
Ur-of-the-Chaldees, 15, 57, 81,
90; soundings, 36–8; site, 151;
walls, *56*, 230; First Dynasty,
103, 110; Royal Tombs, 90, 92,
99, 101, *58*, *59*, 102, 103, 106,
107, 110, 116, 151, *87*, *88*, *90*,
127, 129; Third Dynasty, 99,
150, 151; ziggurat, 151, 152,
104; Mausoleum, 151–3, *105*,
155; other buildings, 153
Urartu, 187, 188, 220
Ur-baba, 147, 149
Urbartutu, 92
Urmia, 22, 32, 188
Ur-nammu, 142, 150, 151, 155,
107, 130
Ur-Nanshe, 106, *68*, 149; (singer)
114, *66*
Ur-ningirsu, 149
Uruk (Warka), 27, 36, 48ff., *17*;
period, 27, 36, 38; terminology,
40, 63, 66; Anu area, 36, *17*, *18*,
49; Eanna Precinct, 36, 38, *17*,
49–51, *20*, 54; White Temple,
36, *17*, *18*, 52, 54; Pillar Hall,
50, *19*, 52; *Riemchengebäude*, 55;
Stone-cone-mosaic Temple, 51,
55
Utnapishtim, 92
Utu, 57
Utu-hegal, 150

Van, Lake, 16, 25, 188
van Loon, M., 29
vaulting, 115, 169, 204

Wadi-al-Natuf, 26
walls, enclosure and defensive, 72,
151, 179, *141*, 224; wall-
tracing, 94; wall-plaques, 114,
67, *68*
Warka, *see* Uruk
Washukkani, 160, 176
Watelin, C. H., 139
weapons, *82*, 127, 177
wheeled vehicles, 106, 128, *86*, *88*,
178
windows, 119
winged bulls, 202, *145*, *146*
wooden vessels, 31
Woolley, C. L., 25, 99ff. and
passim
Wright, H. E., 25
writing, 55, *24*, 87, 90, 111, *157*

Yahya, Tepe, 33, 37, 118
Yarim Tepe, 70, 72, 83
Yorghan Tepe, 176

Zab, Greater, 19, 118
Zab, Lesser, 19, 193
Zagros Mountains, 13, 17, 20, 22
Zarzi, 22, 23, *3*, 25
Zawi Chemi, 22
ziggurats, 39, 49, 203; Ur, 99,
107, 139, 151, 152, *104*, 156,
157; Kish, 105, 106; Ashur,
181, *126*; ʿAqar Quf, *121*, 174;
Babylon, 226, 229
Zigi, 177
Zimrilim, 124, 158; Palace of,
164ff.
Ziusudra, 92
zone sacré, 124
Zu, 144